cities
and
towns
of the
Chesapeake

A Maryland
Guide

Tidewater Publishers
A Division of Schiffer Publishing, Ltd.
4880 Lower Valley Road, Atglen, Pennsylvania 19310

William B. Cronin

Designed by Justin Watkinson
Type set in Franklin Gothic/NewBskvll BT

ISBN: 978-0-7643-4463-3
Printed in China

Published by Schiffer Publishing, Ltd.
4880 Lower Valley Road
Atglen, PA 19310
Phone: (610) 593-1777; Fax: (610) 593-2002
E-mail: Info@schifferbooks.com

For our complete selection of fine books on this and related subjects,
please visit our website at: **www.schifferbooks.com**. You may also write for a free catalog.

This book may be purchased from the publisher. Please try your bookstore first.

We are always looking for people to write books on new and related subjects.
If you have an idea for a book, please contact us at **proposals@schifferbooks.com**.

Schiffer Publishing's titles are available at special discounts for bulk purchases for sales promotions or premiums. Special editions, including personalized covers, corporate imprints, and excerpts can be created in large quantities for special needs. For more information, contact the publisher.

Log canoe race at St. Michael's.

contents

Concord Point Lighthouse at Havre de Grace.

preface

This, my second book about the Chesapeake Bay, surveys the many towns and villages along Maryland's Eastern and Western Shores and complements my earlier book on the islands of the Bay. Both books are written to provide an informative history and photographic summary of the places of interest associated with the Chesapeake for driving and cruising tours.

After retiring from the Chesapeake Bay Institute at Johns Hopkins University, I have had an opportunity to reflect on my thirty-two years on the Bay. During those years on the research vessels *Lydia Louise* and *Maury*, I traveled up every major river in Maryland and Virginia to measure water quality. I also visited many places with friends or alone on my sailboat *Ginger*, named after my beloved Chesapeake Bay retriever. On those journeys, I met the people of the Bay —the watermen, local fire and post office officials, the marina managers, storekeepers, and ordinary citizens — who generously shared their memories and stories with me.

This book reviews all of the towns in the counties along the Maryland Eastern and Western Shores, providing a brief history and references for further information. The major points of interest — the sites and buildings — are described, accompanied by a photograph and map to help the reader to plan a trip to the town. Many of the town descriptions include information concerning events, marinas, lodging, and dining.

I would not have had this cherished lifelong experience on the Bay without the help of family and friends. My professional career on the Bay was supported by the Chesapeake Bay Institute and was initiated by my late brother, Dr. Gene Cronin, the former director of the University of Maryland's Chesapeake Biological Laboratory and an acknowledged expert on the blue crab. This book was completed with the help of my daughter, Wendy Cronin, who drove me to more than one hundred towns around the Bay and compiled the book text and photos. My son, Thomas Cronin, also took on the tasks of visiting the towns and helping with the maps.

I also wish to express thanks to my copy-editor, Ann Jensen, who corrected my spelling, misquoted dates, and prose, and to the efforts of Jesse Marth, of Schiffer Publishing, Ltd., and Jeremy School, the mapmaker. Special thanks also goes to the postmaster of Deal Island and postmistress of Greensboro, as well as to Susan Evans of Smith Island.

Finally, I would like to thank my wife, Elizabeth, for her constant encouragement, which inspired me again and again.

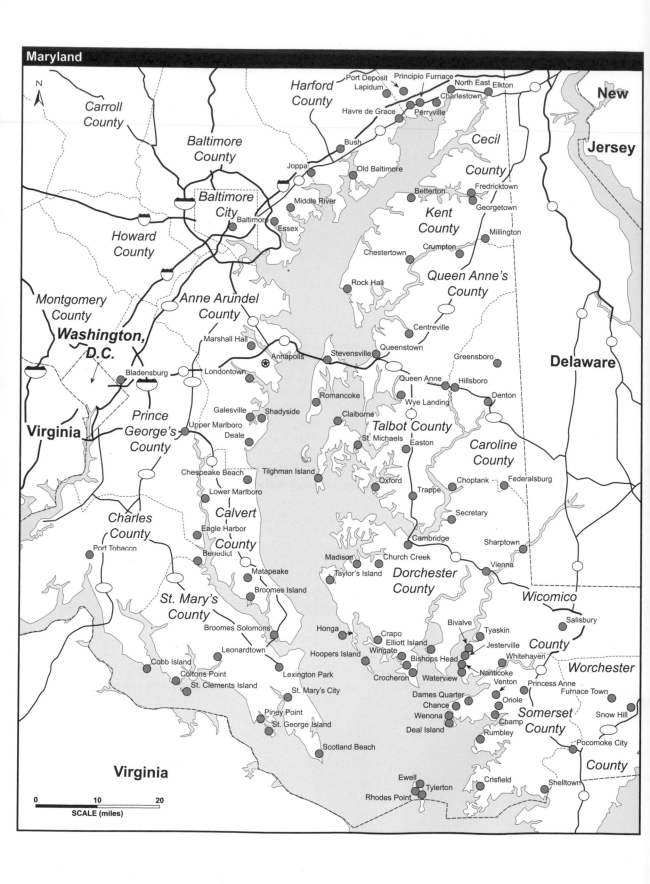

Maryland

N

New Jersey

Delaware

Virginia

Carroll County

Baltimore County

Howard County

Montgomery County

Washington, D.C.

Virginia

Prince George's County

Charles County

St. Mary's County

Anne Arundel County

Calvert County

Harford County

Cecil County

Kent County

Queen Anne's County

Talbot County

Caroline County

Dorchester County

Wicomico County

Worcester County

Somerset County

County

Baltimore City

Port Deposit
Lapidum
Principio Furnace
North East
Elkton
Charlestown
Havre de Grace
Perryville
Bush
Old Baltimore
Joppa
Middle River
Baltimore
Essex
Betterton
Fredricktown
Georgetown
Millington
Chestertown
Crumpton
Rock Hall
Centreville
Marshall Hall
Stevensville
Queenstown
Greensboro
Annapolis
Londontown
Queen Anne
Hillsboro
Denton
Romancoke
Wye Landing
Bladensburg
Galesville
Shadyside
Claiborne
St. Michaels
Easton
Upper Marlboro
Deale
Choptank
Federalsburg
Chespeake Beach
Tilghman Island
Oxford
Trappe
Secretary
Lower Marlboro
Eagle Harbor
Cambridge
Sharptown
Port Tobacco
Benedict
Madison
Church Creek
Vienna
Matapeake
Taylor's Island
Salisbury
Broomes Island
Broomes
Solomons
Honga
Crapo
Elliott Island
Bivalve
Tyaskin
Jesterville
Whitehaven
Leonardtown
Hoopers Island
Wingate
Bishops Head
Crocheron
Waterview
Nanticoke
Venton
Princess Anne
Furnace Town
Cobb Island
Coltons Point
St. Clements Island
Lexington Park
St. Mary's City
Dames Quarter
Chance
Oriole
Snow Hill
Piney Point
St. George Island
Wenona
Champ
Deal Island
Rumbley
Pocomoke City
Scotland Beach
Ewell
Tylerton
Rhodes Point
Crisfield
Shelltown

0   10   20
SCALE (miles)

introduction

Maryland's history followed the waterways of the Chesapeake Bay and its tributaries as European exploration, colonization, and commercial development of their resources created and connected towns and ports. Throughout its early years, Maryland was an integral part of coastal and Bay traffic between North and South and a connection to the West. As a result, the state was crisscrossed by invading waterborne armies of the British during the Revolutionary War and War of 1812. During the Civil War, the Bay carried Northern troops and supplies to and from the South while its rivers and inlets sheltered blockade runners supplying the Confederacy.

The story that William Cronin tells within these pages explores some three hundred years of Maryland and Chesapeake Bay history. He takes us on his exploration of places that aren't always a part of the standard tour guides — this book is an easily portable guide for weekend- or day-trips along area highways and waterways and documents more than one hundred Maryland towns and cities. You'll be guided to well-known and out-of-the-way places with the help of his detailed maps and with addresses, photographs, reviews, and descriptions provided. As he went along, he often found that information on lesser-known sites and interesting places was scarce; this guide is the result of his search for answers. Although it does not cover every location or site, either historic, quaint, or simply interesting, along Maryland's rivers and shores, it will start you on your own journey of exploration of the state's many unique villages, towns, and cities.

One of the unique, but lesser-known towns, is tiny Benedict, where the British landed in 1814 as the first step on their way to burn Washington. You'll find that such towns take you back in time to picturesque settings that offer a distinct contrast to better-known historic cities, such as Annapolis on the Bay's Western Shore and Cambridge on the Eastern Shore's Choptank River.

This book is organized for the traveler, covering the counties on both shores of the Chesapeake. The Eastern Shore includes the coast of the bay, from the northern top of the Bay in Port Deposit, down the East coast to the Atlantic Ocean at Smith Island. The Western Shore includes the coast from Havre de Grace down to the southern tip of the Bay at Scotland Beach. Each chapter is devoted to a county and describes its major cities, towns, or villages, classic architecture, river ferries, and other attractions. Locations within a town are identified on a map with a numbered photograph. Because weather and other conditions on and around the Chesapeake Bay are constantly changing and some marinas, restaurants, places to stay, and events are seasonal, it's important to plan your trip well in advance. It is also possible that some may have closed or moved since the publication of this guide. In this age of the Internet and cell phones, however, it is relatively simple to make advance plans for each stage of your trip.

My father, William Cronin, wrote this guide to help others share his lifetime on the Bay. As a marine scientist for the Johns Hopkins University, Chesapeake Bay Institute from 1950 to 1980, he explored the Bay and its tributaries, collecting scientific data. As he worked and talked with local watermen, he collected a rich and personal history that we have shared in this book. Ultimately, it is the result of the recent four years that my father, my brother Tom, and I spent re-visiting all of the places you'll read about here. We hope, like we did, that you will enjoy the discovery of these sites.

Wendy Cronin,
daughter of the author

Eastern Shore
of the Chesapeake

EASTERN SHORE PLANNERS
list for special occasions

Please check the Internet or call ahead, as dates, locations, and events may change over time.

ONGOING EVENTS

CRUMPTON: Crumpton Fire Department Breakfast: every second Sunday, 410-928- 3956

CENTREVILLE: "Emergence" Coffee House, Queen Anne's County Arts Council; 410-758-2520

ELKTON: Cecil County Farmer's Market, Couthouse Parking Lot: Fridays and Saturdays, April-October; 410-996-8469

Hollingsworth House Tours, Historic Elk Landing, 410-620-6400

ST. MICHAELS: Fresh Farm Market, Church Cove; 410-745-6073

JANUARY

NORTHEAST: New Plays of the American Theater, Cecil College; 410-287-1037

ELKTON: Annual Paper Americana Show, Singerly Fire Hall; 410-398-7735

Elkton's Own Antique Show, 100 Railroad Avenue; 410-398-5076

CENTREVILLE: Baltimore Symphony Orchestra Concert, Mid Shore Symphony Society; 410-758-2343

EASTON: First Night Talbot, New Year's night, downtown Easton; 410-892-8822

FEBRUARY

NORTHEAST: Candlelight Valentine Banquet, Cecil College 410-287-1037

ELKTON: Heart to Heart: A Quilting Discussion, Historic Elk Landing; 410-620-6400

STEVENSVILLE: Cooking Class Getaway, Kent Manor Inn, 410-643-5757

CRAPO: National Outdoor Show, Beach Ground Road, 410-397-8535

MARCH

NORTHEAST: Covered Bridge Theater, Cecil College; 410-287-1037

Girl's Night Out and Day Off, Sandy Cove Ministries; 410-287-5433

CHESTERTOWN: Chestertown Arts League Annual Juried Show, 312 Cannon Street, 410-778-5789

QUEENSTOWN: Ham & Oyster Dinner, Calvary United Methodist Church; 410-827-7113

STEVENSVILLE: Author's Luncheon, Chesapeake Bay Beach Club; 410-634-2497

Artists of the Chesapeake Annual Art Auction; 410-758-2520

Flashlight Egg Hunt, Old Love Point Park; 410-758-0835

APRIL

NORTHEAST: *Note: These three events take place at Cecil College, 410-287-1037*

The Peabody Ragtime Ensemble

Celtic Festival

Cecil Dance Theater

ELKTON: Defender's Day, Historic Elk Landing; 410-620-6400

CHESAPEAKE CITY: Cecil Dance Theater, 2755 Augustine Herman Highway; 410-287-3546

CENTREVILLE: Baltimore Symphony Orchestra Concert, Mid Shore Symphony Society; 410-258-2343

Annual Black Tie & White Boot Affair, Queen Anne's Chamber of Commerce; 410-643-8530

"Made in America" Concert, Queen Anne's County High School; 410-827 -8618

STEVENSVILLE: Bay Bridge Boat Show, Bay Bridge Marina; 410-268-8828

GREENSBORO: Mason Dixon Stones, Greensboro Museum, 114 Sunset Street; 410-479-1750

MAY

PERRYVILLE: Spring Fling, Perryville Chamber of
Commerce, in lot adjacent to Rodgers Tavern
off of Roundhouse Drive, 410-642-6066

NORTHEAST: Flower & Garden Market,
St. Mary Anne's Church; 410-287-5522
Newark Symphony, Cecil College; 410-287-1037
The Underground Season,
Cecil College; 410-287-1037

Chestertown: Chestertown Tea Party,
Memorial Day weekend, Town of Chestertown,
410-778-0500

ROCK HALL: Spring Bike Fest, Rock Hall Bayside
Landing & Park, 410-639-7485

CENTREVILLE: May Mart, Queen Anne's County
High School; 410-827-8618

STEVENSVILLE: Kent Island Day, Stevensville
Downtown Center; 410-643-5358
Chesapeake Wine Festival, Terrapin Nature
Area; 410-739-6943

DENTON: Spring Native Plant Sale,
Adkins Arboretum, 410-634-2847

OXFORD: Oxford Invitational Fine Arts Fair,
Oxford Community Center, 410-226-5904

GREENSBORO: Bill Burton Kids Fishing Derby,
Bill Burton State Park, 410-482-6222

JUNE

NORTHEAST: Girl's Night Out & Day Off,
Sandy Cove Ministries; 410-287-5433
Covered Bridge Theater, Cecil College;
410-287-1037
Annual Flag Ceremony,
Northeast Community College; 410-287-6400
Mid-Atlantic Chevelle Show,
Northeast Community Park; 410-287-6400

ELKTON: Hollingsworth House Tours,
Historic Elk Landing; 410-620-6400
National Marriage Day, 101 E. Main Street;
410-620-5076
Flag Day Celebration, Historic Elk Landing;
410-620-6400
Elkton Classic Car Show, downtown; 410-38-5076

CHESAPEAKE CITY: Canal Day, Historic South
Chesapeake City; 410-885-4215

CHESTERTOWN: *Note: For the events below,
visit the website www.chestertownlions.org/events.*
Chestertown Lions Club Spring Barbecue,
101 Greenwood Avenue, Chestertown
Bay to Bay Ride, Chestertown Lions Club

ROCK HALL: Annual Rockfish Tournament,
Rock Hall Bulkhead, 800-421-9176

CENTREVILLE: Thursdays in the Park Concert Series,
Queen Anne's County Arts Council;
410-758-2520

JULY

CENTREVILLE: Historic Open House,
Historic Consortium of Queen Anne's County,
119 S. Commerce Street; 410-758-3010
Bay Music Festival, Queen Anne's County 4H
Park; 410-604-2100

DENTON: Caroline-Dorchester County Fair,
Caroline County 4-H Park, 8230 Detour Road,
Denton; 410-479-0565
(*Note: This event is sometimes held in August)*

STEVENSVILLE: Kent Island Relay for Life,
Kent Island High School; 410-304-2186
Youth Fishing Derby, Terrapin Park;
410-758-0835
Thursdays in the Park, Kent Manor Inn;
410-758-2520

NORTHEAST: Salute to Cecil County Veterans,
Northeast Community Park; 410-287-5801
Chautauqua, Cecil College; 410-287-1037
Mom and Daughters Weekend,
Sandy Cove Ministries; 410-287-5433

CHESAPEAKE CITY: Summer Music in the Park,
Bohemia Avenue and the Canal; 410-392-4750

ROCK HALL: Annual July Fourth Parade,
Main Street; 410-639-7611
Kent County Watermen's Day,
Rock Hall Bulk-head; 410-639-7733
Rock Hall Yacht Club Log Canoe Race,
22759 McKinleyville Road, 410-639-2182

CENTREVILLE: Thursdays in the Park,
Queen Anne's County Arts Council;
410-758-2520
Historic Open House, Historic Sites Consortium;
410-604-2100

QUEENSTOWN: Independence Day Celebration,
The Aspen Institute, Place Grave Site and Wye;
410-758-3010 (Qachistory.org)
Plantation Manor House, Queen Anne's County
Historical Association; 410-827-1623

STEVENSVILLE: Thursdays in the Park,
Kent Manor Inn; 410-758-2520
Kent Fort Farm's Annual Peach Festival,
Kent Fort Farm; 410-643-1650

FEDERALSBURG: Saturday before 4th,
Patriotic Extravaganza; 410-754-8157

AUGUST

NORTHEAST: All Donzi Poker Run, 410-287-9400
Triathlon, Northeast Community Park;
410-287-7522
Summer's Last Hurrah!, Sandy Cove Ministries;
410-287-5433
ELKTON: British Invasion Day,
Historic Elk Landing; 410-620-6400
CHESAPEAKE CITY: Heritage Day,
South Chesapeake City; 410-885-5088
CHESTERTOWN: Chestertown Threshing Day Dinner,
Turner's Creek Landing, Turner's Creek Park;
410-778-1948
CENTREVILLE: Thursdays in the Park Concert Series,
Queen Anne's County Arts Council;
410-758-2520
Queen Anne's County Fair, Maryland State
Fair Board, 4H Park; 410-758-0267
Historic Open House, Historic Sites Consortium
of Queen Anne's County; 410-604-2100
STEVENSVILLE: Thunder on the Narrows,
Kent Island Yacht Club Grounds; 410-725-6222
DENTON: Caroline Summerfest, River Road,
Denton (www.carolinesummerfest.com)

SEPTEMBER

NORTHEAST: Red Hat Fling,
Sandy Cove Ministries; 410-287-5433
Unity in the Community,
Cecil College; 410-287-1037
CHARLESTOWN: Riverfest in Historic Charlestown;
443-303-4088
ELKTON: Fall Fest: Firefighter's Challenge,
North Street; 410-398-5076
CENTREVILLE: Historic Open House,
Historic Sites Consortium; 410-604 -2100
ROCK HALL: Classic and Custom Car Show,
Bayside Avenue, 410-908-8417
Fallfest, The Mainstay,
5753 Main Street; 410-639-9133
STEVENSVILLE: Pumpkin Patch, Kent Fort Farm,
135 Eastern Lane, 410-643-1650

OCTOBER

PERRYVILLE: Autumnfest, Town of Perryville and
Maryland Office of Tourism; 410-642-6066
NORTHEAST: Girl's Night Out & Day Off,
Sandy Cove Ministries; 410-287-5433
Halloween Party, Northeast Community Park;
410-287-5801
ELKTON: Halloween Parade, Elkton Alliance,
Main Street; 410-642-6066
CHESAPEAKE CITY: Cecil County Harvest Dinner,
Granary Restaurant; 410-275-1603
CHESTERTOWN: Annual Historic Chestertown
House Tour, Kent County Tourism and
Economic Development Office; 410-778-0416
Lion's Club Fall Barbecue,
101 Greenwood Avenue, 410-778-7435
(www.chestertownlionsclub.org)
Wildlife Exhibition & Sale,
Kent County Office of Tourism; 410-778-0416
ROCK HALL: Fall Bike Fest, Rock Hall Bayside
Landing and Park; 410-639-7636
CENTREVILLE: Historic Open House,
Historic Sites Consortium; 410-604-2100
QUEENSTOWN: Ham & Oyster Dinner,
Calvary United Methodist Church; 410-827-7713

NOVEMBER

NORTHEAST: Christmas Tree Lighting,
Northeast Community Park; 410-287-5801
Open House Weekend and Santa House,
North East Chamber of Commerce,
410-287-5801 or 410-287-5252
ELKTON: Antique Bottle Show & Sale,
Singerly Fire Hall; 410-738-9960
The Holiday Arts are Alive! A Festival of Trees
and More!,
300 Newark Avenue; 410-398-5076
Holiday Lighting Ceremony,
Downtown; 410-398-5076
CHESTERTOWN: Emmanuel Church Christmas
Bazaar
410-778-3477
Sultana Downrigging and Tall Ships,
Chestertown Harbor, Kent County Tourism and
Economic Development Office, 410-778-0416
DENTON: Festival of Trees
101 Market Street; 410-479-3500
EASTON: Waterfowl Festival, World's Premier
Art Show & Sale,
starts at Dutchman's Lane; 410-822-4567

DECEMBER

PORT DEPOSIT: Candlelight Tour, Port Deposit
Heritage Corporation, 301-378-3866
(*Note: This event is held every even year.*)

NORTHEAST: Cecil County Christmas Parade,
Main Street, 410-287-5801
Cecil Dance presents "The Spirit of Christmas,"
Cecil College; 410-287-3546

ELKTON: Old Fashioned Christmas with
"The Hollingsworths,"
Historic Elk Landing; 410-620-6400

CHESAPEAKE CITY: Candle Light House Tour,
South Chesapeake City, Town Hall on
Bohemia Avenue; 410-553-0071

CHESTERTOWN: The Annual Holiday House Tour
Kent County Tourism and Economic
Development Office; 410-778-0416

ROCK HALL: Boat Parade and Santa's Arrival,
Rock Hall Harbor, Town of Rock Hall,
410-639-7611

CENTREVILLE: Annual Centreville Christmas Parade,
Centreville Christmas Parade Committee;
410-758-1180
Christmas House Tour,
Queen Anne's County Arts Council; 410-758-252
Christmas Train Show,
4H Park Road; 410-758-8640

DENTON: Denton Holiday Parade and Lighting
of the Green, Market Street,
Town of Denton; 410-479-2050

FEDERALSBURG: Christmas Parade, Federalsburg
Lions Club
North and South Main Street; 410-754-8650

Caroline County

Choptank
2010 Census Population: 129

N. 38 41' W. 75 57'

The village of Choptank is three miles southwest of Preston. The town and river take their names from the Choptank Indians who lived close to what today is Cambridge. With the coming of the English colonists in 1698, the native occupants of the land were displaced and assigned land adjacent to Secretary Creek.

Known variously as Medford's Wharf and Leonard's Wharf, Choptank was a popular docking point for steamers carrying cargo and passengers to and from Baltimore. The once-busy steamboat basin is now only two feet deep. A small fleet of work boats and many more pleasure boats, however, are a common sight on the waters around Cambridge to the south.

ACTIVITIES
Please check the internet or call ahead, as dates, times, and locations may change.

⚓ MARINAS
None, but there is the Choptank Towne Yacht Basin, which offers gasoline and a few transient slips.

Choptank, MD

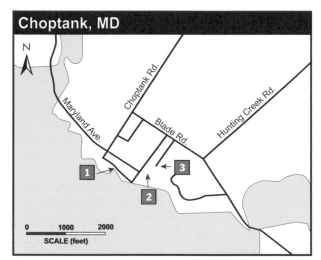

POINTS OF INTEREST
1 CHOPTANK TOWNE YACHT BASIN
2 FORMER OLD SCHOOL,
   Choptank Main Street
3 SMITH'S POINT (VOSHELL PLACE)

Denton

2010 Census Population: 4,418

N. 38 53' W. 75 50'

The town of Denton was established in 1783 near a bend in the Choptank River known as Pig Point. It was the spot designated by the Maryland General Assembly in 1773 as the new county seat. The Revolutionary War postponed construction of a new county courthouse and, when the time came to build one, the town of Goldsboro demanded that it be considered instead. The citizens of Caroline County finally settled the matter in 1790 when they chose Denton instead of Pig Point or Goldsboro.

The county courthouse was completed in 1797 and served for nearly one hundred years. It was finally replaced by the present Victorian-style building, which sits on a public square overlooking the river. It is the only building that survived when the rest of the town was burned during the Civil War. The fire was caused by Fourth of July fireworks set off by Union soldiers camped in town.

Denton had developed as a financial center and, on the eve of the Civil War, boasted three commercial banks. Schooners and other Bay sailing craft and later steamboats carried freight and passengers to and from Denton into the early twentieth century, but eventually couldn't compete with the railroad. Sail-powered vessels continued to carry passengers and some freight into the 1940s. Today, the center of town is distinguished by county government offices and those of lawyers and related businesses.

In the days before World War I, Denton was an important center for horse-racing and a half-mile track in town was very popular. In those early days of the twentieth century, the Brick Hotel was a thriving inn filled with drummers and merchants who did business with the local canneries and shirt factories in the county. At one time, gypsies, who used the village as a way station in their travels, had a large camp just outside of town.

Though many people bound for the beach speed past Denton on Route 404, those who turn aside will find Denton to be a town of provincial charm. It's described locally as the heart in the heart of the country. Places to visit include the Choptank River Heritage Center and Tuckahoe Neck Meeting House in West Denton. Also worthy of note are the historic Caroline County Courthouse and the well-preserved 1883 Schoolhouse, now a Women's Club. Visitors will find a wide variety of eateries to satisfy all tastes and overnight accommodations at the Best Western Denton Inn. For boaters, there's the Choptank Marina on Water Street.

Throughout the year there are a number of events, starting in the spring with the Native Plant Sale at Adkins Arboretum. Come summer, the town is the site of the Caroline County Fair and Caroline Summerfest, and winter is marked by Christmas in Caroline and Denton's Lighting of the Green and Christmas Parade.

MARINAS
- Choptank Marina, Water Street, south of Preston

LODGING
- Best Western Denton Inn, near Denton

RESTAURANTS
- Bullock's Deli, 422 N. Sixth Street, 410-479-0270
- Chesapeake Culinary Center at the Emerson House, 4 S. First Street, 410-479-0015
- China House, 16 Denton Plaza, 410-479-3595
- Colosseum Ristorante and Lounge, 42 Denton Plaza, 410-479-4600
- Joe's Hoagie House, 601 N. 6th Street, 410-479-3384
- La Michhoacana, 18 Denton Plaza, 410-479-9552
- Lily Pad Café And Catering, 4 S. First Street, 410-479-0700
- Market Street Café, 200 Market Street, 410-479-3100
- Snappy's Bar & Grill, Denton Plaza, 410-479-5660
- Subway, 601 Legion Road, 410-479-3344

SPECIAL EVENTS AND ACTIVITIES
Please check the internet or call ahead, as dates, times, and locations may change.
- **May**: Spring Native Plant Sale, Adkins Arboretum
- **August**: Caroline County Fair (www.carolinecountyfair.com) and Caroline Summerfest (www.carolinesummerfest.com)
- **December**: Christmas in Caroline: Lighting of the Green & Christmas Parade

Denton, MD

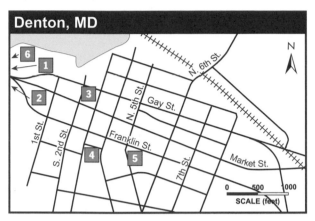

N. 6th St. | N. 5th St. | Gay St. | N. 5th St. | 1st St. | S. 2nd St. | Franklin St. | 7th St. | Market St.

SCALE (feet) 0 500 1000

POINTS OF INTEREST
1 CHOPTANK RIVER HERITAGE CENTER, 10215 River Landing Road, West Denton.
2 ROE AND NICHOLS SHIRT FACTORY, 1885 River Landing Road
3 MUSEUM OF RURAL LIFE, 12 N. Second Street
4 CAROLINE COUNTY COURTHOUSE 1883 SCHOOLHOUSE/WOMEN'S CLUB, 104 S. Second Street
5 TUCKAHOE NECK MEETING HOUSE, West Denton

Federalsburg
2010 Census Population: 2,739   N. 38 412' W. 75 46'

The town of Federalsburg was originally identified as Northwest Fork because of its location on a branch of the Nanticoke River known as Marshyhope Creek. The settlement developed around a general store, opened there in 1789 by Cloudsberry Jones. Another early name, Northwest Forks Bridge, indicates that there was a bridge over the creek in those early days. Politics, not location, played a part in the town's name change when a Federalist Party meeting was held there in the early 1800s.

Located in an area rich with timber, lumber mills flourished in the newly-named town of Federalsburg. It also became a center for shipbuilding, despite the shallowness of the creek. Undaunted, the shipbuilders loaded their hulls on scows to be carried to the deeper waters of the Nanticoke. In addition to milling and shipbuilding, the slave trade was a prosperous business until the Civil War.

A notable landmark in Federalsburg is Exeter, a well-preserved early nineteenth-century house. The use of cypress shingle siding is believed to be unique in Caroline County,

as is the floor plan. Records of the Maryland Historical Trust note that such details indicate "a builder of some sophistication."

The railroad, from Seaford, Delaware, reached Federalsburg in 1868, sparking a new enterprise. The shipping of refrigerated, perishable fruits and vegetables became a mainstay of the local economy and remains so today. The historic train station has been restored as the headquarters of the Maryland and Delaware Railroad Company. The company, formed in 1977, operates a branch railroad line of the former Penn Central Railroad. Today, the railroad operates on more than 120 miles of track. A special train, known as the Hurlock Express, provides rides from Hurlock's historic train station to the one in Federalsburg during the Hurlock Fall Festival.

In recent years, there has been a noticeable influx of people, leading to expansion and development in and around town. Even so, the famed Eastern Shore hospitality and old-fashioned customs characterize life in Federalsburg.

ACTIVITIES
Please check the internet or call ahead, as dates, times, and locations may change.

⚓ MARINAS
• Marina Park, South Main Street; it has four slips for motorboats only.

🛏 LODGING
• Idylwild Farm Bed & Breakfast, Smithville Road, 410-754-91451 (www.idylwildfarm.com)

🍴 RESTAURANTS
• Bloomingdale Quick Mart, 3078 Bloomingdale Avenue, 410-754-8230
• Café Milano, 108 E. Central Avenue, 410-754-0155

Federalsburg, MD

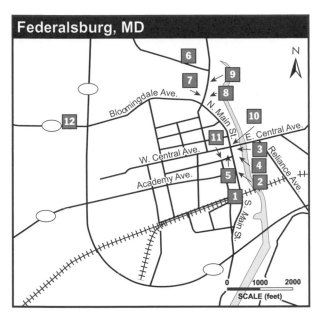

POINTS OF INTEREST

1 FEDERALSBURG, SEAFORD, AND CAMBRIDGE RAILWAY STATION, c. 1870, 160 Railroad Avenue
2 SANDY HILL, 324 S. Main Street
3 DAVIS HOUSE, home of Senator Wilmer Davis, 122 E. Central Avenue
4 DAVIS POULTRY BUSINESS, Davis Lane
5 TOWN HALL, 118 N. Main Street
6 ZION METHODIST CHURCH, 211 Laurel Street

7 EXETER HOUSE,
408 Old Denton Road, 1731
> The original patent was signed to
> Thomas Dill, later rector; it's named after Exeter Cathedral,
> Devonshire, England.

8 HERRING HILL ("IDYLWILD"),
415 Old Denton Road

9 MERRIKAN'S FEED STORE,
501 Old Denton Road

10 CHARLIE WALKER'S HOUSE ("LILLYSHALL"),
516 Old Denton Road; he was a famous local painter.

11 FEDERALSBURG HERITAGE SOCIETY, Covey Williams Alley,
behind the Town Hall off of Morris Avenue
> Built in a renovated garage, this society houses a large
> collection of old pictures and memorabilia about
> Fredericksburg and its history.

12 NICOLITE CHURCH SITE (QUAKER MEETING HOUSE),
Preston Road, 1 mile out of town on the right

Greensboro
2010 Census Population: 1,931   N. 38 59 W. 75 48

In 1732, it was suggested that a town be created at the bridge near the head of the Choptank River, at the "Great Bend," as the S-shaped curve in the river was called. Nothing was done, but that didn't stop Peter Rich. A merchant and innkeeper, Rich patented thirty-one acres at the western end of the bridge and named it "Bridgetown." In 1736, he purchased a two hundred-acre tract adjoining Bridgetown. His land passed to his daughter and her husband, Nathan Harrington, and then to their son, Peter, in 1778. He began selling lots in a new town now called Choptank Bridge. As the story goes, at the end of the American Revolution, returning soldiers changed the town's name again. They called it Greensboro to honor their former commander, General Nathaniel Greene, and, in 1791, the General Assembly made it official.

One of the earliest buildings in town was a four-cell prison housed in a converted brick warehouse belonging to local businessman William Hughett. The building survived well into the nineteenth century and was used at various times to dry tobacco and for making baskets, packing cases, etc. In 1825, it was a tannery and then a drying house; still later, it was a school. Eventually, it fell into disuse and most of its brickwork was removed. Throughout Greensboro's early years, it served the needs of area farmers and was a busy inland port for shipping grain. In 1920, the Helvetia Milk Condensing Company, better known later as Pet Milk, opened one of the largest plants on the peninsula and employed about thirty men.

Greensboro had several churches. One of the earliest is the Catholic Church of the Holy Trinity, which was built in 1875. In 1789, the Methodists built their first church, which was rebuilt and later replaced in 1903 by the one in use today. Greensboro is also distinguished by a number of federal and Victorian homes and buildings. Willow Grove is one of the few Georgian-style houses in Caroline County. It was built by Matthew Driver, Jr., who, with three other members of Congress from Caroline County, ratified the United States Constitution at the Convention held in Annapolis in 1788. It was listed on the National Register of Historic Places in 1972. The Leonard House, which is believed to have been built in 1832 as the parsonage for the Second Methodist Church, was listed on the National Register of Historic Places in 1988.

⬛ MARINAS
- Greensboro Boat Ramp, off Sunset Avenue

⬛ LODGING
- Riverside Restaurant & Hotel, N. Main Street, 410-634-5400
- Holiday Park *(camping and group activities on weekends)*

⬛ RESTAURANTS
- Bodie's Dairy Market, 100 Main Street, 410-482-8124
- Greensboro Deli, 105 Whiteleysburg Road, 410-482-6077
- Greensboro Restaurant, 101 S. Main Street, 410-482-8633
- Harry's, 116 W. Sunset Avenue, 410-482-6758
- La Delizia, 322 N. Main Street, 410-482-8224
- Mr. D's, 610 Sunset Avenue, 410-482-9020

SPECIAL EVENTS AND ACTIVITIES
Please check the internet or call ahead, as dates, times, and locations may change.
- **April**: Mason/Dixon Stones, Saturdays, Greensboro Museum, 114 W. Sunset Street; 410-479-1750
- **May 3rd**: Greensboro Children's Fishing Derby; 410-482-6222

Greensboro, MD

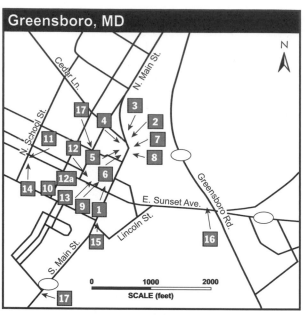

SCALE (feet)

POINTS OF INTEREST

1 BOULAISE HOUSE, 109 N. Main Street
The only surviving townhouse in the town; the two-story wing on the north side is the original 1790 house.

2 COOK-TAYLOR HOUSE, c. 1784, 124 N. Main Street; rebuilt by Robert H. Taylor

3 RIVERSIDE HOTEL, 1912, 204 N. Main Street; newly reopened

4 WYATT-JARMAN HOUSE, mid-1880s, 207 N. Main Street; Jarman was a merchant and cabinet maker

5 CLINTON-JARMAN HOUSE, 205 N. Main Street; he built the Riverside Hotel

6 McCLYMENT HOUSE, 1860, 203 N. Main Street; structurally related to first forms and plans in the county

7 F. ROE HOUSE, 118 N. Main Street; Victorian home of the canner

8 CLINTON PORTER/ANDREW ROE HOUSE, 116 N. Main Street; Roe was a fruit and vegetable packer and a Maryland Senator

9 MT. PLEASANT UNITED METHODIST CHURCH, 1905, 121 Park Avenue

10 BENJAMIN HOUSE, 203 Maple Avenue; a fine example of American farmhouse construction

11 BERNARD HOUSE, c. 1865, 400 W. Sunset Avenue; built by Joseph Bernard, one of Greensboro's leading businessmen

12 LOG CABIN HOME OF GREENSBORO HISTORICAL SOCIETY, 114 W. Sunset Avenue

12a ST. PAUL'S UNITED METHODIST EPISCOPAL CHURCH, 300 W. Sunset Avenue

13 GOLDSBOROUGH HOUSE, 116 W. Sunset Avenue
> Currently being renovated as an upscale restaurant, the house is one of the largest and least altered in the town.

14 MK PORTER HOUSE, c. 1865, 201 W. Sunset Avenue

15 MALONE HOUSE, 204 S. Main Street; built by one of the town's most prominent physicians

16 RIVERDEEN, 13331 Greensboro Road
> Built as a summer home by Addison A. Christian, manager of Gimbel brothers store in Philadelphia, it was used as a maternity hospital during World War II.

17 HARRINGTON HOUSE, c. 1787, 200 Church Street; Peter Harrington is credited with the founding of Greensboro

Cecil County

Charlestown

2010 Census Population: 1,183

N. 39 34' W. 75 58'

Charlestown, on the west side of the Northeast River, was founded with great hopes for growth and prosperity soon to follow. It was selected by the Maryland General Assembly in 1742 for its strategic location at the head of the Bay to become a major shipping center. The original Charlestown Wharf extended three hundred feet into the river and was wide enough to handle three wagons abreast. Near the wharf was a house for inspecting and grading flour before it was shipped. Grains were stored in a large storehouse, three stories high and eighty feet long. The walls of the first floor were thirty-six inches thick. Until silting began to set in, the wharf was a receiving and shipping point for Bay- and even ocean-going vessels. Fishing has also been an important industry in Charlestown, and many barrels of salt herring were shipped from there.

From 1782 to 1787, Charlestown was the county seat. No courthouse was ever built, but there was a small stone jail. Most of the town's citizenry prospered by working the waterfront and providing services needed by those who lived in the town and surrounding countryside. By the turn of the nineteenth century, however, Elkton had eclipsed Charlestown as Cecil County's chief urban center. The town began a slow, but steady, decline that saw little change in its original character.

Today's Historic District, which was approved in 1974, encompasses the original 150 acres, contains about 175 structures, and is bounded by Tasker Street, Ogle Street, Louisa Lane, and the Northeast River. With the exception of a number of Victorian-era structures and others from the late-nineteenth and early-twentieth century, Charlestown is essentially unchanged from its colonial beginnings. Hard times in the early twentieth century resulted in very few new structures being built. Instead, residents altered or added to existing ones.

As is seen elsewhere in towns on the Shore, several of Charlestown's early buildings are of log construction, but because of the availability of stone and clay in the Upper Bay, Charlestown's eighteenth-century buildings display a variety of materials, including log, frame, stone, and brick.

Among the 175 buildings in the Historic District, fourteen are documented to be from the eighteenth century. The largest of those served as inns that filled in colonial days during the popular Charlestown Fair, held each spring and fall. People came to the fairs from Pennsylvania and Maryland's Eastern and Western shores to buy and sell livestock and a variety of goods and enjoy several days of revelry. The town still has its Fair days.

A catalog of a few buildings in the Historic District helps to illustrate the character of life in the town at various times. The 1745 Hamilton House is probably the most intriguing house in Charlestown. It may be the oldest and has escaped any remodeling since it was built. The 1750 Paca House was the home of John Paca, son of Maryland's Governor William Paca. The 1760 Still House on Water Street is one of ten colonial taverns. The Indian Queen, built in 1740, was a tavern for many years. During the French and Indian War, soldiers were quartered there. At its heart, the 1755 Red Lyon was constructed of poplar log planks, some twelve inches wide and five inches thick. At one point, the right half was used as a store. George Washington, who kept meticulous records, noted several stops in Charlestown when he stayed at the brick 1787 Georgian-style mansion. The frame 107 House, built in 1810, is pegged together and the siding is shiplapped, indicating that it may have been built by one of Charlestown's many shipbuilders. It was a Methodist parsonage until recently and several organizations hold their meetings there today. The 1762 Davis House was distinctive enough to appear in a sketch by Benjamin Latrobe, the federal government's *Architect of the Capitol*, made in 1813. Eagle Point, dated 1792, on Conestoga Road, was once a gun club. Finally, the Town Hall and Post Office was built as a school and used until 1861 when it was put to its present use.

ACTIVITIES

Please check the internet or call ahead, as dates, times, and locations may change.

🛥 MARINAS
- Avalon Yacht Basin, Water and Louisa Streets, 410-287-6722
- Charlestown Marina, 4 Water Street, 410-287-8125
- Lee's Marina, 726 Water Street, 410-287-5100
- North East River Marina, 724 Water Street, 410-287-5298

🏠 LODGING
- The Wellwood Club, 523 Water Street, 410-287-6666

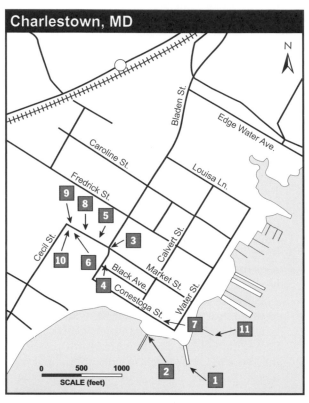

Charlestown, MD

POINTS OF INTEREST

1 COLONIAL WHARF
   Once visited by ocean-going vessels, this is now the site of an inspection house and grain storehouse.

2 EAGLE POINT, Conestoga Road, between Calvert and Water streets, 1791; formerly the Eagle Point Gun Club

3 ST. JOHN'S METHODIST CHURCH, 1856; congregation originally housed in present-day parsonage across the street

4 TOWN HALL/POST OFFICE, 1877
   This building was a school until 1861, then the Town Hall and Post Office.

5 BRICK MANSION, 1787
High-style Georgian architecture;
George Washington recorded several stops there.

6 PACA HOUSE, 1750
Originally one-story, it was the residence of
John Paca, Jr., son of Governor William Paca.

7 THORN HOUSE, c. 1762

8 INDIAN QUEEN, 1740
This early tavern was used during the French
and Indian War to quarter soldiers.

9 RED LYON, 1755
Notable poplar construction; right half housed the Black family
store. This is a fine example of shiplap construction.

10 107 HOUSE, 1810
Probably constructed by ship carpenters; it was formerly a
Methodist parsonage and is now a general meetinghouse.

11 CHARLESTOWN WHARF
It originally ran three hundred into river and
was wide enough for three wagons abreast.

Chesapeake City
2010 Census Population: 673   N. 39 32' W. 75 49'

As early as the seventeenth century, local settlers, including the famous Dutch surveyor Augustine Herrman, recognized the possibility of connecting the Chesapeake Bay with the Delaware River. In the mid 1760s, possible canal routes were surveyed. Not until 1824, after an abandoned start farther north, did construction of the canal begin. At its completion in 1829, only two structures are documented in the town, then known as Bohemia Village. One was a pre-Revolution building known as Chick's Tavern House and a lock house for collecting tolls. The town subsequently grew in response to the needs of the canal operations and commerce.

In 1839, the town's name was changed to Chesapeake City in anticipation of big things to come. It was incorporated in 1849 when the population reached four hundred. By the early twentieth century, the federal government realized the canal's strategic value and bought the canal in 1919. In 1927, the government lowered the canal to sea level. A vertical drawbridge connected the north and south sides of Chesapeake City until July 28, 1942, when the tanker *Franz Klasen* struck the bridge, completely destroying it. The current high suspension bridge was completed in 1949.

Maintaining the canal and attending to the needs of the many commercial and pleasure boats that use the canal are a large part of the city's business, which also thrives on the area's rich history. On the south side of the bridge is the stone Pumphouse, which houses the giant wooden waterwheel that replaced water lost when vessels passed through the canal. It is a national historic landmark. As notably visible as the bridge is the dome of St. Basil's Ukrainian Catholic Church, built in 1920 to serve a small farming community of Ukrainian families. Both the south and north sides of town are distinguished by many restored homes, churches, shops, and galleries. On the North side is a neighborhood of older homes that housed watermen and canal workers. South Chesapeake City celebrates Canal Day every June, summer music in the park in July, Heritage Day in August, and a Candlelight House Tour in December. The city's historical area is on Maryland's Historic Registry. There are many fine restaurants, B&Bs, and marinas for transient and seasonal boat dockage.

⊠ MARINAS
- Bohemia Vista Yacht Basin, 140 Vista Marina Road, 410-885-5402
- Chesapeake Inn & Marina, 505 Second Street, 410-885-2040
  (*Also includes a restaurant*)
- Summit North Marina, 302-8236-1800

⊠ LODGING
- Blue Max, 300 Bohemia Avenue, 410-885-2781
- Inn at the Canal, 104 Bohemia Avenue, 410-885-5995
- Pardon My Garden, 213 Bohemia Avenue, 410-885-5048
- Schaefer's New Canal House, North Chesapeake City, 410-885-2200
- Ship Watch Inn, 410 First Street, 410-885-5300

⊙ RESTAURANTS
- Bayard House Restaurant, 410-885-5040
- Bohemia Café & Bakery, 2nd and George Streets, 410-885-3066
- Canal Creamery, 9 Bohemia Avenue, 410-885-3314
- The Tap Room Seafood Restaurant, 2nd and Bohemia Streets, 410-885-9873
- Village Café, 410 Second Street, 410-885-2294
- Yacht Club Restaurant, 410-885-2267

SPECIAL EVENTS AND ACTIVITIES

Please check the internet or call ahead, as dates, times, and locations may change.

- **April**: Cecil Dance Theater, 2755 Augustine Hermann Highway; 410-287-3546
- **June**: Canal Day Historic South Chesapeake City; 410-885-2415
- **July**: Summer Music in the Park, Bohemia Avenue and the Canal; 410-392-5740
- **August**: Heritage Day, South Chesapeake City; 410-885-5088
- **October**: Cecil County Harvest Dinner, Granary Restaurant; 410-275-1603
- **December**: Candlelight House Tour, South Chesapeake City, Town Hall, Bohemia Avenue; 410--553-0071

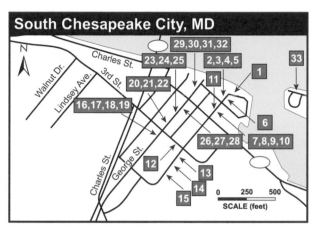

POINTS OF INTEREST – SOUTH CHESAPEAKE CITY, HISTORIC DISTRICT

1 THE OLDE WHARF, 9 Bohemia Avenue
2 BAYARD HOUSE RESTAURANT, 11 Bohemia Avenue
3 CAPTAIN LAYMAN HOUSE, 13 Bohemia Avenue
4 RILEY HOUSE, 15 Bohemia Avenue
5 CROPPER HOUSE, 19 Bohemia Avenue
6 FRANKLIN HALL, 20 Bohemia Avenue

7 J. M. Reed Back Creek General Store, 100 Bohemia Avenue
8 Brady Rees House, 102 Bohemia Avenue
9 Hagar-Kinter House, 106 Bohemia Avenue
10 Chesapeake City Town Hall, 108 Bohemia Avenue
11 Old National Bank (now Dragon Fly),
   109 Bohemia Avenue
12 Trinity Methodist Church, 3rd Street, between Bohemia
   Avenue and George Street
13 William Lindsey House
   (The Blue Max Inn), 300 Bohemia Avenue
14 John Lindsey, 308 Bohemia Avenue
15 Lindsey Clayton House, 310 George Street
16 Araminta Griffith House, 317 George Street

17 Cooling Deschane House, 315 George Street
18 Annie Dunham, 311 George Street
19 Dr. Davis House, 301 George Street
20 Savin Conroy House, 221 George Street
21 Thomas Conroy House, 219 George Street
22 Karsner Cottage, 211 George Street
23 Boulden House, 205 George Street
24 Bryan House, 203 George Street
25 Peaper House, 201 George Street
26 Banks Steele House, 210-212 George Street

CECIL COUNTY

27 BEINSWANGER HOUSE, 208 George Street
28 BEINSWANGER HENN HOUSE, 206 George Street
29 METZ HOUSE, 111 George Street
30 VEAL CONROY HOUSE, 109 George Street
31 FRANCIS KUH HOUSE, 107 George Street
32 JOHN CHANDLER HOUSE, 105 George Street
33 CHESAPEAKE AND DELAWARE CANAL MUSEUM
AND CANAL PUMP HOUSE, 815 Bethel Road

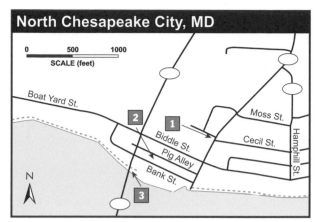

North Chesapeake City, MD

SCALE (feet)
0   500   1000

Boat Yard St.
Moss St.
Cecil St.
Hamphill St.
Biddle St.
Pig Alley
Bank St.

N

POINTS OF INTEREST – NORTH CHESAPEAKE CITY

1 St. Rose of Lima Catholic Church,
   Biddle Street
2 Joseph Schaefer's original house,
   Pig Alley
3 Schaefer's Canal House Restaurant,
   off Route 213

* *The town walking tour has even more historic
   locations. A copy of the walking tour map can
   be found in local shops.*

Elkton

2010 Census Population 15,443

N. 39 37' W.75 50'

The town of Elkton was established between the two creeks that feed the Elk River. First settled by Finns and Swedes, it was known originally as "Head of Elk." The port was a flourishing place, mainly for shipping flour from the Eastern Shore and nearby counties of Pennsylvania. Throughout the 1700s, wheat from Lancaster, Pennsylvania, supported a great number of grist mills along Big and Little Elk Creeks. A pulp mill that once operated there was the third largest in the country. The Elk River was a significant north-south trade route, made even more so when the *Chesapeake*, the first steamboat on the Bay, tied up at Elk Landing.

Zebulon Hollingsworth created Elk Landing, at the head of the Elk River, on two parcels of land he acquired in the early 1700s. He and others built docks and warehouses there as well as an inn that is still standing. Zebulon, Jr., lived through the stirring days of the American Revolution. In August 1777, British General Howe landed at Oldfield Point and marched his 18,000 troops from the Landing to Head of Elk; before going on, he hoped to seize Philadelphia. In 1781, Lafayette loaded his troops onto transports at Head of Elk on their way to America's final victory at Yorktown, Virginia. In 1786, the Cecil County seat of government moved to Head of Elk and the name of the town was changed to Elkton the next year. The British returned to the Chesapeake during the War of 1812 and spread fear throughout the upper Bay until they were turned back at Fort Defiance on the Western bank of the Elk River, thus saving Elkton.

The coming of the New Castle to Frenchtown Railroad, the opening of the C&D Canal in 1829, and the Philadelphia, Wilmington, and Baltimore Railroad in 1837 marked the beginning of Elk Landing's decline. There was a ray of hope that it might be slowed when, in the late nineteenth century, boat builder Henry Deibert launched a number of massive canal boats, releasing them sideways into Little Elk Creek. By 1919, however, silting closed area creeks to boat building and that industry moved to Chesapeake City

A very different industry developed in the early twentieth century. Thanks to laws in New York, New Jersey, and Pennsylvania, as well as a Pennsylvania Railroad stop in Elkton, couples looking to be married avoided the waiting period in those states with a quick trip to Elkton. Until Maryland passed its own law establishing a waiting period in 1938, couples could drive or take a train from New York or Philadelphia to Elkton. They would be met by hustling cab drivers waiting to take them to one of several wedding chapels. Despite Maryland's new law, Elkton continued to be known as America's "Gretna Green." A few chapels are still operating and the town celebrates National Marriage Day every June.

A Wedding Garden is among the historic sites that beckon visitors in Elkton. Year-round the Hollingsworth House at historic Elk Landing is open for tours. Annual Paper Americana and Bottle shows at the Singerly Fire Hall are widely attended, as is Elkton's own "Antiques Road Show" in January. During the summer, the Cecil County Farmers Market is held in the courthouse parking lot. The town regularly celebrates Defenders' Day, Flag Day, British Invasion Day, and, of course, Halloween has its parade. At Christmas, there's a festival of trees and a holiday lights ceremony downtown. Boaters who visit will find a number of marinas to meet their needs. In and around Elkton are many inns, hotels, motels, and restaurants.

⌦ MARINAS
- The Cove Marina, 11 Main Sail Drive, Locust, 410-620-5505
- Elk Haven Marina, 1735 Oldpoint Road, 410-398-4640
- Elk Point Marina, 250 Elk Point Drive, 410-398-6600
- Locust Point Marina, 145 River Road, Locust, 410-392-4994
- Taylor's Marina, 46 River Road, 410-392-3588
- Triton Marina, 285 Plum Point Road, 410-398-7515

⌦ LODGING
- Days Inn, 311 Belle Hill Road, 410-392-5010
- Elkton Inn Motel, 291 E. Pulaski Highway, 410-398-0530
- Elkton Lodge, 200 Belle Hill Road, 410-398-9400
- Hawthorn Suites, 304 Belle Hill Road, 410-620-9494
- Hampton Inn, 2 Warner Road, 410-398-7777
- Knight's Inn, 262 Belle Hill Road, 410-6680
- Motel 6, 223 Belle Hill Road, 410-392-5020
- Sutton Motel, 405 E. Pulaski Highway, 410-398-3830

⌦ RESTAURANTS
- Howard House, North and Main Streets, 410-398-4646
- Judy's Java Firehouse Café, 215 N. Street, 410-996-8648
- Main Street Café, 126 E. Main Street, 410-620-5100
- Moveable Fare & Catering & Café, 420 N. Bridge Street, 410-392-5703
- The Renaissance Restaurant, 156 W. Main Street, 410-398-4241

There are many more out of the central city.

SPECIAL EVENTS AND ACTIVITIES
Please check the internet or call ahead, as dates, times, and locations may change.
- **January**: Annual Paper Americana Show, Singerly Fire Hall, 410-398-7735
  Elkton's Own Antique Road Show, 100 Railroad Avenue, 410-398-5076
- **February**: Heart to Heart: A Quilting Discussion, Historic Elk Landing, 410-620-6400
- **April**: Hollingsworth House Tours, Historic Elk Landing, 410-620-6400
  Defender's Day, Historic Elk Landing, 410-620-6400
- **June**: Cecil County Farmer's Market, Fridays and Saturdays, Courthouse Parking Lot, 410-996-8469
  Hollingsworth House Tours, Historic Elk Landing, 410-620-6400
  National Marriage Day, 101 E. Main Street, 410-398-5076
  Flag Day Celebration, Historic Elk Landing, 410-620-6400
  Elkton Classic Car Show, Downtown Elkton, 410-398-5076
- **July**: Cecil County Farmer's Market (see June description)
- **August**: Cecil County Farmer's Market (see June description)
  Hollingsworth House Tour, Historic Elk Landing, 410-620-6400
  British Invasion Day, Historic Elk Landing, 410-620-6499
- **September**: Cecil County Farmer's Market (see June description)
  Hollingsworth House Tours, Historic Elk Landing, 410-620-6400
  Elkton Fall Fest/Firefighter's Combat Challenge, North Street, 410-398-5076
- **October**: Cecil County Farmer's Market (see June description)
  Hollingsworth House Tours, Historic Elk Landing, 410-620-6400
  Halloween Parade, Downtown Elkton, 410-398-5076
- **November**: Hollingsworth, House Tours Historic Elk Landing, 410-620-6400
  Antique Bottle Show & Sale, Singerly Fire Hall, 410-738-9960
  The Holiday Arts Are Alive! A Festival of Trees & More, 300 Newark Avenue, 410-398-5076
  Holiday Lighting Ceremony Downtown, 410-398-5076
- **December**: Old-Fashioned Christmas with "The Hollingsworths," Elk Landing, 410-620-6400

Elkton, MD

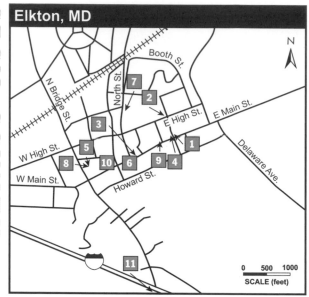

POINTS OF INTEREST

1 HISTORICAL SOCIETY/ARTS COUNCIL, 135 East Main Street

2 LOG CABIN BEHIND THE HISTORICAL SOCIETY

3 ELKTON ALLIANCE AND CHAMBER OFFICE AND WEDDING GARDEN
   The Alliance is a non-profit corporation working with the Town of Elkton to revitalize and preserve the town.

4 MITCHELL HOUSE, East Main Street, 1769-81
   This home of Dr. Abraham Mitchell was done in the early and late Georgian style.

5 CURRENT AMERICAN LEGION HALL, 129 West Main Street, c. 1760
   Home of Col. Henry Hollingsworth, colonel of the Elk Battalion of militia who obtained supplies for American and French forces on their way to the battle of Yorktown during the Revolutionary War.

6 HOWARD HOUSE, 101 West Main Street, 1853; once a bustling tavern.

7 TRINITY EPISCOPAL CHURCH, 105 Bridge Street, 1832
   Gothic-style, the current church was erected and consecrated on St. Barnabas Day, 1867.

8 HOLLINGSWORTH TAVERN, 205 W. Main Street; Generals Hollingsworth and Washington spent time here

9 COURTHOUSE, 129 East Main Street

10 OLD ARMORY, Railroad Avenue at Bow Street, 1915

11 a-c ELK LANDING: a. main house, b. original house (c 1760), c. original boat landing, 590 Landing Lane; the creek is now silted in.

> Elk Landing was the home, trading post, and base of operations of the Swedish-American trader, John Hansson Steelman (1655–1749), who occupied the site between 1693 and 1710. Site was a shipping and supply port for the Continental Army and one of the defense locations during the War of 1812. 410-620-6400.

Fredericktown
2010 Census Not available

Georgetown
2010 Census Not available

In 1736, the Maryland General Assembly created a town on thirty acres of land at the ferry landing on the Sassafras River in Cecil County. It was named Fredericktown in honor of England's Prince Frederick, the ill-fated son of King George II, who died as a young boy. Four days later, the citizens of Kent County petitioned the Assembly for a town on the opposite end of the ferry. They wanted to ship their trade goods from their own wharves on their side of the river. The second town was named Georgetown. In 1747, a tobacco inspector for each county was established in the appropriate town. For the most part, the towns went their separate ways until the French and Indian War in 1754 caused British troops to be quartered in their homes. The following year, some thirty to forty Acadians seeking refuge from Nova Scotia settled in Kent and Cecil Counties, most in tiny Fredericktown.

The towns grew slowly and prospered. Many of their supplies and manufactured goods arrived from Baltimore aboard a weekly packet boat. Everything ran smoothly until the Revolutionary War, which, in 1777, brought three hundred British ships carrying an enormous army to anchor nearby. The British, however, were intent on capturing Elkton at the head of the Bay and spared the two towns. They were not so lucky during the War of 1812, when the British fired artillery and

rockets into Fredericktown. The entire town was looted and burned. Georgetown was taken without a shot being fired. Two dozen businesses, houses, stables, and storage buildings were pillaged and burned. The British burned all but the two houses belonging to the indomitable Miss Kitty Knight.

As the British soldiers, under Admiral Cockburn, approached to set the houses afire, they found Kitty Knight standing in the doorway. "You are about to burn a helpless old lady," she informed them. "I shall not leave. If you burn this house, you burn me with it." They didn't challenge her and went on to set fire to the house next door. Again, she protested, saying that the wind would carry sparks to her house. Reluctantly, they left but not before one of the men struck the door with a boarding axe, leaving a mark that still exists today. Two days later the British sailed away. Today, Kitty Knight's house offers food and lodging to visitors.

Traffic and business eventually went elsewhere and, as a result, Fredericktown and Georgetown remained small hamlets until five marinas for private yachts were built in Fredericktown, bringing prosperity to that community. As pleasure boats took precedence, the fishing fleet declined and with it Georgetown on the other side of the river. Today, only a few fishermen remain.

ACTIVITIES
Please check the internet or call ahead, as dates, times, and locations may change.

■ MARINAS *(all in Georgetown unless otherwise noted)*
- Granary Marina, 14020 Augustine Herman Highway, 410-648-5112
- Duffy Creek Marina, 20 Duffy Creek Lane, 410-275-2141
- Georgetown Yacht Basin, 14020 Augustine Herman Highway, 410-648-5112
- Sailing Associates, 2 George Street, 410-275-8171
- Sassafras Harbor Marina, 410-275-1144
- Skipjack Cove Yachting Resort, 150 Skipjack Road, 410-275-2122
- Sailing Associates, 78 George Street, Cecilton, MD 21913; 410-275-8171

▣ RESTAURANTS
- The Granary & Sassafras Grill, 100 George Street, 410-275-1603
- Kennedyville Inn, 11986 Augustine Herman Highway, 410-348-2400
- Kitty Knight House, 14028 Augustine Herman Highway, Geogetown, 410-648-5200
  (*Note: Also has lodging available.)
- Signals Pub, 150 Skipjack Road, 410-275-2122

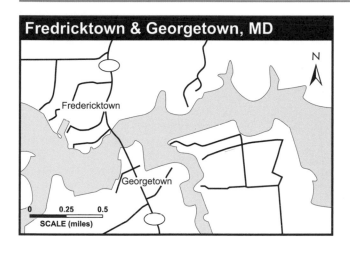

Fredricktown & Georgetown, MD

Frenchtown

The site of Frenchtown, on the Elk River at the head of the Bay, was first settled by Swedes in 1659. They were followed by French Acadians from Nova Scotia, giving rise later to the name Frenchtown. The town grew quickly as a port on a busy water and land route north from Baltimore. It was a prime target during the War of 1812. In April 1813, the British bombarded the town, damaging the wharf, surrounding buildings, and boats in the harbor. Two months later, however, the town had recovered sufficiently to welcome the *Chesapeake*, the first steamboat on the Bay.

An increasing flow of freight, brought to Frenchtown by steamboat, was carried North in wagons to New Castle, Delaware, and then reshipped to Philadelphia. In 1827 the New Castle and Frenchtown Turnpike Company opened a toll road to carry the traffic. The company added a rail line four years later. The first engine, imported from England, had no brakes and must have attracted a crowd every time it approached the town. The engine had to be slowed by roustabouts and porters who caught it and held on until the station master could poke a fence rail in the drive wheels and bring it to a stop.

Within a few years, the two lines consolidated and focused the lens of history on Frenchtown as never before. When the C & D Canal was opened in 1829, the contest between rail, steamboat, and canal was on. The canal, and a new Baltimore to Elkton to Philadelphia rail line opened in 1837, led to the end of the older railroad. Its last train ran in 1854. Soon after, the *Pioneer* and *Ohio*, the remaining steam packets between Frenchtown and Baltimore, ceased to call. The consequence was immediate decline and, finally, complete abandonment. One of the last remaining traces of its former glory was a breakwater of old millstones, which have now all been stolen.

North East

2010 Census Population: 3,572

N. 39 36' W. 75 56'

The earliest date on record for the town of North East is 1716 when a flour mill was erected. Founded in 1719, the Principio Company was operating a furnace and a forge that were part of one of the earliest iron manufacturing companies in the country. The company's furnaces supplied the iron to make the cannon balls and cannon used during the American Revolution and the War of 1812. Thomas Russell, an ironmonger and early manager of the Principio Furnace in Perryville, is buried in the churchyard of the Episcopal Church of St. Mary Anne in North East. The bell tower in the south wall of the church was donated by the Bookings family. The present brick building replaced the original 1742 wooden church, and its congregation is still active in the life of the town. They herald the arrival of spring with the St. Mary Anne Flower and Garden Market in May. Wanderers through the cemetery that surrounds the church will notice crude stone markers identifying the graves of local Native Americans. Another historic church is the North East United Methodist Church. With a congregation that dates from 1781, it is believed to have one of the first, if not the first, parsonage in the state.

Besides the iron furnace, the town of the 1740s consisted of two ordinaries, or taverns, a grist mill, a bake house, and several modest dwellings. The surviving Mill House, adjacent to the mill site, was built in sections, the earliest of which dates from the first quarter of the eighteenth century. Paneling from the house now adorns the Cecil bedroom in Delaware's Winterthur Museum.

The coming of the railroad and the C&D Canal made processing iron closer to the mines more economical and put the survival of the town in doubt, but its citizens rose to the challenge, making the most of the town's rich heritage. Today, you'll find an abundance of antique and gift shops, a full calendar of family-friendly events, a wide array of excellent restaurants, and a waterfront park. Originally a fish house built in 1880, the Upper Bay Museum houses a collection of water-oriented artifacts. A well-known area landmark is the Turkey Point Lighthouse. Standing as a sentinel at the head of the Bay since the colonial days, it is one of the tallest lighthouses on the Chesapeake and was added to the National Register of Historic Places in 2002. Another notable structure is the

Gilpin's Falls Covered Bridge, one of only two surviving covered bridges in the county. Built in 1860, the one hundred-foot span is the longest covered bridge still standing in Maryland. The falls and bridge are named for Samuel Gilpin who operated a flour mill nearby. The bridge was added to the National Register of Historic Places in 2008.

Within the town of North East are many places to visit. One is the old town lockup, on what is now Route 7. The building, like many others, is an excellent example of creative reuse. It was built around 1885 and, until the late 1980s, served as the town hall. The large, frame 5&10 Antique Market, for instance, was originally a hotel. Today it houses a multi-dealer antique market. The Simcoe House, an eighteenth-century log and frame building, has served as both home and offices over the years. Reportedly once the home of a coffin maker, the Hannum House is recognized and recorded on the Maryland Historic Sites Survey. A number of dwellings in North East began life as log houses, often framed on the outside but retaining many of the original structural and interior features. An example is the late eighteenth century colonial-style West House that was once an inn and stage stop. The Federal style is evident in the log-built Reynolds House.

A more recent and vital addition to the town and county is Cecil College, a regional college that offers a variety of academic degree programs. Its students earn associate degrees. They enter the workforce on graduation or continue their education at four-year institutions. The college's theater is the venue for a variety of plays, concerts, and other performances enjoyed by the entire town. A relatively new institution in North East is the Sandy Cove Ministries Chesapeake Lodge, a Christian conference center, campground, and RV park, beautifully situated on the Chesapeake Bay.

The Chesapeake Bay and its waterways attract many boaters who find moorings at several marinas and boat yards in North East. They and other visitors to the town and surrounding area will discover a variety of eateries to satisfy all tastes, from seafood to steaks, gourmet to down-home, and much in between. Worthy of special note: If you happen to be in North East on the second or fourth Sunday of the month during the early morning hours, a home-style breakfast is served at the

North East Fire Station. Comfortable lodging is widely available in North East from modern hotels and inns to the mid-nineteenth century Inn at Northeast Creek, originally the log and frame home belonging to William Roney, a prominent citizen.

The North East Community Park is the scene of many events throughout the year, highlighted by an annual Halloween party and the lighting of a community Christmas Tree. The entire county marks the Christmas season with a parade down the Main Street of North East.

⛵ MARINAS
- Anchor Marina. Inc., Iroquois Drive, 410-287-6000
- Bay Boat Works, 145 Hances Point Road, 410-287-8113
- Jackson Marine Sales, Hances Point, 410-287-9400
- McDaniel Yacht Basin, 15 Grandview Avenue, 410-287-8121
- North East Yacht Sales, 753 Hances Point Road, 410-287-6660
- Wellwood Club Marina, Northeast River, 410-287-6666

🛏 LODGING
- Best Western, 39 Elwoods Road, Exit 100, 410-287-3804
- Comfort Inn & Suites, I-95 & Tr. 2723, Exit 100, 410-287-7100
- Holiday Inn Express, 101 Hotel Plaza, 410-287-0008
- Sandy Cove Ministries Chesapeake Lodge, 60 Sandy Cove Road, 410-287-2683
- William Roney House, 219 S. Main, North East
  (now a bed & breakfast, the Inn at Northeast Creek)

🍴 RESTAURANTS
- Bay Gourmet Seafood & Café, 472 Mauldin Avenue, 410-287-4300
- Empire Restaurant, 111 North East Plaza, 410-287-7988
- Highborne Café, 13 S. Main Street, 410-287-3300
- Knicker's Grille, 1500 Chesapeake Club Drive, 410-287-0200
- Nauti Goose Saloon, 200 Cherry Street, 410-287-7880
- Pier One, 1 N. Main Street, 410-287-6599
- Steak & Main, 1078 S. Main Street, 410-287-3512
- The Victorian Tea Cup Tea Room, 7 Wallace Street, 410-287-9500
- Woody's Crab House, 29 S. Main Street, 410-287-3541

Many other restaurants are nearby within easy driving distance.

SPECIAL EVENTS

Please check the internet or call ahead, as dates, times, and locations may change.

January: New Plays of the American Theatre, Cecil College, Seahawk Drive, 410-287-1037

February: Candlelight Valentine Banquet, Sandy Cove Ministries, 410-287-5433

March: Covered Bridge Theater, Cecil College, Seahawk Drive, 410-287-1037
   Girl's Night Out & Day Off, Sandy Cove Ministries, 410-287-5433

April: Peabody Ragtime Ensemble, Cecil College, Seahawk Drive, 410-287-1037
   Celtic Festival, Cecil College, Seahawk Drive, 410-287-1037
   Cecil Dance Theater, Cecil College, Seahawk Drive, 410-287-1037

May: Flower & Garden Market St. Mary Anne's Church Main St., 410-287-5522
   Newark Symphony Cecil College Seahawk Drive, 410-287-1037
   The Underground Season Cecil College Seahawk Drive, 410-287-1037

June: Girl's Night Out & Day Off, Sandy Cove Ministries, 410-287-5433
   Covered Bridge Theater, Cecil College, Seahawk Drive, 410-287-1037
   Annual Flag Day Ceremony, North East Community Park, 410-620-6400
   North East Garden Tour, Around North East, 410-287-4918
   Mid-Atlantic Chevelle Show, North East Community Park, 410-768-0056

July: Salute to Cecil County Veterans, North East Community Park, 410-287-5801
   Chautauqua Cecil College Seahawk Drive, 410-287-1037
   Moms & Teen Daughters Weekend, Sandy Cove Ministries, 410-287-5433

August: All Donzi Poker Run Riverside Drive, 410-287-9400
   North East Triathlon, North East Community Park, 856-308-7522
   Summer's Last Hurrah!, Sandy Cove Ministries, 410-287-5433

September: Red Hat Fling Sandy Cove Ministries, 410-287-5433
   Unity in the Community, Cecil College, Seahawk Drive, 410-287-1043
   Yesterdays Street Festival, Main Street, 410-287-5600

October: Girl's Night Out & Day Off, Sandy Cove Ministries, 410-287-5433
   Halloween Party, Walnut Street, North East Community Park, 410-287-5801

November: Christmas Tree Lighting, Walnut Street,
   North East Community Park, 410-287-5801
   Open House Weekend Downtown, 410-287-5801
   Santa House, 122 S. Main Street, 410-287-5801

December: Cecil County Christmas Parade, Main Street, 410-287-5801
   Cecil Dance Presents "The Spirit of Christmas," Cecil College, Seahawk Drive, 410-287-3546

North East, MD

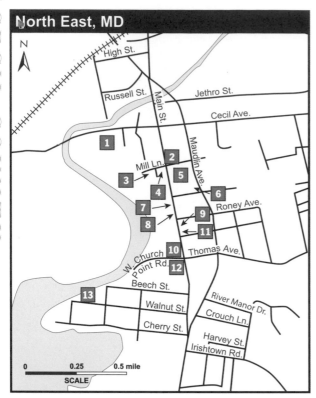

N

0   0.25   0.5 mile
SCALE

POINTS OF INTEREST

1 OLD TOWN LOCKUP, c. 1885, on the old Philadelphia to Baltimore road, today known as Route 7.

2 ANDY ANDERSON'S HOME
   This Victorian-era dwelling, once home of a local hardware store owner, is now a private home.

3 MILL HOUSE; earliest section built in first quarter of the eighteenth century

4 110 S. MAIN STREET; originally served as the post office

5 5&10 ANTIQUE MARKET; originally a hotel, today it is a multi-dealer antique market.

6 SIMCOE HOUSE; log and frame eighteenth century structure

7 REYNOLDS HOUSE;
this log home represents the Federal period

8 THE WILLIAM RONEY HOUSE
This nineteenth century Victorian home is currently
The Inn at North East Creek Bed & Breakfast.

9 HANNUM HOUSE
This home of an early coffin maker is
on the Maryland Historical Sites Survey.

10 ST. MARY ANNE'S CHURCH
This colonial-era church is surrounded by a very early cemetery.
The bell tower was donated by the Bookings family.

11 NORTH EAST UNITED METHODIST CHURCH
Congregation dates from 1781; site of first Methodist parsonage

12 RONEY AND WELLS
This former hardware store closed in 1989. Today it is the
England's Colony on the Bay Gift & Christmas Shop.

13 UPPER BAY MUSEUM; built in 1880 as a fish house,
it houses a collection of water-oriented artifacts.

Perryville

2000 Census Population: 3,762   N. 39 33' W.76 04'

The first visitor to the area was Captain John Smith in 1608. Perryville was first settled in 1632 when Edward Palmer was granted a patent for a settlement on what was then Palmers, now Garrett, Island. In 1695, Lord Baltimore granted George Talbot 31,000 acres of land that included Perryville. At that time, however, it was known as Lower Ferry; in the 1700s, as Susquehanna, and finally, Perryville after Mary Perry Bateman.

During the Revolutionary War, Perryville served as a staging area for the Continental Army. Colonel John Rodgers, who operated the ferry, raised the 5th Company of the Maryland Militia, which became part of the famous Flying Corps in the early stages of the war. Colonel Rodgers' son, John Rodgers, became a Commodore of the American Navy famous for ridding the Mediterranean Sea of the Tripoli Pirates. Commodore Rodgers served with distinction during the War of 1812 and is known as the "Father of the American Navy."

In the 1800s, Perryville was the center point of the Wilmington to Baltimore Rail Line. During the Civil War, the line between Perryville and Baltimore was destroyed. To transport troops and supplies to Annapolis, the Union army took via Perryville the ferry. Perryville continued to serve as a railroad town into the 1900s until the interstate helped Perryville become a highway town.

The town is distinguished by the great number of nineteenth century churches, each unique in its architecture. Perry Point Mansion, built around 1750, has two faces, one toward the driveway, one facing the river. Now a private home, it once sheltered the famous Stump family and later was occupied by the commanding officer of Perry Point Veteran's Hospital.

Perryville's Community Park is the scene of an annual Spring Fling in May; a parade and Autumnfest in the fall. Christmas is celebrated with a tree-lighting Ceremony at Rodgers Tavern.

⬛ MARINAS
- Perryville Yacht Club, 410-642-6364

▣ RESTAURANTS
- Island Inn, 648 Broad Street, 410-642-3448
- Philipchuck's Restaurant, 5408 Pulaski Highway, 410-642-2470
- Rendezvous Bar & Restaurant, 410-642-0015

SPECIAL EVENTS AND ACTIVITIES
Please check the internet or call ahead, as dates, times, and locations may change.
May: "Spring Fling," 410-642-6066
October: "Autumnfest," 410-642-6066

Perryville, MD

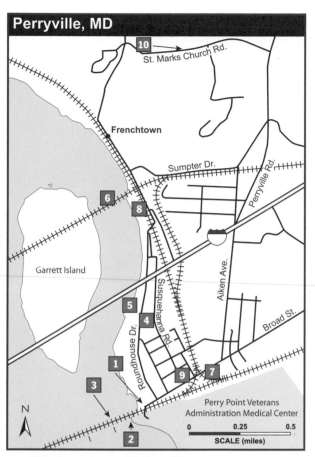

Frenchtown

Garrett Island

St. Marks Church Rd.

Sumpter Dr.

Perryville Rd.

Aiken Ave.

Susquehanna Rd.

Roundhouse Dr.

Broad St.

Perry Point Veterans
Administration Medical Center

0   0.25   0.5

SCALE (miles)

N

POINTS OF INTEREST

1 RODGERS TAVERN, c. 1740
Some famous guests were George and Martha Washington, Lafayette, Rochambeau, Thomas Jefferson and James Madison. Only open for special occasions by the town.

2 SITE OF PHILADELPHIA, WILMINGTON & BALTIMORE BRIDGE; the piers you see now held the bridge.

3 THE PENNSYLVANIA RAILROAD BRIDGE; opened in 1906 and still in use.

4 PERRY POINT MANSION, circa 1750
The structure has two fronts, one on the driveway side and one on the riverside. It was turned over to the Union Army during the Civil War and much damage was done to the stairway and furniture. It was rebuilt by the Stump family and then sold to the U.S. Government in 1918. It served as the superintendent's residence for the hospital built on the grounds. It is now a private residence.

5 SITE OF OWENS CANNING FACTORY; in the 1890s, they canned tomatoes and corn.

6 THE BALTIMORE & OHIO BRIDGE; rebuilt in 1907, it's still in use today.

7 PERRYVILLE RAILROAD STATION
Built in 1905 and restored in 1990 and displays artifacts
of past railroad days in part of the building.

8 PERRYVILLE UNITED METHODIST CHURCH, 325 Susquehanna
Avenue, 1894; built of granite, it has had many names.

9 ST. MARK'S EPISCOPAL CHURCH, 175 St. Marks Church Road,
1844; it replaced a Parish House built in 1798.

10 PERRYVILLE PRESBYTERIAN CHURCH, 710 Broad Street
Built in 1880s and relocated when the railroad was built.
It has the original exposed ceiling beams and an exquisite
stained glass altar window.

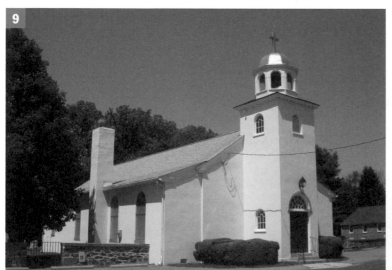

Port Deposit
2000 Census Population: 676   N 39 36' W 76 07'

Captain John Smith visited the then-unnamed site of Port Deposit in 1608 and 1609. Until 1812, the ferry was known by several names, including the Upper Ferry and Creswells Ferry. It and Lapidum, across the Susquehanna River, were the uppermost deep-water ports navigable by ships to be loaded for Baltimore or trans-Atlantic crossings. River barges and wagons loaded with lumber, grain, whiskey, tobacco, and other goods were floated down river to the "port of deposit", hence giving the town its name. When the Susquehanna Canal was completed in 1812, it contributed greatly to the port's growth The Port Deposit Bridge was built in 1818 and remained in service until 1854 when a herd of cattle fell through a span. The rest of the bridge was washed away by a flood in 1857.

Port Deposit is well known for its granite quarry. The first full-scale quarry was opened in 1816–1817, but granite had been used locally before then. The quarry was enlarged in 1829. By 1837, an annual output of about 15,000 perches was reached. Stone was shipped to Philadelphia, Washington, Harrisburg, Baltimore, and Richmond. Philadelphia has twelve churches built of Port Deposit granite, Washington has three, and Baltimore, five. Part of the Naval Academy in Annapolis was built of the Port Deposit stone.

When the first railroad was built in 1832, it contributed to much of the growth of the town. The growth was also stimulated by the local lumber industry. By 1840, 150,000,000 board feet per year were milled and reloaded for shipment on deep-draft vessels.

The most famous Port Deposit resident was Jacob Tome (1810–1898), a principal figure in the banking and lumber businesses. He was the county's first millionaire and its most generous philanthropist. The Tome mansion, no longer standing, was the grandest house in the town. He left a substantial sum for the building of the Jacob Tome School for Boys, which closed in 1941. Its buildings were adapted for use as the Bainbridge Naval Training Center for thousands of recruits before it, too, closed. Carved statues of Jacob Tome and his wife grace the facade of Washington Hall, a former school. In another tribute to Jacob Tome, Adams Hall on Main Street was originally the Jacob Tome Gymnasium. It is now the Town Hall, and, yet another, the Tome Memorial Methodist Church, a gift from Jacob Tome, houses a John Steer organ built in 1910.

The Conowingo Dam, built in 1927, permanently changed the town by terminating all river traffic and decimating the shad and herring fishery. It did, however, stop ice gorges of up to thirty and even fifty feet. The ice gorge of 1910 was the worst in history.

The Old Mill on Main Street may have been the grist mill mentioned in an 1835 survey. Port Deposit was a logical site for such an enterprise, located as it was at the origin of the Pennsylvania-Maryland Canal, the first artificial inland waterway in the United States. The mill was making flour in 1900, brushes in 1905, then again, flour in 1912, and in 1916, sausage and scrapple and general butchering. At one point a section was used to make early-American furniture.

An important historic site is the 1813 Gerry House, where the Marquis de Layfayette was entertained in 1824. It is impressive for the granite slabs used for the columns that support the second story and the cast iron railings embellished with sheaves of wheat, denoting a former owner's pride in being a farmer. The house now belongs to the Port Deposit Heritage Corporation which is restoring it. Finally, the famed Steps, between Main and High Streets, are worthy of a climb for the marvelous view from their top. There are many more sites that contribute to the entire town being placed on the National Historic Registry in 1978.

⛴ MARINAS
- Logan's Wharf, 410-378-3466
- Rock Run Landing, 410-378-3193
- Tome's Landing Marina, 1000 Rowland Drive, 410-378-3384

🏨 LODGING
- Union Hotel (*Also includes a restaurant*), 1282 Susquehanna Road, 410-378-3503
     Note: the restaurant is supposed to have ghosts from the time it was a brothel.
     Creepy ghost children and spirits of dead babies in shoeboxes appear.
- Winchester Hotel, 15 S. Main Street, 410-378-3701

🍴 RESTAURANTS
- Back Fin Blues, 410-378-8878
- C. M. Tugs Grill & Pub, 10 S. Main Street, 410-378-8338
- DiLorenzo's Pizza & Grill, 410-378-2800
- Jumbo Jimmy's Restaurant, 410-378-0045
- Moretti's Café & Grocery, 19 S. Main Street, 410-378-8878
- Old Port Inn, 410-378-2002
- Portside Grill and Restaurant, 600 Rowland Drive, 410-378-4600
- Winchester Tavern, 15 S. Main Street, 410-378-5643

SPECIAL EVENTS AND ACTIVITIES
Please check the internet or call ahead, as dates, times, and locations may change.
- **August**: Port Deposit Heritage Days, 301-378-3866
- **December**: Candlelight Tour, 301-378-3866

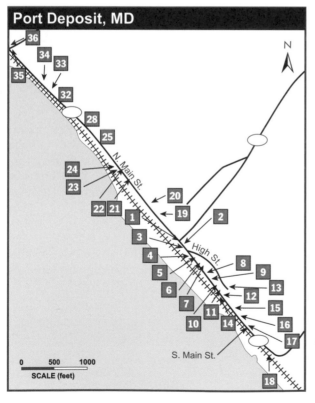

Port Deposit, MD

POINTS OF INTEREST
1 TOWN SQUARE, 1903
     Drinking fountain was built to refresh horses, people, and dogs.
2 GERRY HOUSE, 1813
     Lafayette visited here in 1824. The structure is under restoration by Port Deposit Heritage Corporation.

3 WINCHESTER HOTEL, 15 S. Main Street, c. 1850s–60s
Formerly a candy-making and a dry goods store, now it's Bittner's Restaurant. It was purchased by Robert Cather in 1973.

4 PRESBYTERIAN MANSE, c. 1856; Italianate style

5 RYAN HOUSE, 42 S. Main Street, 1888
Home of former mayor H. F. Ryan, it has since been converted to apartments. The third-floor entrance is three steps below High Street; "gingerbread" design features and seven roofs.

6 Presbyterian Church, 44 S. Main Street, 1902
Granite structure was a gift of James Harvey Roland. It features memorial windows.

7 TOUCHSTONE HOUSE, 46-48 S. Main Street, 1857
Street-level floor for storage, living quarters on upper floor; graceful fence was built by owner's great-grandfather.

8 JOHN SCHAEFFER HOUSE, 50 S. Main Street, 1836; notable roof pediment
Original single-dwelling expanded to eighteen rooms in late 19th century; five fireplaces and two attics; in the 1930s, the house was heated by steam pipes from the lumber mill across the railroad track.

9 BRICK ROW HOUSE, early 1900s, 52-58 S. Main Street
Living quarters on the second floor assured residents safety when ice gorges came down the river.

10 MCCLENAHAN-NESBIT HOUSE, 1880s, 60-62 S. Main Street
A double house built by John McClenahan for his son, John, and daughter, Mrs. Nesbit.

11 ADAMS HALL, 1905, 64 S. Main Street
Now the Town Hall, the building was originally the Jacob Tome gymnasium. It was remodeled in 1983.

12 THE STEPS, from Main Street to High Street, offer a marvelous view from their top

13 (BACKGROUND) MILLER HOUSE, 39 High Street
The house is said to have been constructed from an ark that carried produce down the river. Home of Miss Alice Miller, author of Cecil County, A Study in Local History.

14 FACADE OF WASHINGTON HALL, 1894
Embellished by the figures of Jacob Tome and his wife; carved over the former school's entrance.

15 CARRIAGE AND GAS HOUSE, c. 1850
The street-floor horse stalls are now one large room; the second floor is a home. The building across the railroad tracks was not the Tomes Gas House.

16 Vanneman House, built before 1860
Home of John Vanneman, who owned the wharf opposite his house from which lumber vessels sailed.

17 McCLENAHAN MANSION, c. 1880s, 90 S. Main Street
Clapboard part faces the cliff; newer part was of Port Deposit granite; Queen Anne chimney with ornate decorative corbeling.

18 SNOW'S BATTERY MARKER, opposite 130 Main Street; served with distinction in the Civil War.

19 RUINS OF JEFFERSON HALL, pre-1834
This structure has served as a Roman Catholic Church, bank, schoolhouse, and home; Greek Temple-like center section.

20 ABRAHAMS BUILDING, pre-1867, 38 N. Main Street; a building of many uses, it's now the Water Witch Fire Company

21 58 N. MAIN STREET, early nineteenth century
Water supplied by up-hill spring;
original crane in dining room fireplace.

22 68 N. MAIN STREET, 1884
This Swiss Chalet style was the original office for the
McClenahan Quarry Company. It has a granite vault with
30-inch-thick walls in its present-day kitchen.

23 73 N. MAIN STREET, 1905;
notable Paladian window on third floor

24 75 N. MAIN STREET, pre-1812; it has had eleven different
owners since 1830, six of them women.

25 88-94 N. MAIN STREET; outstanding mansard roof and
ornamentation on dormer windows

26 NESBIT HALL, 1937
Built of Port Deposit granite, it was the second church
constructed by Methodists. It is now a Lion's Club meeting hall.

27 VANNORT HOUSE, 95 N. Main Street
Greek Revival with small porch of Ionic order and tripartite
windows and dormer.

28 PAW PAW BUILDING, 98 N. Main Street
So-named because of paw paw bushes that once flanked the
entrance. The town's first Methodist Church and later the Port
Deposit Academy, a store, and a restaurant; it is now owned
by the Port Deposit Heritage Society and being restored as a
library and museum.

29 TOME MEMORIAL METHODIST CHURCH, 1872, 104 N. Main Street
This gift from Jacob Tome houses a John Steer organ built in
1910. Until recently holes were bored in the floor for drainage
from frequent floods.

CECIL COUNTY

30 METHODIST PARSONAGE, nineteenth century,
101 N. Main Street
> Highly developed jigsaw ornamentation on the porch; houses
> of the same period to the north also have similar porches.

31 McNEILLY HOUSE, pre-1821, 133-135 N. Main Street
> Originally an inn, it was then the town's first Sunday school and
> later the Port Deposit Academy. Appears top-heavy because of a
> World War II addition of top-floor apartments.

32 OLD SORREL, pre-1803, 158-160 N. Main Street;
an old inn and mail stop, it was later a bake shop
with a stone oven in the back wall

33 ST. TERESA'S ROMAN CATHOLIC CHURCH, 1866,
102 N. Main Street
> Served first by priests from Havre de Grace,
> Father Carey from Elkton was the first priest to officiate
> regularly and Father Arnd was instrumental in having poplar
> trees planted along Main Street.

34 BETHEL AME METHODIST CHURCH, 1911, 196 N. Main Street
> The structure burned on November 6, 1966 and the interior
> was completely gutted. Congregation dates to 1848 when slaves
> gathered for a prayer service, meeting later in Rachel Gibson's
> home. Once established, the mission moved to Bethel Hollow,
> south of town. To make way for the Tome School, they met in
> the Church Hall at Rock Run. When it burned, they purchased
> ground for the present building.

35 FIRST BAPTIST CHURCH, c. 1872, 282 N. Main Street
> Until 1902, a Presbyterian House of Worship; an earlier church
> was probably on the same site.

36 OLD MILL, 1815-1830, 300 N. Main Street
> An 1835 survey mentions a grist mill in the area;
> the mill produced everything from flour to brushes,
> furniture, and sausage.

Principio Furnace

2010 Census Not available

Principio Furnace was the first blast furnace in Maryland and one of the first in the nation. The original furnace was built in 1723. The third furnace, built in 1836, was in blast until 1894. It is still standing. There were at least four furnaces over the years. At one time, it was estimated that more than two hundred people were employed by the furnace. Today, however, there is little trace of the large number of buildings associated with the furnace or its employees.

The Maryland furnace exported an estimated 25,000 tons of pig and bar iron to Great Britain between 1718 and 1755. It provided iron for the cannon and cannon balls used by the Americans in the Revolution and the War of 1812. Iron from Principio Furnace went into the manufacture of cannon for the U.S. Navy's first warships and later the frigates Constitution, Constellation, and the United States. The order included twenty-four nine-pounders, twelve six-pounders, and forty twelve pounders. The furnace went through a succession of owners and finally, in 1925, the legacy of iron production at Principio Furnace came to an end. The forge buildings stood until 1942 when they were destroyed by fire.

Abandoned behind "No Trespassing" signs for many years, the furnace could only be viewed from behind a fence. Behind the office building and across a field, you can see the round charcoal kiln and other ruins. To the left is a two-story building that housed machinery. Walk east along the fence, you can see what is left of the 1937 blast furnace. Many other ruins are visible, the most important being the iron master's mansion on the hill. In April 1981, York Building Products purchased the land and is considering plans for preserving the site's historical integrity, promoting its historic significance, and increasing public access with tours by appointment.

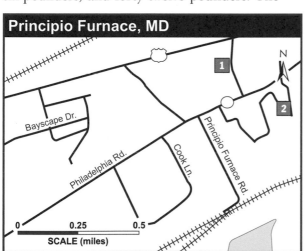

Principio Furnace, MD

Bayscape Dr.

Philadelphia Rd.

Cook Ln.

Principio Furnace Rd.

N

1

2

SCALE (miles)
0   0.25   0.5

POINTS OF INTEREST

1 LOCAL HISTORIC HOME, C. 1840
2 THE FURNACE OFFICE BUILDING, replaced c. 1885

Dorchester County

Bishops Head

1940 Census Population: 225

N. 38 16' W. 76 04'

Bishops Head is a small remote unincorporated town on a peninsula between the Honga River and Fishing Bay in southern Dorchester County. The area is mostly small conifer woods and salt marsh interlaced by small streams and Goose and Tedious Creeks that support a number of crabbing and fishing enterprises. The community and surrounding area are served by St. Thomas United Methodist Church.

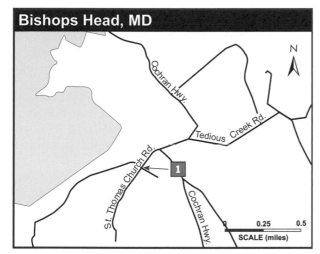

Bishops Head, MD

POINTS OF INTEREST

1 ST. THOMAS UNITED METHODIST CHURCH
Looking much the same today, the structure, built in the late nineteenth century, is the most impressive structure in Dorchester County and is indicative of the impact Methodism had upon the inhabitants of the area.

Cambridge

2010 Census Population: 12,326   N. 38 34' W76 05'

In 1684, the Maryland's General Assembly authorized creation of a town on a river named for a tribe of Choptank Indians, the original occupants of the land. They had been persuaded to move to a reservation upriver some years earlier to make way for English settlers. The Choptank River site chosen for the town was a plantation owned by Daniel Jones. Conveniently located on the south shore of the Choptank River, the site would make an excellent port. The name Cambridge wasn't used until the General Assembly authorized building a courthouse on the site in 1686. It stood alone on High Street until 1692 when an Anglican Church was built nearby. Growth, thereafter, was slow. The next building of note was a tavern that became a center for the sale or barter of ship cargoes brought in from Europe and the West Indies and the products of Eastern Shore plantations. The town and port grew without major incident until the upheaval caused by the Civil War.

Maryland's Governor, Thomas Hicks of Cambridge, was instrumental in keeping Maryland in the Union. Another Cambridge native, Harriet Tubman, earned national and international fame for her work taking Maryland and Southern slaves to freedom in the North via the Underground Railroad. When peace returned, Cambridge began a period of steady growth. By 1890, it numbered more than 4,000 residents and was served by a railroad to Delaware and steamboats to Baltimore. At the turn of the century, Cambridge was second only to Baltimore as an oyster packing center. The town's economy was supported by fruit and vegetable canneries, a thriving ship-building industry, and duck and goose hunting that brought many so-called "sports" to town. Cambridge grew about fifteen percent every ten years until the decade of the 1960s. In 1961, the biggest packer closed down completely, putting 1,500 people out of work, nearly a third of the town. Funds were obtained to build a deep water terminal which deep-sea vessels began to use to deliver frozen tuna for processing. A wide variety of small factories rose to stimulate the town's economy. Racial problems created national interest during the 1960s. In 1992, "Sailwinds Park," a $35 million project to transform the town into a miniature Baltimore, stimulated the economy.

⚓ MARINAS
- Cambridge Municipal Marina, Water Street, 410-228-4031
- Hyatt Regency Chesapeake Bay, 100 Heron Boulevard, 410-901-1234 *(Also includes lodging)*
- Municipal Yacht Basin, Water Street, 410-228-4031

🛏 LODGING
- Best Value Inn, 2831 Ocean Gateway, 410-228-4444
- Cambridge House Bed & Breakfast, 112 High Street, 410-221-7799
- Days Inn & Suites, 2917 Ocean Gateway, 410-228-4444
- Holiday Inn Express, 2715 Ocean Gateway, 410-221-9900
- Inn on Locust Street, 707 Locust Street, 410-961-3321
- Killarney Bed & Breakfast, 102 Killarney Road, 410-901-9899
- Kindred Spirits Family Massage &Cottage Retreat, 102 Hiawatha Road, 410-221-7575
- Lodgecliffe on the Choptank, 103 Choptank Terrace, 410-228-1760
- Mill Street Bed & Breakfast, 114 Mill Street, 410-901-9144

🍴 RESTAURANTS
- Blue Point Provision Company, Hyatt Regency Chesapeake Bay, 100 Heron Boulevard, 410-233-1234
- Cambridge Diner, 21924 Old Route 50, 410-228-8898
- Canvasback Restaurant & Irish Pub, 420 Race Street, 410-221-7888
- Pizza Palace Greek & Italian Restaurant, 600 Sunburst Highway, 410-221-0022
- Pizza Ziva, 411 Academy Street, 410-221-8585
- Spicer's Seafood, Crab Deck & Bar, 802 Woods Road, 410-221-0222

SPECIAL EVENTS AND ACTIVITIES

Please check the internet or call ahead, as dates, times, and locations may change.

March: Annual Harriet Tubman Day, Elks Lodge on Pine Street, 410-228-0401
Sailwinds Park Kite Festival, 410-228-1000

April: Governor's Hall Antique Show and Sale, 410-228-8858
Dorchester Cambridge Cultural Festival 410-228-1000

May: Annual Flower Fair, Outdoors, 410-228-1424
Richardson Maritime Museum Boat Show, 410-221-1871
B&B Sport Aviation Annual Fly-In, 410-221-8000
Jazz Fest and Heritage Day, downtown Cambridge, 410-228-1000
Senior Celebration, 410-228 0190
Antique Aircraft Fly-In, 301-490-6759

June: Annual Juneteenth Celebration, 410-228-0401

July: July 4th, Annual Bay Country Festival, 410-228-0401
Taste of Cambridge, Historic Downtown Cambridge, 410-228-0020
Cambridge Classic Powerboat Regatta, World champion inboards, 410-228-7920

August: Seafood Feast-i-val, 410-228-1211

September: Veterans Recognition Day, 410-228-4692
Model Boat Races, Pink's Pond, 410-228-6029
Annual Boat Docking Contest, 410-397-3631
Choptank Heritage Skipjack Race, 410-228-2142
Cambridge Summer Send-Off, 410-228-1000
Dorchester Showcase, High Street, 410-228-7782
Chesapeake Man Triathlon, 410-964-1246

October: Harvest Festival, Dorchester Historical Society, 410-228-7953
Horn Point Open House, 410-228-8200
Cambridge Coin Show, American Legion Post #91, 410-228-6412
Sailwinds Park Kite Festival, 410-228-1000
Annual Cambridge Schooner Rendezvous, 410-221-7858

November: Grand National Grandtastic Jamboree, 410-228-0111
Annual Festival of Wreaths, Nov. 16th- Dec. 6th, 410-228-8569

December: Christmas Garden of Trains, Cambridge Fire Company, 410-228-4313
Cambridge-Dorchester Christmas Parade, downtown, 410-228-3092
Annual Holiday Candlelight Tour, various locations, 410-221-7868
Bonnie Brook Luminary Display, Bonny Brook Community, 410-376-3563

DORCHESTER COUNTY

Cambridge, MD

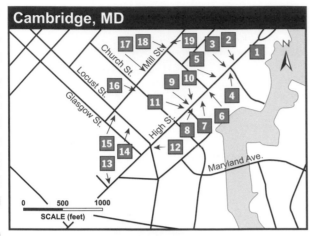

SCALE (feet)

POINTS OF INTEREST

1 THOMAS WILLIAMS HOUSE, 1903, 100 High Street
> Built by the wife of Governor Phillips Lee Goldsborough, it was later owned by Governor Emerson C. Harrison.

2 CHRIST CHURCH RECTORY, 1849, 107 High Street; Federal style parsonage for the Great Choptank Parish

3 JAMES MUSE HOUSE, 1840, 111 High Street
> Built by Dr. James A. Muse in the late Federal/Greek Revival, it was "Victorianized" in 1884. Birthplace of Governor Phillips Lee Goldsborough.

4 WILLIAM MURRAY HOUSE, 1847, 112 High Street
> Built by William Vans Murray, through whose efforts the Lousiana Purchase was made.

5 Joseph Johnson House, 1882, 115 High Street
> Built by Joseph H. Johnson, who is credited with writing Maryland's Oyster Laws.

6 THE LEONARD HOUSE, 1790, 118 High Street
> Together with 120 High Street, it served as a hotel and was home of Maryland's last Federal Governor who voted against the War of 1812.

7 GOLDSBOROUGH HOUSE, 1790, 200 High Street; one of best preserved Federal style structures on the Eastern Shore

8 BRYAN-LeCOMPTE HOUSE, 1803, 204 High Street
> Built by Charles K. Bryan, an artillery captain, and sold to Samuel Woodward in 1842, it has remained in the LeCompte family for four generations.

9 DORCHESTER COUNTY COURTHOUSE, 1854, 206 High Street
  In front is a bell that was taken from a Mexican monastery in 1846 and used as a fire alarm.

10 THE BAYLY HOUSE, 1755, 207 High Street
  Relocated across the bay from Annapolis, it has been in the Bayly family for six generations.

11 JOSIAH BAYLY LAW OFFICE, 1796, 213 High Street; oldest surviving lawyer office in town

12 CHRONICLE BUILDING, 302 High Street

13 SYCAMORE COTTAGE, 417 High Street

14 RECTORY FOR ZION METHODIST CHURCH, 1889, 610 Locust Street; second story was added in 1908

15 612 LOCUST STREET
  Original church, 1802 to 1846, was named Garretson's Chapel, for his first sermon he was arrested and put in the Cambridge jail. The present church, originally built in 1911, was rebuilt after a fire in 1950. Gothic Revival style.

16 312 MILL STREET, 1912
  Home of Captain Levi Phillips, founder of the Phillips Packing Company. It features eight fireplaces and twenty-two rooms. The original Zion Church stood on this site from 1802 until 1846.

17 305 MILL STREET

Former home of Governor Emerson C. Harrington, who helped establish the Claiborne-Annapolis Ferry. His support of prohibition threw Maryland into an uproar.

18 201 MILL STREET

Built on the site of the Cambridge Academy, which was incorporated in 1812 and destroyed by fire in 1902. A fine example of an early nineteenth century school building.

19 115 MILL STREET, 1923; Colonial Revival style

Built by W. Grayson Winterbottom, who was instrumental in founding the Phillips Packing Company, one of the largest produce manufacturing companies in the Eastern United States

Note: There are many more historic houses in Cambridge. Get a copy of Historic Walking tour of Cambridge, Maryland, by the Dorchester County Department of Tourism to find them all.

Church Creek

2010 Census Population: 125

Church Creek was one of the first five towns to be established in Dorchester County by an act of the General Assembly. It was first named Dorchester Town in unfulfilled anticipation of becoming the county seat. Then it was called White Haven for a time before its present name was adopted. During the eighteenth century, the town was the center of the county's shipbuilding industry until the adjacent forests of pine and oak were depleted. The first church in Dorchester County, Old Trinity Church, was established circa 1675, just west of the town. The tile floor, altar table, and exterior brick walls are all original. Thomas King Carroll, Maryland's governor in 1830, is buried in the churchyard, as is Anna Ella Carroll, known as the "silent member" of President Lincoln's cabinet. Many Revolutionary War soldiers are also buried there. Within the town, on the grounds of the White Haven Methodist Church, is Dorchester's bicentennial tree, believed to be over three hundred years old. It is also called the "Treaty Oak", said to be a place where a treaty with Indians was made in 1650. Many of the residents commute to work in Cambridge and Cambridge Wire Belts, Inc. is a major industry in the immediate vicinity. Several "in home" businesses thrive in and around the town.

ACTIVITIES

Please check the internet or call ahead, as dates, times, and locations may change.

LODGING

• Loblolly Landing & Lodge, 2142 Liners Road, 410-397-3033

DORCHESTER COUNTY

DORCHESTER COUNTY

Church Creek, MD

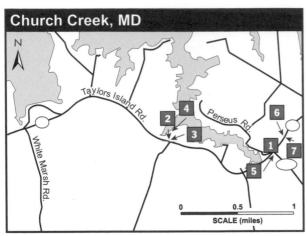

POINTS OF INTEREST

1 Church Creek post office,
   4681 Golden Hill Road
2 Old Trinity Church,
   Old Trinity Church Road
3 Trinity Church original sanctuary,
   Old Trinity Church Road
4 Trinity Church graveyard,
   Old Trinity Church Road
5 Church Creek volunteer fire department,
   Church Creek Road at Golden Hill Road
6 Whitehaven Methodist Church, 1920
   Church Creek Road
7 Historic tree behind Whitehaven
   Church, 1920 Church Creek Road

*Also search for Gibson House, home of Daniel T. Owen, an abolitionist and delegate to the 1860 Republican Convention that nominated Lincoln, and Wyvill House, just West of Church Creek, home of Dr. Dorsey Wyvill, one of the founders of the Medical and Chirurgical Faculty of Maryland in 1799.

Crapo

1940 Census Population: 160

N. 38 19' W. 76 08'

This village is near Lakes Cove of the Honga River. In 1866, the site was called Woodland Town, replacing "Woodland," an apt but hardly inspiring moniker. The townspeople wanted a more modern name and, after much study, decided on a derivative of the French crapeau, meaning amphibian. The proper pronunciation is "Cray-po," which the natives prefer over the vulgar pronunciation. Crapo honors the multitude of frogs that abound — and bound — throughout this marshy land.

⊡ LODGING

• Caroline's Stonehouse, 2411 Lakesville Crapo Road, 410-397-8500

SPECIAL EVENTS AND ACTIVITIES

Please check the internet or call ahead, as dates, times, and locations may change.
February: National Outdoor Show, Beach Ground Road, 410-397-8535

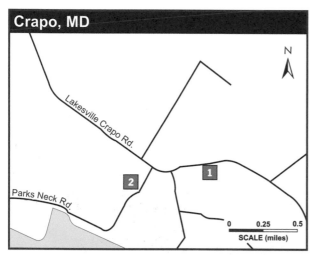

Crapo, MD

POINTS OF INTEREST

1 CRAPO POST OFFICE, 2568 Lakesville Road
2 ABANDONED BOAT RAILWAY, Asquith Island Road at the waterfront

DORCHESTER COUNTY

Crocheron
1914 Census Population: 12

N. 38 15' W. 76 03'

Crocheron is a hamlet on Hog Island, near the point where Tedious Creek meets Fishing Bay. This community of watermen is named for Nathan Crocheron who settled there in the mid-nineteenth century. Many of the residents are descended from the inhabitants of Holland and Bloodsworth Islands who had to evacuate when rising sea levels and erosion inundated them. Some also moved their houses. Eugene Crocheron was the postmaster in 1902.

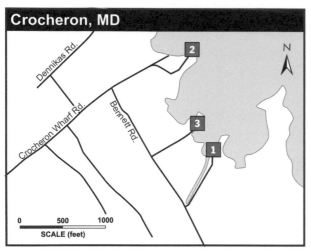

Crocheron, MD

Dennikas Rd.

Crocheron Wharf Rd.

Bennett Rd.

N

0 500 1000
SCALE (feet)

POINTS OF INTEREST

1 POWLEY'S MARINA, 2000-2019 Wingate Bishops Head Road, 410-397-8188
2 OLD SEAFOOD PACKING HOUSE, 2000-2019 Wingate Bishops Head Road
3 CROCHERON WATERMAN'S CRAB BOAT THE *WE TWO II*, Crocheron Wharf Road and Bennett Road

Elliott Island (Elliott's Island)

2010 Census Population: 52

N. 38 19' W. 76 00'

Elliott Island, lying between the Nanticoke River and Fishing Bay, is a mile and a half long and varies in width. The island is roughly a quarter of a mile to a mile of above sea level with its arable land separated by thousands of acres of tidal-marsh meadows interwoven with creeks and ponds known as the Dorchester Everglades. As early as 1642, the area's Nanticoke Indians were crossing the Bay to attack St. Mary's City, but by 1799, they had disappeared. The first ship known to have stopped at the island was in 1697. The earliest known patent holder was John Edmonson, who assigned his land to a William Smith. By the 1690s planter John Elliott held land on both sides of Fishing Bay. Elbert Elliott, the last surviving Elliott, died in 1967.

It's known that a log roadway existed to the island as early as 1734 but getting there was never easy. That may have encouraged islanders to ally themselves with the British during the American Revolution. They became picaroons, or pirates, who slipped in and out of the marshes to raid area plantations. They hit the home of John Elliott, Jr. at least twice.

Sloops, bugeyes, log canoes, and schooners were built on the island The first recorded builder was the third John Elliott as early as 1757.

They built their boats by rack-of-eye, or what they called "winchum-squinchum," meaning without plans or formal models. For a brief period in the 1880s, steamboats linked Elliott's Island with the outside world, but that lasted only a few years until ice took out the pier. The island became known as "The Land That Time Forgot" and was generally only reached by water. Isolation was only one of the islanders' problems. Mosquitos were a constant problem and there were several serious epidemics.

Methodism arrived on the island with camp meetings and in 1854, Davis Methodist Episcopal Church was built. The first school was built two years later. The island got its first post office in 1883. Early in the twentieth century a long line of poles brought electricity to the island, which greatly helped its tomato canneries, button manufacturing, and businesses that catered to hunters of ducks, "turkles," and muskrats. In the decades following 1948, the population gradually declined. In many ways, it remains what an old islander once called "a little democracy, with few rules and laws, but with certain rights and privileges respected: not tied up in knots with civil government."

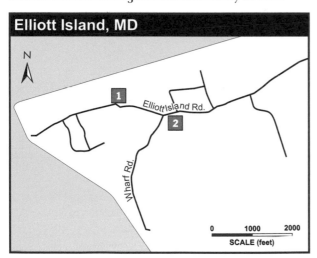

POINTS OF INTEREST

1 ELLIOTT ISLAND VOLUNTEER FIRE DEPARTMENT, 2317 Elliott Island Road

2 ELLIOTT ISLAND UNITED METHODIST CHURCH, near 2310 Elliott Island Road

Honga

The village of Honga occupies a section of shore along the Honga River, which is more estuary than river. Speculation on the name's origins ranges from a word the Rappahannock Indians called Captain John Smith to an abbreviation of the Powhatan Indian word for "goose," *kahunge*, or a misspelling and mispronunciation of "hunger." The village could be related to an early settlement on the site of a nearby county park that was called Plymouth. It is recorded as having been laid out on "Phillips his pointe" to serve as a port of entry for tobacco so that plantation owners would not have to travel to larger towns to have their tobacco inspected. In 1707, the tobacco inspector was available at the Plymouth warehouse only three days a week. Finally, in 1773, the warehouse was sold and the name "Plymouth" disappeared from the records and the village we know today as Honga supports oyster and sport fishing industries.

Hoopers Island

2010 Census Population: 428

Hoopers Island is really three islands: Upper Hoopers Island (N. 38 20' W. 76 14'), Middle Hoopers Island (N. 38 126', W. 76 11'), and Lower Hoopers Island, which is no longer occupied. There was once a village named Applegarth on Lower Hooper Island, but the hurricane of 1933 wiped out the bridge and what little that remained of it. The islands are named after Col. Henry Hooper, whose son was a Revolutionary War commander of the Dorchester Militia. The residents of the islands were originally farmers, but now make their living from the Bay. Because the first settlers were Catholics, the first church was St. Mary's Star of the Sea; erected in 1692, it was replaced by the present church in 1872.

Henry Hooper was granted one hundred acres on Hooper's Island near the "Hungar," now Honga River. Captain John Smith called the nearby Hooper Strait "Limbo" after he encountered a severe storm there while exploring the Bay. The storm blew out his sails, which were replaced by ones made from the shirts of the crew.

There are several small towns on the islands, and Hoopersville, on the Middle Island, has two small packing houses. Fishing Creek and Honga, on the Upper Island, both have dock facilities. A county park occupies the ancient site of Plymouth, where the bridge crosses to Upper Hooper Island. In 1748, the General Assembly ordered a tobacco warehouse to be erected there; it lasted until 1773, when it was sold. Recently many retirees have built vacation homes on the islands, and some even live there year-round.

Now closed, the Phillip's Seafood Factory was the birthplace of Phillip's Crab Houses and Restaurants in Maryland.

DORCHESTER COUNTY

ACTIVITIES

Please check the internet or call ahead, as dates, times, and locations may change.

⛴ MARINAS
- Hoopersville: docking at packing houses only
- Fishing Creek and Honga: town docks only

▣ RESTAURANTS
- Old Salty's Restaurant, 2560 Hoopers Island Road, 410-397-3752

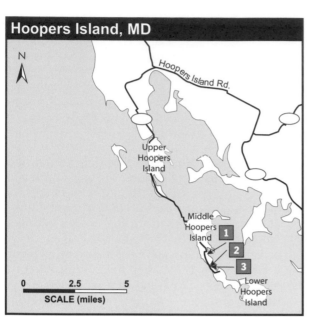

Hoopers Island, MD

N

Hoopers Island Rd.

Upper Hoopers Island

Middle Hoopers Island

Lower Hoopers Island

0   2.5   5
SCALE (miles)

POINTS OF INTEREST
*Note: All of these are located on Hoopersville Road.
1   HOOPERSVILLE COMMUNITY HALL
2   HOOPERS ISLAND MEMORIAL CHURCH
3   BRIDGE TO HOOPERS ISLAND

Madison

2010 Census Population: 204

N. 38 31' W. 76 13'

The village that today bears the name of President James Madison (1809–1817) was settled about 1760. It was originally called "Tobacco Stick," a name that provides a much more compelling tale. It is said that an Indian accused of being a miscreant was fleeing a posse of angry settlers. He managed to elude them by vaulting over a creek near their settlement using a long tobacco stick. Another town legend concerns a wild, white mule, called the Devil by locals, that galloped through the marshes at night until one night he sank in the bog. Later, a town drunk claimed to have seen the mule's ghost one night, and subsequently gave up drinking and became a minister.

Madison's location on the Bay made its homes and farms an easy prey for raiding British ships. One winter raid involved local soldiers who captured the Becky Phipps, a British ship locked in the ice. Today, the ship's canon stands in a park at the entrance to Taylor's Island. The town's sole industries are an oyster packing plant and a restaurant-marina.

ACTIVITIES

Please check the internet or call ahead, as dates, times, and locations may change.

⬛ MARINAS

• Madison Bay Sea & Sea
• Madison Canning Road, 410-228-4111

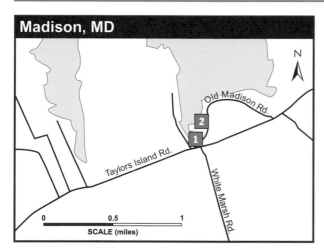

Madison, MD

POINTS OF INTEREST

1 MADISON UNITED METHODIST CHURCH, 1213 Old Madison Road
2 VOLUNTEER FIRE COMPANY, 1154 Taylors Island Road

DORCHESTER COUNTY

Secretary
2010 Census Population: 535   N. 38 37' W. 75 57'

Secretary is a small fishing village on the Warwick River. It has a mixed lineage, but takes its name from the position held by Henry Sewall, original owner of the land and Secretary of Maryland under Governor Charles Calvert in 1661. Secretary did not become a town until 1883, however, when it was surveyed and the first lot sold.

The most significant building on the site of the future town is believed to have been Carthegena Manor, built in the early eighteenth century. Its original, fine interior paneling was moved to the Brooklyn Museum of Art when the house was modernized. The building was long associated with Lady Jane Sewall, widow of Henry Sewall, who became the wife of Lord Baltimore, but the estimated 1720 date of its construction makes it more likely the home of Henry Trippe, whose son, Captain Henry Trippe, was a county burgess, sheriff, and deputy commissary from 1733 to 1742. The manor house was sold in the latter half of the nineteenth century.

Most of Secretary's residents engaged in oystering for a livelihood. The original oyster packing house eventually gave way to a major fruit and vegetable packing business. The twentieth century brought a number of significant changes, including incorporation in 1900. Not long after that, the addition of a steamboat wharf made the town a major stopping place of various steamboat lines from Baltimore. It was noted for sending more Eastern Shore vegetables to Baltimore than any other point on the peninsula.

In the 1800s, the first county almshouse, interestingly named "Sunnyside," was built across Secretary Creek from Carthagena. The first religious service was conducted in one of the wharf houses. The year 1886 saw construction of the first Methodist Church, followed in 1892 by the Methodist Protestant Church and the Roman Catholic Church. Local children depended on private tutors for their schooling until 1939, when a modern brick school was built.

⚓ MARINAS
• Town Dock (18 rented slips)

🍴 RESTAURANTS
• Suicide Bridge Restaurant, 410-943-4689
This famous restaurant is about two miles away and also gives a replica steamboat tour of the Choptank River.

SPECIAL EVENTS AND ACTIVITIES
Please check the internet or call ahead, as dates, times, and locations may change.
September: Riverfest takes place over Labor Day weekend

Secretary, MD

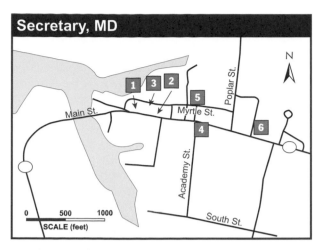

N

POINTS OF INTEREST

1 SECRETARY GENERAL STORE,
   107 Main Street; 410-943-0808
2 UNITED METHODIST CHURCH,
   142 Main Street
3 ST. LUKE'S CHURCH, 124 Main Street
4 OUR LADY OF GOOD COUNCIL CHURCH,
   410-943-4300
5 SECRETARY VOLUNTEER FIRE DEPARTMENT
   15 Myrtle Street
6 CARTHAGENA, formerly My Lady Sewell's
   Manor; this is private property

Taylor's Island

2010 Census Population: 173

DORCHESTER COUNTY

Taylor's Island and the village on it were named for Thomas Taylor, who received a grant for the land in 1662, before Dorchester became a county. Settlers from the Bay's Western Shore were farming there as early 1659. Later residents built ships until the virgin timber was depleted in the early 1850s. Since then, the principal occupations were commercial fishing, sport fishing, hunting, and farming. A tomato packing plant prospered on the island until the 1950s. There were also grist mills at Oyster Creek, Hooper Point, and near the mouth of St. John's Creek.

A major landmark on the island is the historic Grace Episcopal Church. It is part of a complex of three frame buildings. The Gothic-style church was built in the late nineteenth century and was listed on the National Register of Historic Places in 1979. The second building in the group is a twenty-foot by thirty-foot frame chapel of ease dating from the early nineteenth century. Dorchester County's first school house was moved to its present site by the Grace Foundation in 1955.

A very different island landmark is the cannon from the British ship *Dauntless's* tender. In 1814, during the War of 1812, men from Madison and Taylor's Islands captured the eighteen-man crew of the ship's tender when it became trapped in the ice. The cannon was named for Lt. Phipps, commander of the tender, and Becky, a slave whom they had taken prisoner. The cannon was last fired to celebrate President Wilson's election. It caused more of a spectacle than anticipated when it blew up. Islanders were no more daunted than was the ship from which the cannon came and subsequently reassembled it. The cannon stands today as a silent monument commemorating the 1814 event. In 1802, a ferry operated between the mainland and the island; in 1805, it connected Taylor's Island with Meekin's Neck over Slaughter Creek. A modern bridge now spans the creek.

Slaughter Creek isn't named for an event, but for Thomas Slaughter, who was a member of Captain Rodger Mackeele's pirate crew. A similar unsavory connection also gave Punch Island its name. During Prohibition, the island was a deposit point for moon shiners. Today's remaining working watermen share the island with retirees and vacationers who have built homes there. There are still many old homes and farms on or near the island. Visit the Taylor's Island old schoolhouse, now a museum, at 4212 Hooper Neck Road.

ACTIVITIES

Please check the internet or call ahead, as dates, times, and locations may change.

MARINAS
- Bucks & Ducks, LLC, 1345 Hoopers Island Road, 410-320-4550

LODGING
- The Island House B&B, 513 Taylor's Island Road, 410-228-2184

RESTAURANTS
- The Island Grill, 514 Taylor's Island Road, 410-228-9094

Taylors Island, MD

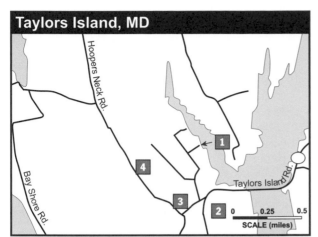

POINTS OF INTEREST

1 THE BECKY-PHIPPS CANNON
Captured from the British Tender to the ship, the *H.M.S. Dauntless*, it is mounted at the entrance to Taylor's Island on Taylor's Island Road.

2 TAYLOR'S ISLAND VOLUNTEER FIRE DEPARTMENT, 501 Taylors Island Road

3 TAYLOR'S ISLAND METHODIST CHURCH, Hooper Neck Road

4 GRACE EPISCOPAL CHURCH, 4401 Hooper Neck Road

DORCHESTER COUNTY

Vienna

2010 Census Population: 271

The small riverside village that came to be known as Vienna was designated in 1706 by Maryland's General Assembly as a site for future development to promote trade. The region was first mentioned nearly one hundred years earlier by Captain John Smith during his 1608 exploration of the Bay. The land was a portion of ten thousand acres along the north shore of the Nanticoke River, patented in 1664 as Nanticoke Manor. The name of the village, originally called Emporer's Landing, came from that of the Nanticoke chief, or emperor, Vinnacokasimmon. More or less, pronounced Vee-enn-na, it became Vienna.

In 1768, the town became the center of the region's Custom District. A Custom House, built in 1791, operated until 1866. It has been restored and is still standing. Wharves and warehouses ran along the shore. Shipbuilding and cotton were the local economy's main supports. Behind and to the left of the Customs House are the remains of the warehouse used for steamship docking in the 1840s. Vienna was raided by the British at least five times during the Revolutionary War and a local resident, Levin

Dorsey, was killed in 1781, the only casualty of the war in Dorchester County. To the right of the Customs House are the remains of the breastworks used to defend the town during the Revolution and the War of 1812. During the Civil War, Southern blockade runners came up the Nanticoke, where Confederate sympathizers outfitted them with food and supplies for the beleaguered South.

A ferry that had been established to cross the river in 1671 operated until 1828 when a wooden bridge was built. At about the same time, steamboats appeared on the Bay and their captains considered the bridge a menace. It was taken down and, by 1860, the ferry had resumed operation. Increased development brought more residents who found the ferry inadequate to meet their needs and a second bridge was built in 1931. Since the late 1980s, a new bridge and bypass have made life and travel in the area easier.

Present-day Vienna may no longer be a commercial hub, but the town has changed very little. Much of its early architecture survives and has been restored.

⊟ MARINAS
• Waterfront Park, with docking

⊟ LODGING
• The Tavern B&B, 111 Water Street, 410-376-3347

⊟ RESTAURANTS
• Nanticoke Inn, 113 Ocean Gateway, 410-376-3006

SPECIAL EVENTS
Please check the internet or call ahead, as dates, times, and locations may change.
April: Nanticoke River Shad Festival, 410-543-1999
September: Annual Native American Festival, 410-376-3889
December: Vienna Luminaries and House Tours, 410-221-1450

Vienna, MD

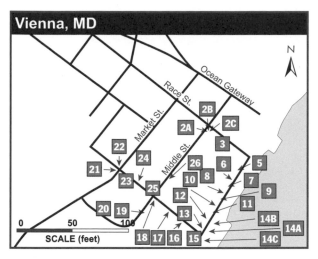

POINTS OF INTEREST

1. VIENNA HERITAGE MUSEUM, 303 Race Street
2. **a-c** CIRCA-1900 HOMES, 100 Middle Street
3. FERRY TOLL HOUSE, between Middle and Water Streets, 1860; it was used until 1931
4. DR. S.S. EWELL HOUSE, late 1700s
   This structure housed the doctor's practice for nearly fifty years. Four of five original fireplaces remain, as do the chestnut beams and mortise and tenoned floor joists.
5. 105 WATER STREET, before 1877; similar to the Wright House next door
6. CAPT. C. E. WRIGHT HOUSE, 1835-1850; this structure still has many ship's fittings and hardware.
7. 109 WATER STREET, 1860-1870; original widow's walk was destroyed by fire
8. Tavern House, 111 Water Street, mid to late 1700s
   Now a Bed & Breakfast, the structure has six fireplaces and its original post and beam construction.

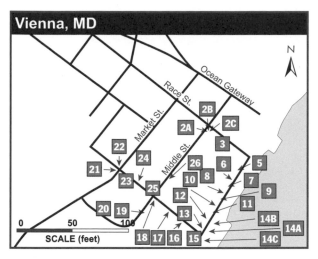

9 113 WATER STREET, 1810-1850
Restored saving original pegged rafters and cornice braces;
mortised studs and sills; dove-tailed floor joists; and fireplaces.

10 115 WATER STREET, early 1800s
This structure was sold in 1802 for "7 slaves, six horses,
1 yoke of oxen,1 head of sheep, 70 bales of cleaned wheat,
and 1 crop of corn."

11 117 WATER STREET, 1810-1850; late federal period,
retains many original features.

12 119 WATER STREET, c. 1800; the building's
construction indicates the work of shipbuilders.

13 THOMAS HOLIDAY HICK'S HOUSE, c. 1828
Governor Hicks is credited with keeping Maryland
in the Union despite local Southern sympathies.

14 a-c. CUSTOMS HOUSE, OLD WAREHOUSE,
and STONE BREASTWORKS, c. 1768.
The Customs House served until 1865 when Baltimore became
Maryland's commercial center. The town was invaded by the
British during the American Revolution and the War of 1812.

15 NANTICOKE MANOR HOUSE, late 1700s, 110 Church Street
The original section, now in the rear,
was the first brick house in Vienna.

16 METHODIST EPISCOPAL CHURCH AND CEMETERY
This was the site of three early Methodist churches.
Grave markers date from the 1850s
and some descendants still live in Vienna.

17 112 CHURCH STREET, c. 1800; one of Vienna's oldest homes

18 114 CHURCH STREET, c. 1855; once owned by Dr. George Bunting, founder of the Noxema Company

19 THE MEADOW, 204 Middle Street
> The name was chosen from three names found in an old deed. It is noted for its two stained-glass windows and what was once a stable in the rear.

20 HUGHES CEMETERY, Middle Street
> Headstones in this African-American cemetery date from 1859 to 1918.

21 201 MARKET STREET, late 1700s
> Though mostly obscured by foliage, this is one of the oldest buildings in Vienna. It features chestnut ceiling beams, hand-hewn sills, and early fireplaces and mantles.

22 127 MARKET STREET, c. 1870
> This structure features elaborate cornice above the central window of the second floor with carved brackets and turned drop-finials.

23 VIENNA METHODIST CHURCH, 206 Church Street
> Alterations date from 1849, 1882, and 1901; formerly the Methodist Protestant Church, it is now known as the United Methodist Church.

24 ST. PAUL'S EPISCOPAL CHURCH SITE, 1709, 203 Church Street
> The original building's foundation is located in the Protestant Episcopal Cemetery on Chapel of Ease Road.

25 Pearcy's Purchase, 125 Middle Street, c. 1790
> One of Vienna's oldest structures, it features exposed ceiling beams and working fireplaces.

26 120 MIDDLE STREET
> Architectural features include a hyphen and kitchen in line with the street and main part of the house, and two exterior brick chimneys on its gable ends and on the outside of the kitchen.

Wingate

2010 Census Not available

N. 38 17' W. 76 07'

Wingate is a center for oyster shucking and seafood packing nineteen miles south of Cambridge. Nearby is a small promontory called John's Point, which was the site of an early county seat of Dorchester County. The town was named for its first postmaster, Urim G. Wingate, in 1902, a red letter year in its history. For the first time, it had a post office, a postmaster, and an official name.

Two seafood packing companies operate in Wingate. For years the town was known as the home of Bronza Parks, a widely known builder of Bay boats. Among the more than four hundred boats that he built were a number of skipjacks, including the *Rosie Parks*, *Martha Lewis*, and *Lady Katie*. Bronza's career was cut short when he was killed by Willis C. Rowe. The man had commissioned him to build a small skipjack and, when the finished price for the boat was more than he'd expected, he shot the boat builder three times.

Note: I had been a captain of the Chesapeake Bay Institute's research vessels for many years and was acquainted with Bronza Parks. Before his death, he had just completed a research vessel for the Institute.

⌂ LODGING
• Wingate Manor B&B, 2335 Wingate-Bishop's Head Road, 410-397-8717

Wingate, MD

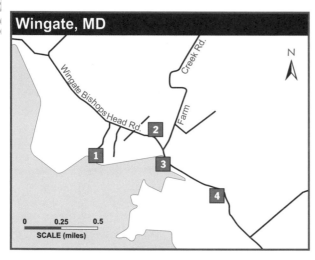

POINTS OF INTEREST
1 WINGATE'S SMALL HARBOR
2 CRAB POTS AT WINGATE
3 WINGATE MANOR
  2335 Wingate-Bishop's Head Road;
  now a Bed and Breakfast, 410-397-8717
4 PICTURESQUE ABANDONED WATERMAN'S
  HOUSE OUTSIDE OF WINGATE

Kent County

Betterton

2010 Census Population: 345

Today's Betterton was first known as Crew's Landing, for Edward Crew, owner of fifty acres and a wharf on the Sassafras River in the early eighteenth century. The small fishing hamlet remained a quiet village until 1851 when Richard Turner built Ellwood there for himself and his wife, the former Elizabeth Betterton. Turner soon became the town's most prominent citizen. By 1860, he was operating a busy mill and warehouse and eventually, built a steamboat wharf below the bluff where now there is a picnic pavilion. Over the next twenty years, Bay steamers brought vacationers to the community, which became a thriving summer resort, boasting twelve hotels, dance pavilions, and a bathing beach. Not surprisingly, the village was renamed Betterton in honor of Mrs. Turner. The Betterton post office was established in 1885, as the resort continued to grow. In 1906, it was incorporated.

The coming of automobiles, trucks, and good roads doomed the steamboat, and in 1962, the company declared bankruptcy and by so doing, brought on the end of an era. By the mid 1980s, Betterton had become a residential community of pleasant homes overlooking the Sassafras River and the Bay. A few dilapidated and abandoned hotels remained, inviting demolition. The five-acre waterfront park near the mouth of the Sassafras River is the largest public beach in Kent County. Seven hundred feet of the shoreline are accessible with a five-hundred-foot boardwalk, three hundred feet of sandy beach for swimming, a bathhouse and public restrooms. The river's freshwater, flowing into the upper Chesapeake, keep the waters there free of sea nettles and is inviting to swimmers all summer long. A flat-surfaced jetty is available for fishermen and a public landing and pier or boaters. There are many old homes to see today. One older inn, Bay Cliff, is now a comfortably large residence. The two tulip poplars gracing the front lawn are said to be the largest in Maryland. Ellwood Farm was a home built for Richard and Elizabeth Betterton Turner in 1851, southwest corner of Howell Point Road. There once was a conducted tour but that no longer runs.

ACTIVITIES

Please check the internet or call ahead, as dates, times, and locations may change.

⛴ MARINAS

None, but the public is allowed to use the free dock, which includes nine transient slips, for one night.

Betterton, MD

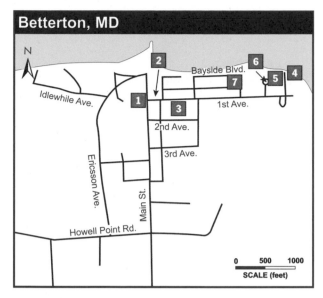

POINTS OF INTEREST

1 SHADY LAWN COTTAGE; formerly an Inn, now privately owned.

2 THE ROYAL SWAN BUILDING, c. 1905
This Victorian-style, turreted structure was formerly the Bayside Inn. It was purchased by the Royal Swan Club in 1931 and is now a private residence, located on Betterton's highest point between 1st and 2nd Avenues.

3 THE "COURTIN' BRIDGE";
this bridge spans a ravine on the south side of Betterton at the shore.

4 THE ORIGINAL STEAMBOAT PIER:
the remains are visible at low tide.

5 EVERGREEN KNOLL, 130 1st Avenue
These summer rentals are the oldest family-owned and operated retreat in Kent County.

6 PRECIOUS BLOOD CATHOLIC CHURCH, 1916
Now abandoned, the structure was commonly photographed for postcards.

7 BETTERTON UNITED METHODIST CHURCH, 300 Main Street

Chestertown

2010 Census Population 5,252   N. 39 12' W.76 04'

Because Chestertown's harbor was a better port of entry, it replaced New Yarmouth, ten miles downstream, as the county seat. Briefly called New Town, the village took the name of the river on which it lies. Chestertown has served as Kent County's seat of government since 1706. Throughout the centuries, it has been a Royal Port of Entry, the scene of its own Revolutionary War Tea Party, and the hub of a thriving agricultural and seafood packing area during the heyday of steamboats on the Chesapeake.

High Street, the town's main thoroughfare, runs from the river to the center of town where it intersects Cross Street. There, the early 1697 Courthouse and other public buildings and businesses were located. Aside from being the county seat, the town developed rapidly in the eighteenth century as the area's center of trade, especially for agricultural products. In the early days, the local economy had been dependent mainly upon tobacco, but in 1760, a dramatic shift to wheat production brought prosperity to a growing population and stronger ties with Philadelphia in the years just before the American Revolution, 1773-1775.

Washington College, the first college chartered in the nation after the Declaration of Independence, added new distinction to the town. Founded by William Smith in 1782, it was named "in honorable and perpetual memory of General Washington." George Washington authorized the "College at Chester" to use his name and gave the school a gift of fifty guineas and his commitment to five years of service on the college's Board of Visitors and Governors.

Following a period of decline and relative stagnation after the Revolution, the town's fortunes began to rise. In 1860, the existing courthouse was built. Fruit-growing and the coming of the railroad in 1872 partially account for the construction of a number of buildings that still characterize the town's center, where there is now a public park with an ornate fountain dating from 1899. It marks the site of a solidly-built market house, the armory, and the first firehouse.

◪ MARINAS
- Scott's Point Marina, 410-778-2959
- Chestertown Marina, Inc., 410-778-3616
- Chester River Marine Services, 410-778-2240

◪ LODGING AND RESTAURANTS
All these places have restaurants; contact information is the same for both lodging and restaurant
- April Inn, 407 E. Campus Avenue, 410-778-3603
- Bittersweet Guest Suites, 239 High Street, 410-778-2300
- Brampton Bed & Breakfast Inn, 25227 Chestertown Road, 410-778-1860
- Comfort Suites Chestertown, 100 Scheeler Road, 410-810-0555
- Hill's Inn Bed & Breakfast, 114 Washington Avenue, 410-778-1926
- Imperial Hotel, 208 High Street, 410-778-5000
- White Swan Tavern, 251 High Street, 410-778-2300

SPECIAL EVENTS
Please check the internet or call ahead, as dates, times, and locations may change.
May: Memorial Day Weekend: Chestertown Teaparty
October: Annual Historic Chestertown House Tour, 410-778-3499
October/November: Sultana Downrigging, and tall ships
December: Annual Chestertown Holiday House Tour

And if you have time....
- Visit an art gallery, as there are several artists in residence
- Try the bookstore; Chestertown has a good stock
- Take a ride on the *Sultana* schooner, 410-778-5954
- Take a guided tour of Kent County, 410-778-2829

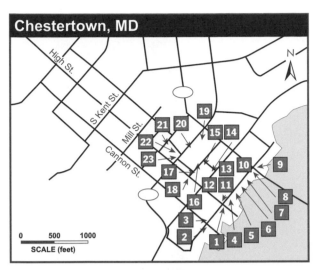

Chestertown, MD

SCALE (feet)
0   500   1000

POINTS OF INTEREST

1 THE CUSTOM HOUSE
   An official Port of Entry in 1706, the original Custom House is no longer standing. The present Custom House was built in 1746 and it celebrates Maryland's revolutionary "Tea Party" every year.

2 210 S. WATER STREET; built in 1847, now fully restored

3 HYNSON-RINGGOLD HOUSE
   This homestead was built in two sections. In 1932, the interior of the East Room was removed to the Baltimore Museum of Art. Today, it is the home of the president of Washington College.

4 WIDEHALL, c. 1770, 101 N. Water Street
   This homestead was built by Thomas Smythe, who is said to have been Kent County's wealthiest citizen.

5 103 N. WATER STREET, c. 1796;
the facade is a notable waterfront landmark

6 RIVER HOUSE, c. 1780, 107 N. Water Street
This structure is a fine example of the homes built
just after the Revolutionary War.

7 WATKINS-BRYAN HOUSE, c. 1740, 109 N. Water Street;
2-1/2-story home of an early local merchant.

8 PERKINS HOUSE, 115 N. Water Street;
likely built by Simon Wicks in the late 18th century.

9 201 N. WATER STREET; in 1805, a wooden bridge
and small toll house were built on this site.

10 FRISBY HOUSE, c. 1770, 110 N. Water Street;
noted for its wide, interestingly capped chimneys

11 WICKES HOUSE, 102 High Street; Five-bay,
gabled-roofed house with dormers and fifteen fireplaces.

12 BUCK-BACCHUS HOUSE, c. 1735, Queen and High Streets
Built by John Buck, a shipping merchant,
the structure was probably used as a warehouse.

13 NICHOLSON HOUSE, 111 N. Queen Street
Nicholson was the youngest of three brothers,
all of whom were prominent in the infant
U.S. Navy during the American Revolution.

14 GEDDES-PIPER HOUSE, 101 Church Ally
This structure was owned by several merchants,
one of whom was Collector of Customs. His ship,
the brigantine Geddes, was the scene of the
Chestertown Tea Party before the Revolutionary War.

15 LAWYER'S ROW, 113 Court Street;
a series of small, street-side offices

16 MASONIC BUILDING, c. 1835, Park Row and Court Streets;
identified by three Masonic emblems

17 STAM'S HALL, Court and High Streets
Stam, a druggist and merchant, had a flourishing business
on the ground floor and a place for public entertainment and
gatherings on the second floor.

18 WHITE SWAN TAVERN, 1733, 231 High Street
Built as a residence, it became a tavern in the 1790s,
and a general store in the 1850s. It was reopened as
a tavern in the 1970s, and in 1981 opened as a B&B,
restored to its 1795 appearance.

19 CHRIST METHODIST CHURCH, Mill and High Streets; one of
the most richly ornamented church buildings in town.

20 KENT COUNTY OFFICES, 1901, 400 High Street
Erected as a public school, it is open today as a
prime example of colonial revival architecture.
A visitor center is on the second floor.

21 THE COURTHOUSE, nineteenth century, 103 N. Cross Street
Front section of the structure was built in 1860;
a colonial revival addition was added in 1969.

22 EMMANUEL EPISCOPAL CHURCH, Cross Street and Park Row
The original structure was built between 1767 and 1772
as a chapel of ease, but has had several modifications since.
To show the separation from England, it was called the
Protestant Episcopal Church.

23 FOUNTAIN PARK, 1899
This horse water trough, located on the Cross Street side of
the park, was crowned by Hebe, Goddess of Youth and Beauty.

Millington

2010 Census Population: 643

Millington was originally called Head of Chester and then Bridgetown after Gilbert Falconer divided the land into fifty acre parcels and constructed a bridge there in 1748. The sparse settlement grew and, by 1798, was extending into land owned by Richard Millington, who built one of the first houses. It was in 1798 that the residents applied to Maryland's General Assembly for the right to establish and regulate a market. By 1827, the community was officially named Millington in honor of its first citizen, and continued to prosper to the present day. With the advent of the Kent and Queen Anne's Railroad, Millington became known for peaches, which it shipped in large quantities for some time.

ACTIVITIES

Please check the internet or call ahead, as dates, times, and locations may change.

◎ RESTAURANTS
- Two Tree Restaurant, 401 Cypress Street, 410-928-5887
- Millington Pizza, 189 Sasssafras Street, 410-928-3239
- Tailgate Market Deli, 198 Sassafras Street, 410-928-3136

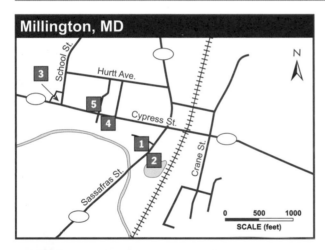

POINTS OF INTEREST

1 GRIST MILL, Sassafras Street, 1766; open on special, occasions
2 OLD MILLINGTON SCHOOL, 350 Cypress Street; now apartments
3 FORMER MILLINGTON RESIDENTIAL ACADEMY, at School Street; now a private home
4 FORMER HOTEL, 396 Cypress Street; being renovated
5 5. PARADISE HOUSE, 401 Cypress Street; carefully restored, rear portion built in 1699, front in 1744.

Rock Hall
2010 Census Population: 1,310

N. 39 08' W. 76 14'

One of the first settlements in Kent County, the town was formerly known as Rock Hall Crossroads. Just a dirt path in 1675, the town's Main Street was part of the first road in Kent County. Travel by water in those days was preferable to long journeys over the rough roads of the times, and its location made Rock Hall a hub of colonial travel on the Chesapeake Bay. During the Revolutionary War, Tench Tilghman took the ferry from Annapolis to Rock Hall, on his way to Philadelphia, with the news of Cornwallis's surrender at Yorktown. The Annapolis-to-Rock Hall ferry was one of many that linked segments of Post Road, which led from the Carolinas to New England. Among the thousands who traveled that route were George Washington, Thomas Jefferson, and James Madison.

Rock Hall experienced a building boom in 1889 that was spurred by a family of carpenters who, according to a persistent legend, used the timbers that washed down the Conemaugh River from Johnstown in that year's great flood. The two-story frame dwellings are recognized by their decorated corner posts, attic dormers, and comfortable front porches.

Today, with fifteen marinas, the harbor is a favorite destination for pleasure boaters and local fishermen. Oysters, crabs, clams, and fish are shipped from Rock Hall all over the state and often as far as New England. The town itself is a typical turn-of-the-century community. Away from the active harbor, its main street has modest storefronts. Their overhanging balconies supported by iron posts give the street a nostalgic appeal. Visitors have a variety of dining, recreation, and shopping options. The Rock Hall Trolley Company runs a loop around the center of the town every hour. A $2.00 ticket is good for rides all day, with a stop off for refreshments at the old-fashioned soda fountain in Durding's Store.

For a listing of places to eat, stay, and see, turn to the next page.

◰ MARINAS

- Gratitude Marine, 5924 Lawton Avenue, 410-639-7011
- Haven Harbor Marina, 20880 Rock Hall Avenue, 410-778-6697
- Hill's Marina, 4866 Skinners Neck Road, 410-639-7267
- Long Cove Marina, 22589 Hudson Street, 410-778-6777
- North Point Marina, 5639 Walnut Street, 410-639-2907
- Osprey Point Marina, 20786 Rock Hall Avenue, 410-639-2663
- Rock Hall Landing Marina, 5657 Hawthorne Avenue, 410-639-2224
- Rock Hall Marine Railway, 5676 South Hawthorne Avenue, 410-639-2263
- Sailing Emporium, 1144 Green Lane, 410-778-1342
- Spring Cove Marina, 21035 Spring Cove Road, 410-639-2110 *(*Note: Lodging is also available)*
- Steamboat Landing, 4800-4802 Skinners Neck Road, 410-639-7813
- Swan Creek Marina, 6043 Lawton Avenue, 410-639-7813

◰ LODGING

- Bay Breeze Inn, 5758 N. Main Street, 410-639-2061
- Black Duck Inn and Dock Side Café, 21906 Chesapeake Avenue, 410-639-2478
- Carriage House, 5877 Coleman Road, 410-639-2855
- Inn at Huntingfield Creek, Huntingfield Manor, 4928 Eastern Neck Road, 410-639-7779
- Inn at Osprey Point *(*Note: Also has a restaurant)*, 20786 Rock Hall Avenue, 410-639-2663
- Inn at Swan Haven Bed & Breakfast, 20950 Rock Hall Avenue, 410-639-2527
- Mariner's Motel, 5681 S. Hawthorne Avenue, 410-639-2291
- Moonlight Bay Marina & Inn, 6002 Lawton Avenue, 410-639-2660
- North Point Marina Hotel, 5639 Walnut Street, 410-639-2907
- Swan Point Inn *(*Note: Also has a restaurant)*, 20658 Wilkins Avenue, 410-639-2500
- Tallula's on Main, 5750 N. Main Street, 410-639-2956

◰ RESTAURANTS

- Bay Leaf Gourmet, 5757 Main Street, 410-639-2700
- Bay Wolf Restaurant, 21270 Rock Hall Avenue, 410-639-2000
- Chessie's Restaurant and Carry-Out, 21321 Rock Hall Avenue, 410-639-7727
- Durding's Store, 5742 Main Street, 410-778-7957
- Ford's Seafood, 6262 Rock Hall Road, 410-639-2032
- Fur, Fin and Feather, 20895 Bayside Avenue, 410-639-2686
- Muskrat Alley Café, 5877 Coleman Road, 410-639-2855
- Old Oars Inn, 5781 N. Main Street, 410-639-2541
- P. E. Pruitt's Waterside Restaurant, 20899 Bayside Avenue, 410-639-7454
- Rock Hall Snack Bar, Route 20, 410-639-7427
- Waterman's Crab House, 21055 Sharp Street, 410-639-2261

SPECIAL EVENTS AND ACTIVITIES

Please check the internet or call ahead, as dates, times, and locations may change.

May: Spring Bike Fest, Rock Hall Bayside Landing & Park
June: Annual Rockfish Tournament, Rock Hall Bulkhead
July: July 4th Parade, meets at Main Street
   Kent County Waterman's Day, Rock Hall Bulkhead
   Rock Hall Yacht Club Log Canoe Race, 22759 McKinleyville Road
September: Fall Fest, Main Street
October: Fall Bike Fest, Rock Hall Bayside Landing & Park
December: Boat Parade and Santa on Main Street, Rock Hall Harbor

Rock Hall, MD

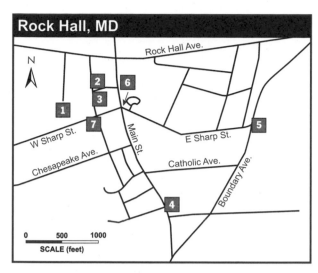

Rock Hall Ave.

W Sharp St.

Chesapeake Ave.

Main St

E Sharp St.

Catholic Ave.

Boundary Ave.

0   500   1000

SCALE (feet)

POINTS OF INTEREST

1 CHESTER RIVER KAYAK ADVENTURES, 5758 Main Street; 410-639-2001

2 JT's ROCK HALL INN, 5769 N Main Street; 410-639-ROCK

3 MAINSTAY PERFORMING ARTS CENTER, 410-639-9133

4 ROCK HALL MUSEUM, 410-639-7611

5 ROCK HALL WATERMAN'S MUSEUM, 20880 Rock Hall Avenue; 410-778-6697

6 TOLCHESTER BEACH REVISITED MUSEUM, 5753 Main Street; 410-708-2496

7 DURDING'S DRUG STORE, 5742 Main Street; a mainstay for generations

Queen Anne's County

Centreville
2010 Census Population: 4,285

Centreville is a perfect example of small town America. Lovers of period architecture can stroll tree-lined streets and study good examples, from simple and austere colonial homes to gracious Victorian-era dwellings with wraparound porches. The first settlement was known as Chester Mill and dates back to the establishment of St. Paul's Parish in 1692. Because it was equally accessible to all county residents, the town became the county seat of government in 1782, and the name was changed to Centreville. The Episcopal Church at 301 S. Liberty Street was built in the early 1700s at a cost of over 15,000 pounds of tobacco.

⬚ LODGING
- Hillside Motel, Route 213 N (south end of town), 410-758-2270
- Rose Tree Bed and Breakfast, 116 S. Commerce Street, 410-758-3991

⬚ RESTAURANTS
- Coliseum Pizza, 112 N. Commerce Street, 410-758-1800
- Doc's Riverside Grill, 511 Chesterfield Avenue, 410-758-1707
- Hillside Steak & Crabhouse, Route 213 (south end of town), 410-758-1300
- Julia's, 122 N. Commerce Street, 410-758-0471
- Sugar Magnolia Café, 101 S. Commerce Street, 410-758-8572

SPECIAL EVENTS
Please check the internet or call ahead, as dates, times, and locations may change.

January–March: "Emergence" Coffee House, Queen Anne's County Arts Council, 410-758-2520

Baltimore Symphony Orchestra Concert, Mid Shore Symphony Society, 410-758-2343

March: Artists of the Chesapeake, Queen Anne's County Arts Council, 410-758-2520

April: "Emergence" Coffee House, 3rd Annual Poetry Contest, Queen Anne's County Arts Council, 410-758-2529

Baltimore Symphony Orchestra Concert, Mid Shore Symphony Society, 410-758-2343

Annual Black Tie and White Boot Affair, Queen Anne's Chamber of Commerce, 410-643-8530

"Made in America" Concert, Queen Anne's County High School, 410-827-8618

May: May Mart, Queen Anne's County Courthouse Lawn, 410-758-1858.

June: Historic Open House, Historic Consortium of QAC, 119 S. Commerce Street, 410-758-3010

Bay Music Festival, Queen Anne's County 4-H Park, 410-604-2100

June–August: Thursdays in the Park, Concert Series, Queen Anne's County Arts Council, 410-758-2520

July: Historic Open House, Historic Sites Consortium of QAC, 410-604-2100

August: Queen Anne's County Fair, Maryland State Fair Board, 4-H Park, 410-758-0267

Historic Open House, Historic Sites Consortium of QAC, 410-604-2100

September: Historic Open House, Historic Sites Consortium of QAC, 410-604-2100

October: Fall Artisan's Festival, Centreville Rotary Club, 410-758-0030

"Emergence" Coffee House, Queen Anne's County Arts Council, 410-758-2520

November: "Emergence" Coffee House, Queen Anne's County Arts Festival, 410-758-2520

December: Annual Centreville Christmas Parade, Centreville Christmas Parade Committee, 410-758-1180.

Centreville Christmas House Tour, Queen Anne's County Arts Council, 410-758-2520

Christmas Train Show, 4-H Park Road, 410-758-8640

QUEEN ANNE'S COUNTY

Centreville, MD

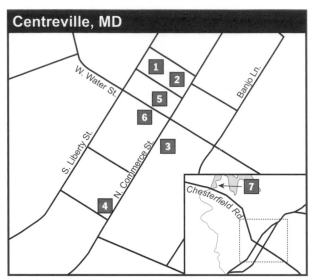

POINTS OF INTEREST

1 County Courthouse, 1792,
100 Courthouse Square
> The landscaping includes a tree planted
> in June 1977 by Her Royal Highness
> The Princess Anne. Tours are available.
> Call 410-758-0216 for more information.

2 QUEEN ANNE'S STATUE,
Courthouse Square

3 WRIGHT'S CHANCE, c. 1744
> Early plantation house moved from
> original site patented in 1681. Restored by
> the Queen Anne's Historical Society and
> open by request the first Saturday of each
> month, May to October, 10:00 a.m.
> to 3:00 p.m. For information,
> call 410-604-2100.

4 TUCKER HOUSE, c. 1792
> Built on the second lot sold in the
> Centreville, it is one of the oldest houses
> in town. Open by request on the first
> Saturday of each month, May to October,
> 10:00 a.m. to 3:00 p.m. For information,
> call 410-8604-2100.

5 BLUE LANTERN INN, 110-112 S.
Commerce Street, c. 1792-1798

6 ST. PAUL'S EPISCOPAL CHURCH,
301 S. Liberty Street, c. 1692
> The church was built at its current
> location in 1834 and by 1909 had been
> remodeled three times.

7 DOCK AT CENTREVILLE

Crumpton

2010 Census Population: Not available

Crumpton, on the banks of the Chester River, was known in the nineteenth century as McAllister's Ferry. Crossings were made aboard a simple barge hauled between the river's banks. The village grew around the ferry landing, spreading over the farm of William Crumpton. In 1858, James Shepard and Maurice Walsh of Salem, New Jersey, bought the tract and laid out the town, by then known as Crumpton. In the days of the steamboats on the Bay, Crumpton was the point on the Chester River where they turned around to return to the Chesapeake. It enjoyed a brief period of prosperity during the latter part of the nineteenth century.

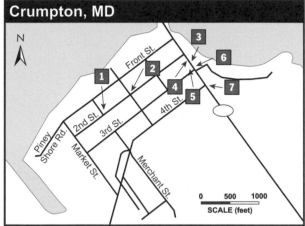

POINTS OF INTEREST

1 VAN TINE HOUSE, c. 1875
   The exterior dental cornice can be found on several area houses and suggests a common builder, NE corner of Front and Merchant Street.

2 HAMAN HOUSE; earliest known date of house appears on an 1877 map

3 HARRISON HOUSE, 1883; it's the largest and most distinctive house in Crumpton

4 CRUMPTON HOTEL; built in the 1860s when the town was first laid out, early Victorian

5 OLD POST OFFICE

6 RUBSAMEN HOUSE
   This structure is notable because it is built on locally-made concrete blocks, which are an early example of such construction.

7 HARTLEY HOUSE, c. 1865
   One of the finest examples of Victorian architecture surviving in Crumpton, it retains almost all of the exterior trim, a bracketed cornice, and a one-story porch with single brackets applied against scrolled fascia. The paneled entrance features sidelights, a transom, and paneled shutters.

Matapeake

2010 Census Population: Not available

N. 38 57' W. 76 21'

Matapeake is Algonquian for "water, a current, or an expanse of water," as is the case of the small town by that name on the shores of the Chesapeake. It was also the name taken by a tribe of Native Americans who lived and hunted in the area of Mattapex Neck and Indian Springs. The quiet little town is known primarily as the Eastern Shore terminus of a ferry that crossed the Bay from Sandy Point, just north of Annapolis on the west side. A trip on the ferry was a particular favorite of businessmen who relished a good whiskey and a game of cards while their wives enjoyed the Bay air. This ended when the Chesapeake Bay Bridge opened in

1952 — Matapeake became a forgotten village and has remained so ever since.

The Bayfront village had a reprieve of sorts in 1981 when the state of Maryland chose it as the site for a giant model of the Chesapeake Bay. The 8.6-acre, fixed-bed model is housed in a fourteen-acre building and was built to a horizontal scale of 1:1000 and a vertical scale of 1:100. It was designed and used to simulate the Chesapeake's tidal heights and currents, salinity distributions, and freshwater flows. Though the model was initially very successful, it proved too expensive to operate and was closed down and put into storage.

POINT OF INTEREST

1 Dock at Matapeake State Park, 201 Clubhouse Drive

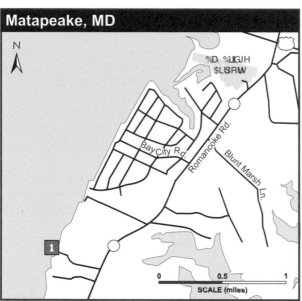

Matapeake, MD

Queen Anne – Hillsboro

Queen Anne and Hillsboro are two immediately neighboring towns separated by a tributary of the Choptank River. Hillsboro lies in Caroline County, while Queen Anne lies both in Queen Anne's and Talbot Counties. The three county lines meet at the Tuckahoe State Park.

Queen Anne
2010 Census Population: 222

Queen Anne/Talbot County
N. 38 55' W. 75 57'

Named for Anne, Queen of England from 1702 to 1714, the village of Queen Anne is divided by Tuckahoe Creek, named for marsh plants that grow in the area. Native Americans made bread from Tuckahoe's roots. Aside from dividing the town, Tuckahoe Creek also forms part of the boundary between Queen Anne's and Talbot Counties.

Along the highway south of Queen Anne a marker calls attention to the fact that the former slave and abolitionist Frederick Douglass was born and lived for six years on a farm near there. Pastoral best describes this area today, but once, though it's hard to believe, this quiet small town was a center of rural industry and owes its existence to a railroad that established a depot on the spot in 1867. The town grew around the depot and the railroad that served a granary and flour mill, tomato and other canneries, a lumber mill, a milk cooling station, and large poultry farms. A second depot was added in 1896 when the Maryland, Delaware, and Virginia Railroad came to the Shore. Today, the train has gone the way of the steamboats that once stopped at Queen Anne.

At the same time that passenger train service was flourishing, so was travel by steamboat. For many, in the late nineteenth and early twentieth centuries, steamboat travel was much more comfortable than traveling on the roads. They often made an excursion of it, spending a day traveling the rivers and Bay just for the pleasure of it. In 1878, the Maryland Steamboat Company began running the *Highland Light* and the *Kent* that offered nightly service from Queen Anne to Baltimore and many stops on the Eastern Shore. Over the next decade, the fleet expanded with the *Avalon*, *Tred Avon*, *Ida*, and *Joppa*, but, like the trains, steamboat passenger service couldn't survive the coming of the automobile. The *Joppa* was the last; she stopped running in 1932.

Following World War II, the changes were relentless and rapid. By 1960, passenger trains were also gone. Today, the two-lane highways that crisscross Queen Anne's County carry their traffic through Queen Anne and the surrounding countryside. They are narrow enough to encourage passersby to slow down and enjoy the views.

Hillsboro
2010 Census Population: 164

Caroline County
N. 38 92' W. 75 94'

For a small village, Hillsboro has a remarkably long history. Records show the community had a chapel as early as 1694. Since the middle 1700s, there has been a bridge over Tuckahoe Creek, which meanders through the state park and Queen Anne and skirts Hillsboro. Near the bridge is the house said to have been built by Francis Sellers, a merchant in the 1780s. The town also supported a tobacco warehouse and tavern. Because steamboats couldn't make

it all the way to Hillsboro, smaller boats carried goods and freight upstream to the town. Hardly a backwater, in 1797, Hillsboro boasted an academy that provided the children of white farmers with a classical education. In the late 1900s, it became a county school. Worth looking for along Tuckahoe Road south of town is a colonial era brick house begun by Charles Daffin and finished with Victorian Gothic detailing.

QUEEN ANNE'S COUNTY

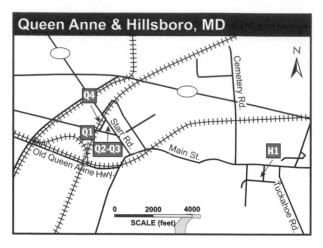

Queen Anne & Hillsboro, MD

Cemetery Rd.

N

Q4

Starr Rd.

Q1

Q2-Q3

Main St.

Old Queen Anne Hwy.

H1

Tuckahoe Rd.

0   2000   4000
SCALE (feet)

Q1

Q2

Q3

Q4

POINTS OF INTEREST – QUEEN ANNE

Q1 OLD RAILROAD BRIDGE, over Alternate Route 404

Q2-Q3 GIBSON'S STORE, Park Avenue at Starr Road, 1912; the current sign says it all

Q4 REMNANT OF RAILROAD TRACK, RAILROAD AVENUE; THIS TRACK SERVED THE MANY MILLS AND CANNERIES IN THE AREA.

POINTS OF INTEREST – HILLSBORO

H1 HILLSBORO UNITED METHODIST CHURCH, Maple and Main Streets

H1

Queenstown
2010 Census Population: 664

N. 38 59' W. 76 09'

In 1658, Lord Baltimore granted Colonel Henry Coursey as much land as he could cover on a map with his thumb. His grant took in most of the land that would become Queenstown. The Colonel quickly made a treaty with the Iroquois nation that assured him of peace in the region. Queen Anne's Town, as it was named in honor of England's new monarch, eventually became Queenstown and, in 1707, the Queen Anne's County seat. A brick courthouse was built in 1708. Its middle section served as the jail until 1749. The field behind the building, known as "Gallows Field," was the scene of public hangings. In the eighteenth century, Queenstown was a prominent shipping center where area farmers took their corn, wheat, hemp, and tobacco to be shipped to market by steamboat. A post office was opened in 1800.

During the War of 1812, the town was of sufficient importance to attract an attack by the British army. The force of 1,400 men landed in two groups. One group was routed by a local force of eighteen men and retired to their ships. The other group never engaged the citizens. They went ashore on the wrong side of Queenstown Creek and hadn't the means to cross. They, too, left without accomplishing their goal.

Today, a nationally acclaimed golf course and one of Maryland's largest designer outlet centers attract people to Queenstown and, in time, it is hope more will come to explore the town and its historic sites.

⊡ LODGING
- The Manor House, 511 Pintail Point Farm Lane, 410-827-7029
- Queenstown Inn Bed & Breakfast, 7109 Main Street, 410-827-3396 (*Includes a restaurant*)

◻ RESTAURANTS
- Captain Jim's, Route 50
- Ivy Market Cafe, 7109 Main Street, 410-827-3397
- Potter's Pantry, Route 18, 410-827-8846

SPECIAL EVENTS
Please check the internet or call ahead, as dates, times, and locations may change.
March: Calvary United Methodist Ham & Oyster Dinner, 410-827-7113
July: Independence Day Celebration, The Aspen Institute, Pace Grave site and Wye Plantation Manor House, Queen Anne's County Historical Association, 410-758-1623
October: Calvary United Methodist Church Ham & Oyster Dinner, 410-827-7713

QUEEN ANNE'S COUNTY

Queenstown, MD

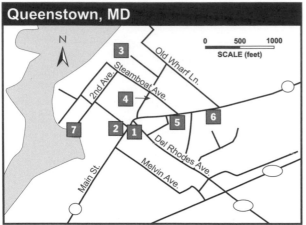

N

SCALE (feet)
0   500   1000

Old Wharf Ln.
2nd Ave.
Steamboat Ave.
Main St.
Del Rhodes Ave.
Melvin Ave.

POINTS OF INTEREST

1 COLONIAL COURTHOUSE, Route 18 and Del Rhodes Avenue, c. 1708
First courthouse in the county. Tours available by request. For more information, call 410-827-7646.

2 CANTERBURY HOUSE, 6923 Main Street, circa 1850

3 BOWLINGLY
Surveyed in 1858 for James Bowling, the house was built in 1733. The British attack in 1813 at Bowlingly was defeated. It was bought in 1897 by Queen Anne's Railroad Company, which turned it into a hotel and amusement park. The large porches were the refuge of many who used the railroad.

4 NATIONWIDE AGENCY
Once a post office and a bank, it is the only building in the county with a cast iron front.

5 CAROLINE WILSON HOUSE
A relatively plain example of a house type that first appeared on the shore in the 1850s and persisted into the nineteenth century. It represents a distinct departure from earlier dwellings in that the chimneys were located on the interior parlor walls, flanking the stair hall.

6 ST. LUKE'S EPISCOPAL CHURCH, c. 1890
A fine example of a small frame parish church, 7208 Main Street.

7 QUEENSTOWN DOCK, bottom of 2nd Avenue

Romancoke

2010 Census Population: Not available

Romancoke is an unincorporated community on Kent Island. The name comes from an Algonquian word for "circling of the water." Until the Chesapeake Bay Bridge was built in 1952, the town was the eastern terminus of the Romancoke–Claiborne Ferry that linked the Eastern and Western Shores. Today Romancoke is mostly residential and is part of the Stevensville postal district. The old ferry dock has become a fishing pier.

POINT OF INTEREST

1 FISHING PIER; one-time ferry dock

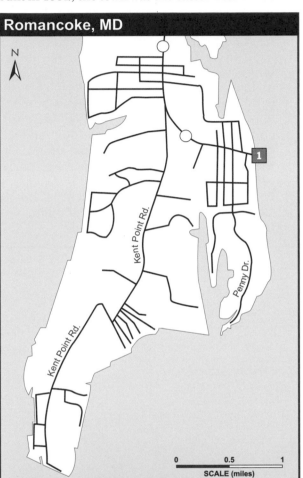

Stevensville

2010 Census Population: 6,803

N. 38 59' W. 76 19'

Stevensville occupies a land grant belonging to Francis Stevens in 1694. Stevens Adventure, as he called it, remained farmland until 1850 when James and Charles Stevens sold their two farms for the development of a town. Early residents of Kent Island and Stevensville were watermen, farmers, cannery workers, and those who owned or worked in small businesses. By 1877, the town consisted of a post office, residential streets, several churches, stores catering to residents and visitors, and two hotels. One was originally a pre-Civil War boarding house, the other accommodated travelers from the Matapeake, Love Point, and Broad Creek ferry landings.

The turn of the twentieth century brought the railroad from Queenstown on the shore to Love Point on Kent Island, north of Stevensville. At nearby wharves, cargoes of produce and seafood were loaded aboard waiting vessels of steam and sail for their trip across the Bay to Baltimore markets. The return trips brought everything from manufactured goods to mail. The town continued to grow, and within a decade had two schools and was served by a number of doctors, a blacksmith, and a saw mill. It continued to flourish until the late 1940s when the railroad stopped its passenger and freight service. Thereafter, little changed in the town itself. In the 1950s, the Chesapeake Bay Bridge brought some new businesses and residents, but mainly ensured that Stevensville would keep its early charm as cars sped by on their way to the Shore and ocean beaches. Today, side roads and overpasses provide passage for residents from one side of Route 50 to the other. The highway also enables new residents to commute to the Western and Eastern Shores from housing developments scattered across Kent Island. As for Stevensville, it is still a close-knit community that retains an aura of bygone days.

▰ MARINAS
- Angler's Marina (Big Owl Dock Bar), 410-827-6717
- Bay Bridge Marina, 410-268-8828
- Mears Point Marina, 410-827-8888
- Queen Anne Marina, 410-643-2021

▰ LODGING
- Kent Manor Inn & Restaurant, 500 Kent Manor Drive, 410-643-5757
- Land's End Manor on the Bay B&B, 232 Prospect Bay Drive West, 410-827-6184
- Maria's Love Point B&B, 1710 Love Point Road, 410-643-5054

▰ RESTAURANTS
- Big Bats Café, 216 St. Clair Place, 410-604-1120
- Cracker Barrel, 115 Blue Jay Court, 410-643-3841
- Hemingway's, Pier
- Kentmore Restaurant, 910 Kentmore Road, Exit 37 (Route 8); 410-641-2263
- R's Americantina, 410 Thompson Creek Mall, 410-643-7700
- Ram's Head Shore House, 800 Main Street, 410-643-2466
- Red Eye's Dock Bar, 428 Kent Narrows Way North, 410-827-3937
- Rustico Restaurant & Wine Bar, 401 Love Point Road, 410-643-9444

SPECIAL EVENTS AND ACTIVITIES

Please check the internet or call ahead, as dates, times, and locations may change.

February: Cooking Class Getaway, Kent Manor Inn, 410-643-5757

March: Author's Luncheon, Chesapeake Bay Beach Club, 410-634-2497
   Artists of the Chesapeake Annual Art Auction ($50), 410-758-2520
   Flashlight Egg Hunt, Old Love point Park, 410-758-0835

April: Bay Bridge Boat Show, Bay Bridge Marina, 410-268-8828

May: Kent Island Day, Stevensville Downtown Center, 410-643-5358
   Chesapeake Wine Festival, Terrapin Nature Area, 410-739-6943

June: Kent Island Relay for Life, Kent Island High School, 410-304-2186
   Youth Fishing Derby, Terrapin Park, 410-758-0835

June–July: Thursdays in the Park, Kent Manor Inn, 410-758-2520

July: Kent Fort Farm's 14th Annual Peach Festival, Kent Fort Farm,

August: Thunder on the Narrows, Kent Island Yacht Club grounds, 410-725-6222

October: Weekends, Pumpkin Patch at Kent Fort Farm, 410-643-1650

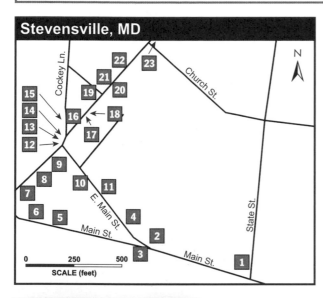

Stevensville, MD

SCALE (feet)
0   250   500

POINTS OF INTEREST

1 THE DUNN HOUSE, c. 1910,
   Route 18 entering E. Main Street;
   was built for a cannery owner

2 KENT ISLAND FEDERATION OF ART,
   c. 1900, 200 block of E. Main Street;
   exhibits work of artists and craftsmen,
   Wednesday through Sunday

3 CAPTAIN EUGENE HERBERT HOUSE,
   c. 1870, 200 block of E. Main Street
      The captain followed the coastal trade
      from Maine to North Carolina.

4 COCKEY HOUSE, c. 1870,
   200 block of E. Main Street;
   once served as a parsonage and library.

5 LEGG FARM HOUSE,
   200 block of E. Main Street
      Third oldest building in Stevensville,
      it was once owned by Bloody Point
      Lighthouse keeper Moses Legg and
      his wife.

6 PRICE-RINGGOLD HOUSE, 200 block of East Main Street
Home of Marian Price Stewart, a founding member of the
Kent Island Heritage Society, until her death in 1991.

7 CAPTAIN "JIM ED" JONES HOUSE, 300 block of Love Point
Road, 1880; destroyed by fire and rebuilt in 1882.

8 SCHOOLHOUSE, 300 block of Love Point Road, 1870;
two teachers taught grades 1 through 4 in its two rooms

9 CHARLES STEVENS STORE, 300 block of Love Point Road,
c. 1865; one of the first stores in town, now a bakery

10 GROLLMAN'S ORIGINAL DRY GOODS STORE,
200 block of East Main Street, 1870

11 CHRIST CHURCH AND RECTORY, 200 block
of East Main Street, 1880; houses the oldest
Episcopal congregation in the United States

12 ORIGINAL STEVENSVILLE POST OFFICE, East Main Street
at Love Point Road; now an Acme Market

13 JENNIE LEGG DRY GOODS STORE, Love Point Road at Cockney
Lane; town's second oldest building, now a furniture store.

14 CRAY HOUSE, 1809, Cockney Lane
The oldest house in Stevensville, it is now the
headquarters for the Kent Island Heritage Society.

15 STEVENSVILLE TRAIN STATION, 1894, Cockney Lane;

16 moved from Love Point in 1988 and restored.

17 COUNTRY STORE, c. 1900, 400 block of Love Point Road
Original German siding probably salvaged from the Johnstown
Flood of 1889. The owner's brother, a judge, once held court in
a corner of the store.

18 HOME OF DR. C. PERCY KEMP AND DR. J. E. H. LEWIS, 1880-1890, 400 block of Love Point Road; formerly a drugstore, it's now a dance studio.

19 STEVENSVILLE POST OFFICE BUILDING, pre-1877, 400 block of Love Point Road; it's now used by a variety of businesses.

20 STEVENSVILLE BANK, 1903-1907, 400 block of Love Point Road; a bank until the 1960s and then occupied by a variety of businesses.

21 METHODIST CHURCH AND PARSONAGE, c. 1864, 400 block of Love Point Road; now the Ye Olde Church House Antique Shop.

22 LOWERY HOTEL, c. 1860, 400 block of Love Point Road
Once met the needs of travelers from the Matapeake, Love Point, and Broad Creek ferry landings.

23 H. GOODHAND HOTEL, 400 block of Love Point Road; identified on 1877 map, once known as Skinner's Boarding House

24 PRICE HOUSE, 1915, 500 block of Love Point Road
The cupola was used as a lookout for enemy planes during World War II.

Somerset County

Champp

2010 Census Population: Not available

N. 38 10' W. 75 48'

Champ is a small, unincorporated community once identified as St. Peter's Peninsula. The name change came about when an optometrist, J. Frank Beauchamp, petitioned for a post office to bear his name. The postal authorities, who preferred a shorter name, agreed if the doctor would agree to shorten it. As the story goes, he suggested Champ, which they accepted.

Today, the loosely-knit village is set in an uncongested area of natural beauty with river and bay waterfront and the bounty they offer. A soft-shell crab hatchery is the community's single identifiable industry. Landmarks are St. James Methodist Church and the community dock.

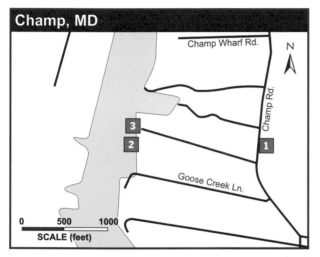

POINTS OF INTEREST

1 ST. JAMES METHODIST CHURCH, intersection of State Highway 627 and Champ Road
2 SOFT SHELL HATCHERY; no longer in use
3 CHAMP TOWN DOCK

Chance
2010 Census Population: 353   N. 38 11' W. 75 57'

Like Champ, this community had its share of trouble with the postal service. Some say that the name came from a nearby land patent of that name. The prevailing story is that when residents requested a post office, the postal service rejected the name Rock Creek, which had been suggested by Captain James Whitlock. The Captain came back with the half-facetious suggestion of "Chance," thinking that there was little chance of it being accepted. He was wrong. The original name lives on, however, in the local Rock Creek M.E. Church, built in 1900. The word is that Chance is the place that serious crabbers go for crab pots and the community has several marinas.

ACTIVITIES

Please check the internet or call ahead, as dates, times, and locations may change.

⊠ MARINAS
- Scott's Cove Marina, 10551 Eldon Willing Road, 410-784-2363 (*Also listed for Deale Island*)
- Windsor's Marina, 23407 Deal Island Road

◎ RESTAURANTS
- Island Seafood
- Lucky's Last Chance General Store, 23724 Deal Island Road, 410-784-2722

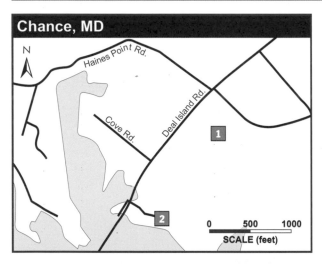

Chance, MD

N

Haines Point Rd.

Cove Rd.

Deal Island Rd.

1

2

0   500   1000
SCALE (feet)

POINTS OF INTEREST
1 ROCK CREEK M. E. CHURCH, c. 1900, Deal Island Road (Route 363)
2 NEW CRAB POTS; in preparation for the season.

Crisfield

2010 Census Population: 2,726   N. 38 59' W. 75 51'

The first inhabitants of the area were Pocomoke and Annemessex Indian tribes of the Algonquin Nation. In 1666, a three hundred-acre tract was granted to the area's first English settler, Benjamin Sommers. Others followed and what began as a fishing village grew to become a town named "Somers Cove" in honor of its first resident. Crisfield is the southern-most city in Maryland and geographically Apes Hole, a section of the Crisfield area, is the southernmost point of the state. By the nineteenth century, the town had become a center for the distribution of seafood along the East Coast. Crisfield became a boomtown and its Goodsell's Alley was notorious for its abundance of brothels and saloons, where fist-fights and gunfights were common. The town was once known as the Dodge City of the East.

In 1866, a Princess Anne attorney, John W. Crisfield, was instrumental in bringing the railroad to the Crisfield seaport and the town was renamed in his honor. The arrival of the railroad meant that Crisfield seafood was being shipped all over the United States and was known as "The seafood capital of the world." By 1904 Crisfield was the second largest town in Maryland, second only to Baltimore.

Crisfield continues to be famous for its seafood, particularly the Maryland crab. It abounds with restaurants, seafood packing houses, and seafood distribution companies. The town has recently seen a burst of condo construction, but with no growth in population. It is the home of Somers Cove Marina, one of the largest marinas on the East Coast, with 450 slips. Nearby Jersey Island was once connected to the mainland with an unusual bridge, which opened by one section rolling over the other. It was destroyed to create an entrance to the marina.

Charter and head-boat fishing opportunities are plentiful. Information on what's available in the town and area is available at the J, Millard Tawes Historical Museum and Visitor's Center.

Local landmarks include Goodie's Boat Yard, onetime site of the M. C. Bard marine blacksmith shop that made single-cylinder motors for the local watermen; the Metompkin Soft Shell Crab processing plant enables visitors to a first hand look at the modern methods used to process and ship this delicacy; the Metompkin Bay Oyster Company is one of three remaining oyster houses out of an original 150 seafood processing houses;

Boats from Crisfield visit Smith and Tangier Islands daily and offer overnight trips to Norfolk in the summertime. Nearby Jane's Island State Park offers hiking, camping, picnicking, swimming, boating, and fishing.

⚓ MARINAS
- Somers Cove Marina, 410-968-2501

🛏 LODGING
- The Cove, 218 Broadway, 410-968-2220 *(Also includes a restaurant)*
- My Fair Lady B&B, Main Street, 410-968-0352
- Paddlewheel Motel, 701 W. Main Street, 410-968-2220
- Pines Motel, 127 Somerset Avenue, 410-968-0900

🍽 RESTAURANTS
- Circle Inn, 4012 Crisfield Highway, 410-968-1965
- Gordon's Confectionary, 831 W. Main Street, 410-968-0566
- Lynn's Kitchen Gourmet Chinese Restaurant, 103 N. Fourth Street, 410-968-3888
- Maho's Restaurant, 410-968-2835
- Mi Pueblito Grill, 333 W. Main Street, 410-968-9984
- Olde Crisfield Restaurant, 204 S. Tenth Street, 410-968-2722
- Pizza Shoppe, 65C Richardson Avenue, 410-968-0333

SPECIAL EVENTS

Please check the internet or call ahead, as dates, times, and locations may change.
May: Soft Shell Spring Fair, Chamber of Commerce, P.O. Box 292, 410-968-2500
July: Fireworks, Somers Cove, 410-968-2500
  Just Folks Festival, City Dock, 410-968-2787
  Annual J. Millard Tawes Crab & Clam Bake, 410-968-2500
August: Annual Hard Crab Derby & Fair, 410-968-2500
December: Christmas Parade, Chamber of Commerce, 410-968-2500

Crisfield, MD

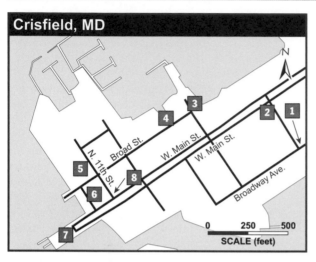

POINTS OF INTEREST

1 THE J. MILLARD TAWES HISTORICAL MUSEUM, 1983, end of Ninth Street; in memory of the fifth governor of Maryland

2 CHARLIE ADAMS CORNER, WATERMAN'S INN, and the METOMPKIN SEAFOOD BUILDING, N. Eleventh Street
  Looking east up Main Street, the entire median strip was once the railroad line through the city.

3 GOODIE'S BOAT YARD, 900 Broad Street
  The M. C. Bard marine blacksmith shop once stood here. The shop made single cylinder motors for the local watermen.

4 METOMPKIN SOFT SHELL CRABS, 101-105 Eleventh Street
  You may see first-hand the modern methods used to process and ship this delicacy.

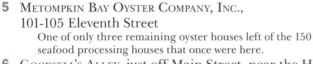

5 METOMPKIN BAY OYSTER COMPANY, INC.,
   101-105 Eleventh Street
      One of only three remaining oyster houses left of the 150
      seafood processing houses that once were here.

6 GOODSELL'S ALLEY, just off Main Street, near the Harbor
      A notorious section of the city. Brothels and saloons used to
      abound, and fist-fights and gunfights were once common.
      Crisfield was once known as the Dodge City of the east.

7 DEPOT AREA, Main Street at the Harbor
      This was the terminus of the railroad. Steamboats would also
      unload here. Up to five trains were common; ferries to Smith
      and Tangier islands leave from here throughout the year.

8 JP TAWES AND BROS. HARDWARE STORE, 1100 W. Main Street;
   a well-known town store

* Jersey Island was the site of the old drawbridge, and is worth a visit.
**A Crisfield walking tour leaves from the Museum at 10 a.m., Monday
   through Saturday, Memorial Day to Labor Day, 410-968-2501

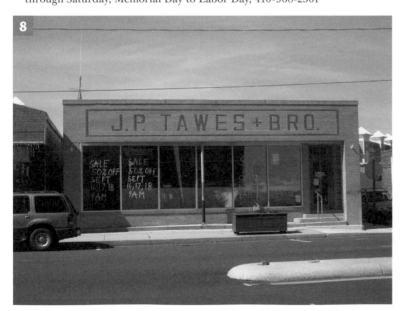

SOMERSET COUNTY

Dames Quarter

2010 Census Population: 167

N. 38 11' W. 78 54'

In 1670, the village known as Dames Quarter, its name appeared to be spelled Damnd Quarter. One supposition is that it was close to Devil's, later Deal, Island, and referred to the land or quarter of the damned. Two more likely possibilities could be that it was named for John Dames, who lived in the area in 1780, or for Captain Frederick Deames, who was in the area in 1781. Whatever the association, by 1794 the village was being called Dames Quarter.

At the turn of the twentieth century, the twenty-one-acre community became a resort that rivaled Ocean City at that time. In 1950, when that resort closed, George and Loraine Henry bought the land and opened a club with a restaurant, stage, and dance hall. They called it Henry's Beach, which operated until 1991.

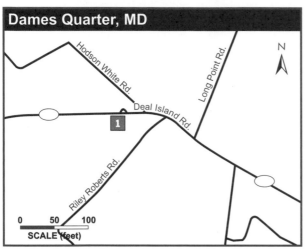

Dames Quarter, MD

Hodson White Rd.

Long Point Rd.

Deal Island Rd.

1

Riley Roberts Rd.

N

0   50   100

SCALE (feet)

POINT OF INTEREST

1 SOMERSET UNITED METHODIST CHURCH, Deal Island Road at Hodson-White Road

Deal Island

2010 Census Population: 471

Deal Island is the name of the village on Deal Island. In the eighteenth century, the island was known for pirates who preyed on shipping in the Tangier Sound and the lower Bay. At that time, it was called Devil's Island, a name that lasted until the American Revolution when the pirates harassed rebel shipping. Finally, Maryland raised a navy, defeated the pirates, and stopped the raids. Illegal smuggling was practiced during the Civil War by Confederate sympathizers with fast schooners that could dodge the blockading Federal gunboats. The blockade runners did a flourishing business until 1863 when a fleet of shallow draft gunboats put an end to their trade. By 1900, Deal Island was the second-largest town in Somerset County, boasting a population of 1,500 residents, five general stores, two blacksmiths, a gristmill, a sail loft, and a veterinary surgeon.

About fifty-four percent of the island is marshland. The islanders are nearly all watermen who have followed traditional jobs for many generations. Religion came to the island in the form of Methodism. According to tradition, an elder in the church changed the name to Deal. The most famous of several preachers was Joshua Thomas, "The Parson of the Islands," who came from Tangier Island. He started holding camp meetings in 1828. More than two hundred boats and steamers brought crowds to the wooden shelters set up for the occasion. The grounds were lit at night by fire stands, which were bonfires set atop piles of mud and sand. The tradition of the camp meeting continued through the twentieth century when began to be held under a roofed pavilion named for Joshua Thomas. He is buried near his little chapel behind St. John's United Methodist Church, one of three on the island. By 1850, the population was five hundred. Almost gone are the Chesapeake Bay skipjacks, which once numbered more than two thousand. Only thirty-three are left and, in 2002, Deal Islanders owned five: the *Fannie L. Dourghety*, *Ida May*, *Somerset*, *Crisfield*, and *Caleb Jones*. Boat-builders were busy at both boatyards. An itinerant boat builder and several individuals also built skipjacks, including the *E. C. Collier*, now preserved at the Chesapeake Bay Maritime Museum in St. Michaels, and the *Minnie V.*, operated by the Maryland Historical Society.

⌧ MARINAS
• Scott's Cove Marina, 10551 Eldon Willing Road, 410-784-2428

⌧ RESTAURANTS
• Billy Anderson Seafood, 315 Richard Webster Road, 410-784-2300
• Corbins Seafood, 23386 Deal Island Road, 410-784-2400

SPECIAL EVENTS AND ACTIVITIES
Please check the internet or call ahead, as dates, times, and locations may change.
September: Labor Day Skipjack Races and Festival, 410-784-2799

SOMERSET COUNTY

Deal Island, MD

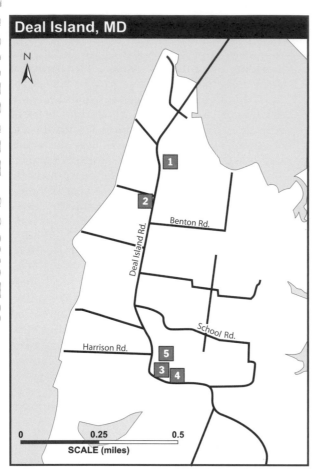

N

Benton Rd.

Deal Island Rd.

School Rd.

Harrison Rd.

1
2
5
3
4

0   0.25   0.5

SCALE (miles)

POINTS OF INTEREST

1 DEAL ISLAND BANK, 1908,
   Deal Island Road south of Hotel Road
2 DEAL ISLAND – CHANCE VOLUNTEER FIRE
   DEPARTMENT, 10090 Deal Island Road
3 ST. JOHN'S METHODIST CHURCH,
   8960 Deal Island Road
4 JOSHUA THOMAS CHAPEL,
   Deal Island Road north of Junction
   with Tangier Island Road
5 OLD ST. JOHN'S CHURCH WITHOUT A STEEPLE
   Aboveground graves were used to
   protect the interred from high water.
   The Somerset Cemeteries Project writes:
   "This historically significant church
   and cemetery is in serious distress, and
   the Joshua Thomas Chapel itself is in
   imminent danger of being condemned.
   An effort is underway to make repairs to
   the chapel and cemetery."

Oriole
2010 Census Population: Not available

Sometime around 1880, a leading citizen petitioned the Post Office Department to name his community St. Peter's, but there was another St. Peter's and they had to choose another name. Because large flocks of orioles nested in the village trees, the townspeople named it Oriole. It could, later, be associated, at least in name, with Baltimore, the home of a popular baseball team, the Oryuls.

During the 1880s, boat-building was the principal occupation. In their heyday, a good number of the more than 2,000 skipjacks on the Chesapeake were built in Oriole. In 2008, only thirty-three of the original boats survived. Of that thirty-three, four were built in Oriole: the *Hilda M. Willig*, *Nellie L. Byrd*, *Sigsbee*, and *Thomas Clyde*. Many of the surviving skipjacks have been converted to carry passengers.

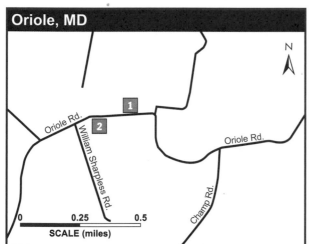

Oriole, MD

POINTS OF INTEREST
1 ORIOLE ST. PETER'S UNITED METHODIST CHURCH, 27160 Oriole Road
2 QUAINT, EARLY VICTORIAN DOUBLE-STEEPLE HOUSE IN ORIOLE, 27072 Oriole Road

Princess Anne

2010 Census Population: 3,290

N. 38 12' W. 75 42'

The hamlet of Princess Anne is at the head of the Manokin River in an area prized for the opportunities it offers hunters, fishermen, photographers, kayakers, and nature lovers. Created in 1733, it was named for Princess Anne, daughter of King George II, and today serves as the county seat of Somerset County. By the mid-eighteenth century, the town had gained considerable importance in trade on the Manokin River that was navigable as far as the bridge at Princess Anne. Local trade was increased later by the southward extension of the railroad. Much of the town's architectural heritage has been preserved. About fifty acres of the old town, containing an estimated three hundred structures, is entered in the National Register of Historic Places. Among them are the first Manokin Presbyterian Church building, erected in 1756 to serve the congregation established about 1683; the Washington Hotel, dating from 1797; John W. Crisfield's mid-nineteenth century home, known as Somerset House, and his law office; the Colonel George Handy House, built in 1805; and St. Andrew's Episcopal Church, c. 1 767-73, which originally served as the chapel-of-ease for Somerset Parish. In the 1980s, Manokin River Park opened and features the 1870 election house that was relocated to the park at the same time. Princess Anne is also notable as the location of the Eastern Shore campus of the University of Maryland.

▣ LODGING
- Econo Lodge, 10936 Market Lane, 410-651-9400
- The Hayman House B&B, 30491 Prince William Street, 410-651-2753
- Princess Anne Motel, 205 Mt. Vernon Road, 410-651-1900
- Washington Hotel Inn, 11784 Somerset Avenue, 410-651-2525 (*Also includes a restaurant*)

▣ RESTAURANTS
- Peaky's Restaurant & Lounge, Mt. Vernon Road, 410-651-1950
- Spikes Pub & Subs, Mt. Vernon Road, 410-651-9124

SPECIAL EVENTS AND ACTIVITIES
Please check the internet or call ahead, as dates, times, and locations may change.
April: Annual Daffodil Show, S. Somerset Avenue, 410-651-9636
   Horse Show, Civic Center, 410-651-2408
May: Princess Anne Expo & Antique Auto Championship, 410-968-1171
August: Horse Show, Civic Center, 410-6511-3185
   Somerset County Fair, Washington High School, 410-651-3802
October: Scottish Irish (Celtic) Festival, 410-651-0757
   Olde Princess Anne Days, 410-651-1705
   Princess Anne Country Craft Show, Manokin Park, 410-546-0454
December: Christmas Antiques Show, Civic Center, 410-546-3027
   A Princess Anne Christmas, Manokin River Park, 410-651-0757
   Christmas Candlelight Tour, Prince William Street, 410-651-2762

Princess Anne, MD

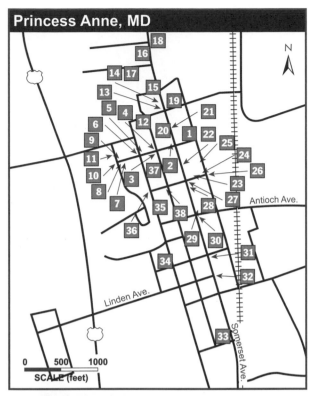

SCALE (feet)

POINTS OF INTEREST

1 OLD PRESBYTERIAN CHURCH LECTURE HALL, c. 1860, 30548 Prince William Street; originally used by the Manokin Presbyterian congregation

2 SOMERSET COUNTY COURTHOUSE, 1904-05, 30512 Prince William Street
Georgian Revival, it replaced the second original building erected in 1832-33.

3 C. H. HAYMAN HOUSE, 1898, 30491 Prince William Street
This large Queen Anne-style frame house provides an interesting display of Victorian and Colonial Revival designs.

4 DOUGHERTY HOUSE, c. 1835 or 1837, 30400 Prince William Street; a combination of Greek Revival and mid-nineteenth century cottage architecture

5 JUDGE LEVIN T. H. IRVING HOUSE (EPISCOPAL RECTORY), 30480 Prince William Street, c. 1850; Greek Revival

6 TEACKLE GATEHOUSE, c. 1805, 30466 Prince William Street; one of two entrance buildings that housed slaves and hired help.

7 FONTAINE-FITZGERALD HOUSE, c. 1852, 30459 Prince William Street; Greek Revival

8 FRANCIS BARNES HOUSE, c. 1853-54, 30449 Prince William Street; well-designed example of a bracketed house

9 RUFUS PARSONS HOUSE, c. 1858, 30448 Prince William Street; unusual example of Greek Revival

10 TEACKLE MANSION, 11736 Mansion Street, 1802, 1818-19; a highly elaborate Federal Style architectural example

11 SETH VENABLE HOUSE (SIMPLICITY), 11748 Prince William Street; built by Seth Venable, a local carpenter, for him and his family

12 WILLAM GEDDES HOUSE (TUNSTALL COTTAGE); oldest dwelling in Princess Anne

13 CHARLES JONES HOUSE, c. 1780, 11816 Somerset Avenue; located on Lot 3, one of the original thirty lots

14 WOOLFORD-ELZEY HOUSE, 11828 Somerset Avenue, c. 1788, c. 1840; the core dates to the eighteenth century, later the exterior was altered

15 ELECTION HOUSE, c 1870, and MANOKIN RIVER PARK, Somerset Avenue; the old election house was relocated here when the park was opened in the late 1980s.

16 MANOKINM PRESBYTERIAN CHURCH, 11890 Somerset Avenue, 1756, 1871-72; 1888; the original congregation was established about 1683

17 NUTTER'S PURCHASE, c. 1800, 30455 Flurer's Lane; erected as part of a tanning complex.

18 LINDEN HILL, c. 1835, 11923 Somerset Avenue; Federal-Greek Revival telescope form

19 METROPOLITAN UNITED METHODIST CHURCH, 1886; Gothic Revival

20 Washington Hotel, 1797, 11784 Somerset Avenue; modifications done in 1838 and later

21 John W. Crisfield Law Office, c. 1847-48, 11787 Somerset Avenue; antebellum frame commercial architecture

22 Old Bank of Somerset, c. 1884, 11739 Somerset Avenue; unusual combination of Gothic Revival and Romanesque architecture

23 John W. Crisfield House (Somerset House), c. 1852 and earlier; late Federal/Greek Revival

24 Anna I. Haines House, c. 1909, 30560 Washington Street; brick townhouse

25 The Laura House, c. 1905, 11728 Beechwood Street; modest Victorian

26 Colonel George Handy House, 1805-06, 11719 Beechwood Street; frame sheathed with original weatherboards and a sawn log smokehouse

27 Boxwood Gardens, c. 1850, corner of Somerset and Washington Streets

28 General George Handy House, c. 1845; remodeled Greek Revival

29 Joshua W. Miles House (Hinman House), c. 1890; elaborate Queen Anne style

30 William W. Johnson House, c. 1834-35, 11653 Somerset Avenue; finely detailed Federal Style

31 Levin Woolford House, c. 1853, 11601 Somerset Lane; only example of the Second Empire in town

32 WATERS HOUSE, c. 1859, 11571 Somerset Avenue; erected well south of the original thirty lots

33 FRANK COLLINS HOUSE AND DAIRY BARN, c. 1910 and earlier, 11510 Somerset Avenue
Colonial Revival detailing; dairy barn that predates the house.

34 CASSIUS DASHIELL HOUSE, 1896, 1160 Beckford Avenue; displays intricate Victorian sawn work

35 BECKFORD AVENUE TENANT HOUSES, c. 1870, 11679 and 11685 Beckford Avenue; erected for the workers on the Beckford property.

36 BECKFORD, c. 1803, 11692 Beckford Avenue; a fine example of a Flemish bond house with Federal details

37 ST. ANDREW'S EPISCOPAL CHURCH, c. 1767-73, 1859, 1896; originally chapel-of-ease for Somerset parish

38 LITTLETON LONG HOUSE, c. 1830, 11696 Church Street; Federal/Greek Revival

* A walking tour can be found at:
http://www.townofprincessanne.com/heritage-history.html

Rumbley
2010 Census "Frenchtown-Rumbley" Population: 100   N. 38 06' W. 75 51'

Rumbley Village is named after nearby Rumbley Point. Back in 1953, Mr. William McLane, the postmaster at Manokin, explained that the town was so named because the waters of nearby Tangier Sound made a rumbling noise. Many villagers disagreed, and it is most likely named for Henry and Lydia Rumbly who settled in the area in 1790. Several small villages similar to Rumbley developed along the shores of Tangier Sound and the Chesapeake Bay to fill the need for modest watermen's housing close to where they worked. Most of the houses in the village are two stories and face the water. In several instances, the watermen's work sheds or shanties are near their dwellings, vividly illustrating the residents' close attachment to the water.

ACTIVITIES
Please check the internet or call ahead, as dates, times, and locations may change.

⌇ MARINAS
- Goose Creek Marina, 410-651-1193
  Directions: Rt. 13S to Md. Rt. 413 toward Crisfield.
  Turn Right on Rt. 361W and go eight miles to the Village of Rumbley.

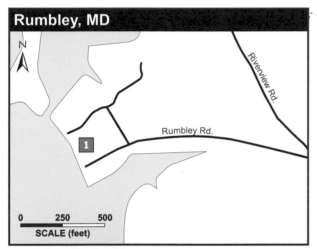

Rumbley, MD

Riverview Rd

Rumbley Rd.

1

0   250   500
SCALE (feet)

POINT OF INTEREST
1 THOMAS W. BLAKE HOUSE SITE, c. 1860
Destroyed by fire in the 1980s, the oldest crab house in Rumbley is located in front of this site (now Goose Creek Marina).

Shelltown

2010 Census Population: Not available

SOMERSET COUNTY

The name Shelltown came from the large shell deposits along the riverbank. Native Americans of the Archaic Period who camped in the area of Shelltown left large heaps, or middens, of discarded oyster shells. Surviving shell heaps are often many feet thick and cover thousands of square feet. Shelltown owes its name to one such remnant of the past. The village houses face the main street that connects Shelltown Road and the wharf. The small community is composed of a dozen frame and recently built brick structures. The Cropper Store is the only commercial building. A few buildings date from the third quarter of the nineteenth century, but most were erected during the early twentieth century. Even though the existing dwellings date from relatively modern times, the existence of a village is documented as early as the late eighteenth century.

Shelltown, MD

N

Williams Point Rd.

Shelltown Rd

Peters Point Ln.

Veronica Ln.

1

0   0.25   0.5

SCALE (miles)

POINTS OF INTEREST

1 DOCK AND FISHING AREA

Shells used to be highly visible here, but may now be covered by silt.

Smith Island – Ewell
2010 Census Population: 276   N. 37 58' W. 76 01'

Smith Island is the only populated off-shore island in Maryland. It was named for Henry Smith who was the island's largest landholder in 1679. There are several islands, most of which are predominately salt marsh with an elevation of less than four feet, and three communities: Ewell and Rhodes Point, connected by a single lane road, and Tylerton, accessible only by boat. In the last 150 years the island has lost 3,300 acres of wetlands and restoration efforts are planned for the next fifty years.

People traveling to Smith Island can reach it only by boat. Ferries connect it to Point Lookout on the Western Shore of the Chesapeake and Crisfield on the Eastern Shore. Visitors find rooms in a guesthouse and enjoy seafood meals. They are also charmed by the hardy islanders' livelihood working the water, their devotion to the Methodist Church, and their local dialect.

The customs and atmosphere are similar to the West Country of England, principally from settlers from Cornwall and Wales who arrived during the early Elizabethan period. A special treat is the Smith Island Cake featuring eight to fifteen thin layers filed with creme, frosting and/or crushed candy bars. It has been designated the official dessert of Maryland.

Despite concession to modern amenities and a grudging acceptance of tourism, the residents do exactly as their forebears did; they steadfastly fish the surrounding waters for oysters and crabs. Visitors have a choice of charter boats: the *Captain Jason I* and *Captain Jason II* (410-425-5931); the *Island Belle II*, (410-968-1118); and the *Captain Tyler II* (410-425-2771) from Somers Cove Marina and Reedville, Virginia. KOA Campground (410-453-3430).

⬛ MARINAS
• Smith Island Marina, Ewell, 410-425-4220

⬛ LODGING
• Bayside Cottage, Rhodes Point, 410-905-6041
• Chesapeake Fishing Adventures B&B Tylerton, 410-968-0175
• Chesapeake Sunrise B&B, Ewell, 410-425-4220
• Fisherman's Rest Cottage, Ewell, 410-4525-2095
• Inn of Silent Music, Tylerton, 410-425-3541
• Pauline's House, Tylerton, 410-771-4040
• Susan's on Smith Island, Ewell, 410-425-2403

⬛ RESTAURANTS
• Bayside Inn, Ewell, 410-425-2771
• Drum Point Market, Tylerton, 410-425-2108
• Ruke's Seafood Deck, Ewell, 410-425-2311

SPECIAL EVENTS AND ACTIVITIES
Please check the internet or call ahead, as dates, times, and locations may change.
May: Smith Island Day, Crisfield-Smith Island Cultural Alliance, 410-425-3351
September: "A Taste of Smith Island" Dinner,
    boat leaves Crisfield for Ewell 6 p.m., 410-425-3351

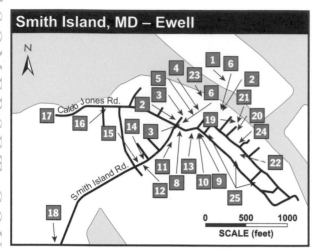

Smith Island, MD – Ewell

POINTS OF INTEREST – EWELL

1 GOAT ISLAND; released about thirty years ago, they are a herd of about forty.

2 VERIZON MICROWAVE TOWER; brought phone service to the island.

3 SMITH ISLAND MARINA, end of Smith Island Road

4 BAYSIDE INN RESTAURANT, Smith Island Road; serves visitors from tour boats during the summer season

5 BIKE AND CART RENTAL FOR TRAVEL AROUND THE ISLAND, Smith Island Road

6 SMITH ISLAND VISITORS CENTER AND MUSEUM, 20846 Caleb Jones Road; provides an excellent history of the island

7 RUKE'S STORE, Caleb Jones Road across from the Visitors Center
    A mainstay where watermen share stories, movies are shown, and other social events occur.

8 EWELL UNITED METHODIST CHURCH, 20851 Caleb Jones Road; the religious and social center of the island

9 WOODEN KEEL REMAINS OF 60-FOOT BUGEYE *C. S. TYLER*, Caleb Jones Road at Somers Road

10 WILSON-BUTLER TABERNACLE, Caleb Jones Road at Somers Road; site of annual camp meeting the last weekend in July and the first weekend in August

11 EDDIE T. EVANS BALL PARK, Caleb Jones Road at Somers Road

12 EWELL SCHOOL & LIBRARY, Smith Island Road

13 RECREATION CENTER, Caleb Jones Road at Somers Road

14 EWELL FIRE DEPARTMENT, Smith Island Road

15 MIDDLETON HOUSE, Caleb Jones Road; now headquarters for the Martin National Wildlife Refuge

16 SUSAN'S ON SMITH ISLAND B&B, 20759 Caleb Jones Road, 410-425-2403
Great views of waterfowl and Goat Island. Susan Evans is a lifetime Smith Islander and Smith Island cake for dessert is guaranteed.

17 PITCHCROFT, past end of Caleb Jones Road
Site of the first house on the island. A British soldier is buried there and the British flag, donated by the United Kingdom, flew over him until 1965. He is supposed to be buried standing up and facing England.

18 THE EXTENSIVE MARSH BETWEEN EWELL AND RHODES POINT
Once a dumping ground for trash, old cars, etc., the marsh and its wildlife are now protected by a major cleanup effort by Islanders.

19 HARBOR SIDE GROCERY

20 THE ISLAND BELLE MAIL BOAT AND DOCK
The mail boat runs daily between Ewell and Crisfield, piloted by Captain Otis.

21 A FAVOURITE PASTIME GIFT SHOP, Caleb Jones Road

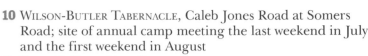

22 EWELL POST OFFICE, Caleb Jones Road

23 THE SMITH ISLAND BAKING COMPANY,
storefront on Caleb Jones Road
It's from here that Smith Island cakes are shipped all over the
world. The mailing address is 4065 Smith Island Road.

24 PUMP HOUSES; provide clean drinking water to Islanders.

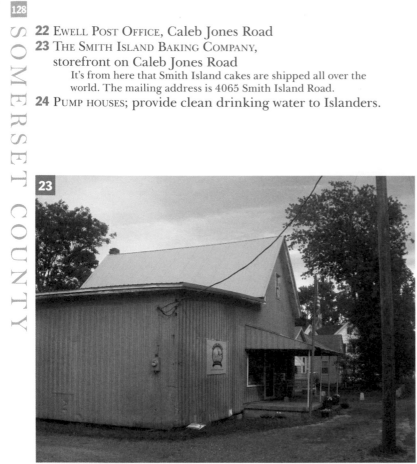

Smith Island, MD – Rhodes Point

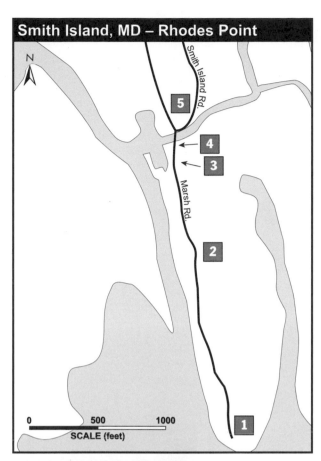

POINTS OF INTEREST – RHODES POINT

Originally called Rogue's Point for the pirates who frequented there.

1 MARINE RAILWAY
2 CALVARY UNITED METHODIST CHURCH
3 VAUGHN HOFFMAN MEMORIAL BUILDING; named for the only islander killed in World War II
4 CLINIC BUILDING

   Visiting nurses come to the island, but most medical care is provided in Crisfield. A helicopter pad is available for helicopters to transport emergency patients.

5 HUGE OLD HOUSE, previously abandoned (photo), but currently undergoing complete renovation.

Smith Island, MD – Tylerton

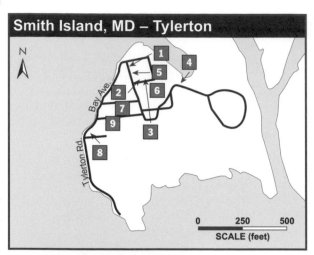

SCALE (feet) 0 250 500

POINTS OF INTEREST – TYLERTON

1 CHESAPEAKE BAY FOUNDATION EDUCATIONAL CENTER, Bay Avenue, 410-268-8816
2 TYLERTON POST OFFICE, 20846 Center Street
3 DRUM POINT MARKET, 21162 Center Street; they have good crab cake lunches
4 TYLERTON CO-OP, 123 Wharf Street; Tylertown's only crab picking house
5 UNION METHODIST CHURCH AND CEMETERY, Center Street and Union Church Street
6 TYLERTON SCHOOL; Maryland's last one-room schoolhouse closed in 1996
7 FIRE DEPARTMENT AND COMMUNITY CENTER, Tuffs Street
8 INN OF SILENT MUSIC B&B, 2955 TYLERTON ROAD; open most of the year
9 OLDEST HOUSE ON THE ISLAND, Tuffs Street at Tylerton Road
   Built early nineteenth century, moved to Tylerton from a now non-existent island in the early decades of the 20th century.

Venton

2010 Census Population: Not available

N. 38 12' W. 76 46'

A village once described as a "rundown hamlet" is still called by its old name of Habnab, though it became Venton in 1921. The name Venton was considered "more dignified" in contrast to the former name, which suggested a possible real estate venture taken "freely, at random." Unfortunately, after the name change, Venton was often misconstrued with the more familiar Denton. Habnab was the name of a tract of land patented in the seventeenth century. "Habnab" is an old English variation of the now familiar term "hobnob." In 1940, the population was 210 individuals. There were three stores, a post office, and two churches. Now nearly all are gone, with a few residences remaining today.

Wenona

2010 Census Population: Not available

N. 38 08' W. 75 58'

The name Wenona is the Sioux Indian word for "first born child" and was chosen by the U.S. Post office for this small island village. The residents' white frame houses are ranged along a strip of land about a mile wide, bounded on its western side by water and marshland. Nearly all of them make their living by catching, packing, and shipping oysters and crabs, trapping muskrats, and catering to hunters and fishermen. The simple, quiet life of the area has attracted retirees and vacationers. The village is the smaller of the two on the island, but it is the site of the main harbor. By 1877, the village had fifty houses and a growing population that leveled off at the turn of the century. Today, there are about eighty houses. Its most famous residents were several generations of the Brown family who were sail makers famous for their skipjack sails. The business closed in the 1970s and by 1988 had been torn down.

ACTIVITIES

Please check the internet or call ahead, as dates, times, and locations may change.

⚓ MARINAS

• Only tie-up piers are available in the dredged harbor.

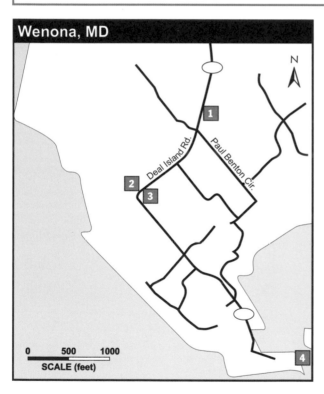

Wenona, MD

N

0   500   1000
SCALE (feet)

POINTS OF INTEREST

1 Quaint painting of the original Wenona church, with the original graveyard in the background
2 New St. Paul's United Methodist Church, Deal Island Road (Route 363)
3 Faith Independent Church, Deal Island Road (Route 363)
4 Town Dock and Skipjack

Talbot County

Claiborne
2010 Census Not available

Claiborne is a small village in Eastern Bay. It is named in honor of Captain William Claibourne who operated a trading post on Kent Island in 1631, thus establishing the first settlement in Maryland. The town itself was created by the Baltimore & Eastern Shore Railroad in 1886 as a ferry landing. In 1940, it became the eastern end of the Romancoke-Claiborne ferry. Both the railroad and ferry are long gone. The Chesapeake Bay Bridge, built in 1952, turned Claiborne into a quiet residential community.

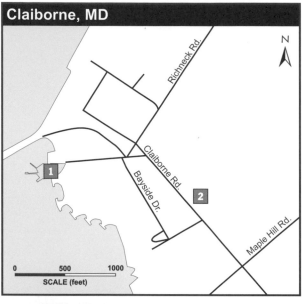

Claiborne, MD

POINTS OF INTEREST
1 CLAIBORNE PIER, Claiborne Landing Road
2 CLAIBORNE UNITED METHODIST CHURCH, 10403 Claiborne Road

Easton

2010 Census Population: 15,945

N. 38 46' W. 76 04'

The town of Easton grew inland from the water. Life there centered around the water and around a religious institution and a court of justice. The first was the Friend's Meeting House, established in 1682-1683; then came the Courthouse in 1711. The town was known early as Talbot Court House and later Talbot Town. Not until 1788 did the community attract the attention of Maryland's General Assembly which appointed a commission to lay out a town. The legislature also appropriated funds to improve the Courthouse for use as a sub-capital for the Eastern Shore.

Easton was also the location of the cathedral of the Episcopal Diocese of Easton. The town is distinguished by numerous Eastern Shore "firsts": Easton had the Shore's first newspaper, first bank, and first gas plant. It also had the first steamship line and the first airplane flight to Baltimore. An appreciation for education and the arts reflects the character of the town, county, and surrounding area that harks back to earlier days when Easton developed as the "Colonial Capital of the Eastern Shore." That heritage is still evident in the wide use of the colonial-style of architecture in new construction.

⚓ MARINAS

- Campbell's Boatyard at Jack's Point, 106 Richardson Street, 410-226-5105
- Cutts & Case, 306 Tilghman Street, 410-226-5416
- Easton Point Marina, 975 Port Street, 410-822-1201
- Hinkley Yacht Service, 202 Banks Street, 410-226-5113
- Mears Yacht Haven, 502 E. Strend Street, 410-5450
- Oxford Boatyard, E. Strand Street, 410-226-5101
- Oxford Yacht Agency, 317 S. Morris Street, 410-226-5454
- Schooner's Landing, 314 Tilghman Street, 410-226-0160

🛏 LODGING

- Ashby "1663" Bed & Breakfast, 410-8224235
- Bishop's House, 214 Goldsboro, 410-820-7290
- Comfort Inn, 8253 Ocean Gateway, 410-820-8333
- Day's Inn, 70180 Ocean Highway, 410-822-4600
- Econo Lodge, 8175 Ocean Gateway, 410-820-5555
- Gross Coate 1658, 11300 Gross Coate Road, 410-919-0802
- The Tidewater Inn, 101 E. Dover Strect, 410-822-1300

◻ RESTAURANTS

- Acapulco, 201 Marlboro Avenue, 410-763-9060
- Amish Market, 101 Marlboro Avenue, 410-822-8989
- Applebee's, 899 Ocean Gateway, 410-770-9882
- Bagel Bakery, 113 Marlboro Avenue, 410-763-7310
- Bartlet Pear Inn, 28 S. Harrison Street, 410-777-9882
- The BBQ Joint, 216 E. Dover Street, #201, 410-690-3641
- Captain's Ketch, 316 Glebe Road, 410-820-7717
- Chili's Bar & Grill, 28587 Marlboro Avenue, 410-763-7077
- China Buffet, 218223 Elliot Road, 410-763-7707
- Coffee Cat/Night Cat, 1 Goldsborough Street, 410-822-3347
- Darnell's Grill & Catering, 22 N. Harrison Street, 410-770-5534
- Easton Diner, 8451 Ocean Gateway, 410-819-0535
- General Tanuki's Restaurant, 25 Goldsboro Street, 410-819-0707
- Giovanni's Italian Delight, 8117 Ocean Gateway, 410-770-6993
- Giufridda's Pizza, 810 Dover Street, 410-819-3296
- Good Time Charlie's, 101 Marlboro Avenue, 410-822-3426
- Hong Kong Kitchens, 201 Marlboro Avenue, 410-822-7688
- House of Hunan, 102 Marlboro Street, 410-820-4015
- Hunter's Tavern at Tidewater Inn, 101 E. Dover Street, 410-822-1300
- In Japan Restaurant, 410-229-8380
- Inn at 22 Dover/Peacock Restaurant, 410-450-7600
- The Inn at Easton, 28 S. Harrison Street, 410-822-4910
- Jin Jin Chinese Restaurant, 6. N. Washington Street, 410-820-0011
- Lazy Lunch, Located behind #28 South Washington Street, 410-770-3447
- Ledo's Pizza, 108 Marlboro Avenue, 410-819-3000
- Legal Spirits, 42 E. Dover Street, 410-820-0065
- Martini's Restaurant, 14 N. Washington Street, 410-820-4100
- Mason's Gourmet, 226 Harrison Street, 410-822-3204
- Night Cat, 5 Goldsborough Street, 410-786-2750
- Olde Town Creamery, 96 Goldsborough Street, 410-820-5223
- Osteria Alfredo, 210 Marlboro Street, 410-822-9088
- Out of the Fire, 22 Goldsborough Street, 410-770-4727
- Pasnera Bread, 8933 Ocean Gateway, 410-767-8230
- Peacock Restaurant & Lounge, 202 E. Oliver Street, 410-819-8007
- Pizza Italian Market, 218 N. Washington Street, 410-820-8281
- Plaza Trapata, 7813 Ocean Gateway, 410-770-8550
- Portofino Restaurant Italiano, 4 W. Dover Street, 410-770-9200
- Restaurant Columbia, 28 S. Washington Street, 410-770-5172
- Roberto's Pizza & Italian, 101 Marlboro Avenue, 410-770-3500
- Rusticana Pizza, 33219 Marlboro Avenue, 410-820-7422
- Scossa Restaurant & Lounge, 8 N. Washington Street, 410-822-2202
- Soda Fountain at Hill's Drugstore, 30 E. Dover Street, 410-822-9751
- Sonic, 8475 Ocean Gateway, 410-725-6222
- Washington Street Pub, 200 N. Washington Street, 410-829-9011
- Waterview Grill at the Easton Club, 28449 Clubhouse Drive, 410-820-9270
- The Wedge, 17 Goldsboro Street, 410-770-3737
- Wildflower Café, 12 W. Dover Street, 410-822-9067
- Zambino's Pizza, 606 Dover Road, 410-822-4911

SPECIAL EVENTS AND ACTIVITIES

Please check the internet or call ahead, as dates, times, and locations may change.

January: First Night Talbot, downtown Easton, New Year's night, 11 S. Harrison Street, 410-770-8000

May: Talbot County restaurant Week, city-wide, dining extravaganza, 410-822-4653

November: Waterfowl Festival, World's Premier Art Show & Sale, 410-822-4567

November-December: Festival of Trees, 101 E. Dover Street, 410-819-FEST

Easton, MD

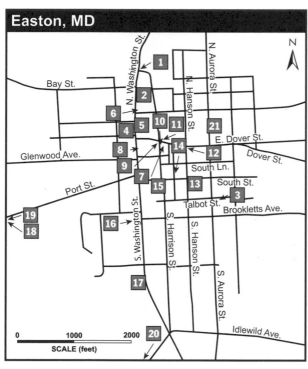

POINTS OF INTEREST

1 COLONIAL-STYLE SHOPPING CENTER
2 2. THOMAS PERRIN SMITH HOUSE, 1803, 119 N. Washington Street
   Early home of the first newspaper on the shore, it's now the Chesapeake Bay Yacht Club.
3 THE BRICK HOTEL, 1812, 401-412 S. Talbot Street; once the shore's leading hostelry, now an office building
4 TALBOT COUNTY COURTHOUSE, 1711; it has been extensively remodeled over the years
5 SHANNAHAN & WRIGHTSON HARDWARE BUILDING, 1791, 12 N. Washington Street; the oldest store in Easton
6 FIRST MASONIC GRAND LODGE, 114 N. Washington Street, 1783; the first one in Maryland.

7 TALBOT COUNTY FREE LIBRARY, 100 W. Dover Street

8 HISTORICAL SOCIETY OF TALBOT COUNTY,
25 S. Washington Street

9 AVALON THEATER, 40 E. Dover Street, 1921;
year-round schedule of cultural events

10 THE BULLITT HOUSE, 1801, 102 E. Dover Street;
one of Easton's most beautiful homes,
now the Mid-Shore Community Foundation

11 TIDEWATER INN, 1949, 101 E Dover Street;
"The Pride of the Eastern Shore"

12 THE INN AT EASTON, 1790, 202 E. Dover Road;
one of Easton's three-bay brick buildings

13 ACADEMY ART MUSEUM, c. eighteenth century,
106 South Street; free and open to the public

14 TALBOT COUNTY WOMEN'S CLUB, c. eighteenth century, 18
Talbot Lane; purchased in 1943 and completely restored

15 CHRIST CHURCH, 111 S. Harrison Street;
built in 1840 of Port Deposit granite.

16 Memorial Hospital, early 1900s, 219 S. Washington Street; one of the finest on the shore

17 Third Haven Meeting House, 1682, 405 S. Washington Street
   The oldest meetinghouse in the United States, it was rebuilt in 1990.

18 Easton Point Marina, 975 Port Street

19 Boat Ramp, Port Street

20 Talbot Country Club, 1910, 6142 Country Club Road

21 Foxley Hall, 1795, 24 N. Aurora Street; one of the most distinguished residences in town.

Oxford

2010 Census Population: 651

N.38 41' W. 76 10'

Oxford is one of the oldest towns in Maryland. Although settled some twenty years earlier, Oxford marks the year 1683 as its official founding — it was that year the General Assembly identified the settlement as Oxford when it designated it an official port of entry and laid out as a town. Until the American Revolution, Oxford was one of the colony's chief international shipping centers and served many of the large tobacco plantations in the area.

A prominent early citizen of Oxford was Robert Morris, Sr., an agent for a Liverpool shipping firm who greatly influenced the town's growth. His son, Robert Morris, Jr., became known as "the financier of the American Revolution." Other Oxford residents of importance were Jeremiah Banning, a sea captain, hero, and statesman; the Reverend Thomas Bacon, who wrote the first compilation of the laws of Maryland; Matthew Tilghman, often called the "father of statehood"; and Colonel Tench Tilghman, who carried the news of Cornwallis's surrender at Yorktown to the Continental Congress at Philadelphia.

The American Revolution marked the end of Oxford's glory. No longer did great numbers of ocean-going ships call at the port, and tobacco, the mainstay of local export trade, was replaced by wheat as a cash crop. Businesses went bankrupt, cattle grazed in the streets, and the population dwindled. Oxford slipped into what has been called its "long slumber" for nearly one hundred years. After the Civil War, however, the port's economy recovered and enjoyed a new prosperity. Improved methods of canning and packing brought business back to the town, opening a national market for oysters made possible by the coming of the railroad and steamboats. Business was booming, houses were going up everywhere, and tourists and boaters arrived in droves, but it was not to last. The oysters played out, the packing houses closed, and the steamships and railroad disappeared.

Oxford has remained a picturesque waterman's town that experienced a resurgence from a thriving economy supported by tourism and leisure water-related activities, foremost of which is sailing. The U.S. Bureau of Commercial Fisheries Biological Laboratory has built a facility to study oyster culture and diseases. Research here may revive the oyster industry.

MARINAS
- Bollard Yachts, LLC, 26106B Bachelor's Harbor Drive, 410-226-0390
- Campbell's Bachelor Point Yacht Club, LLC, 410-226-5592
- Campbell's Boatyard @ Jack's Point, 410-226-5105
- Campbell's Town Creek Boatyard, LLC, 109 Myrtle Avenue, 410-226-0213
- Cutts & Case, 306 Tilghman Street, 410-226-5416
- Eastern Shore Electric Boats, Campbell's Bachelor Point Yacht Harbor, 410-226-5300
- Hinckley Yacht Services, 202 Banks Street, 410-226-5113
- Mears Yachrt Haven, located at the entrance to Town Creek,
  it's home to the Oxford Yacht Club, 410-226-5450
- Oxford Boatyard & Yacht Sales, 402 E. Strand, 410-226-5101
- Oxford Yacht Agency, 317 S. Morris Street, 410-226-0223
- Shipshape, 208 E. Pier Street, 410-226-5479
- Town Creek Marina, 410-226-0207
- Tred Avon Yacht Sales/Charters, 102 S. Morris Street, 410-226-5000

LODGING
- The 1876 House Bed & Breakfast and Limousine Service, 110 N. Morris Street,
  410-226-5496
- Combsberry, 4837 Evergreen Road, 410-226-5353
- Nichols House, 217 S. Morris Street, 410-226-5799
- Oxford Inn & Pope's Treasures, 504 S. Morris Street, 410-226-5220
- Robert Morris Inn, 314 N. Morris Street

RESTAURANTS
- Latitude 38 Bistro and Spirits, 26342 Oxford Road, 410-226-5303
- Mill Street Grill, 101 Mill Street, 410-226-0400
- Pier Street Restaurant and Marina, Inc., W. Pier Street
- Pope's Tavern, 506 S. Morris Street, 410-226-5220
- Schooners's Landing, Foot of Tilghman Street, 410-226-0160

SPECIAL EVENTS AND ACTIVITIES
Please check the internet or call ahead, as dates, times, and locations may change.
April: 4th Saturday, Annual Oxford Day, throughout the town
May: Memorial Day Weekend, Oxford Invitational Fine Arts Fair, Oxford Community Center
June: 1st Saturday, Cardboard Boat Races
December: 1st Saturday, Lighted Boat Parade with Santa

TALBOT COUNTY

Oxford, MD

N

E. Stroud Rd.

Tilghman St.

Factory St.

South St.

S. Morris St.

S. Morris St.

E. Pier St.

S. Morris St.

```
0      500    1000
SCALE (feet)
```

POINTS OF INTEREST

1 OXFORD TOWN MUSEUM, 101 S. Morris Street, located in the heart of town, next to Town Hall

2 THE ACADEMY HOUSE, 1848, 205 N. Morris Street; built for the officers of the Maryland Military Academy.

3 BARNABY HOUSE, 1770s, 212 N. Morris Street; features pine woodwork, corner fireplace, and a hand-made staircase.

4 GRAPEVINE HOUSE, 1798, 305 N. Morris Street
The grapevine in front of the house was brought from the Isle of Jersey in 1810.

5 ROBERT MORRIS INN, corner of North Morris Street and The Strand
Once said to have had the best crab cakes in Maryland by Chesapeake author James Michener.

6 U.S. BUREAU OF COMMERCIAL FISHERIES BIOLOGICAL LABORATORY, 904 S. Morris Street
Established in 1960 to study oyster culture and diseases with the hope that its research will revive the oyster industry.

7 OXFORD-BELLEVUE FERRY, N. Morris Street and The Strand
Believed to be the oldest privately-owned ferry in the country, it was started in 1683, discontinued after the American Revolution, and resumed in 1836.

St. Michaels

2010 Census Population: 1,029   N. 38 47' W. 76 13'

The town of St. Michaels began in 1778 as a development scheme by James Braddock, the factor, or agent, for a Liverpool firm of merchants. Braddock began to purchase land in the vicinity of St. Michaels Church, probably Christ Episcopal Church built in 1677. His land extended from Church Creek to the main road, now Talbot Street. At the time of his last purchase in 1779, he held more than two hundred acres, which he had divided into lots. When he died in 1782, he had sold thirty-seven lots. Among those who settled in the town were house carpenters, shipwrights, wheelwrights, blacksmiths, planters, watermen, and mariners. Very early in its history it was known for its shipbuilding.

St. Michaels is best known perhaps for the log canoe, a unique Chesapeake Bay craft developed in the 1880s. At the height of the oyster boom on the Bay, there were approximately 1,500 built. The remaining fourteen canoes are used exclusively for racing. Today the Miles River Yachting Club is the home port of the log canoe racing fleet. Some of the famed Baltimore Clippers were also built in St. Michaels.

One of the town's most notable citizens was Frederick Douglass, who devoted his life to the abolition of slavery. He died in 1895 at the age of seventy-eight. The town is popularly known as "The town that fooled the British." During the War of 1812, when the townspeople were warned of a bombardment by the British fleet, they hung lanterns in trees beyond the town. They succeeded in fooling the British who overshot the town. Only one house was hit, and it's known today as the "Cannonball House."

Through most of the nineteenth century, the steamboat was an important means of travel on the Chesapeake Bay. Several steamboats, including the *Champion*, *Olive*, *Nelly White*, *Emma Giles*, *Dreamland*, *Jane Mosely*, and *Louise*, provided passenger and freight service to and from St. Michaels. The harbor was also filled with skipjacks and other oyster boats delivering their catch to the town's two shucking and four packing houses. Crabbing also employed a number of St. Michaels watermen in the early 1900s. Seafood wasn't the only industry: tomato canning supported two canneries located on Navy Point, site of the Chesapeake Bay Maritime Museum today.

Along Talbot Street beautiful old homes have been revitalized and now house antique and specialty shops, restaurants, bed and breakfast inns, and other businesses. River cruises are available in the *Patriot*. Regardless of the mode of transportation you use to reach St. Michaels, it is a beautiful historic town that welcomes visitors from all over the world.

⛵ MARINAS

- Chesapeake Bay Maritime Museum; working boatyard, no services, 213 North Talbot Street, 410-745-2916
- Higgins Yacht Yard, 203 Carpenter Street, 410-745-9303
- St. Michael's Harbor Inn Marina, 101 N. Harbor Road, 410-7345-9001
  (*Includes lodging, spa, and the Shore Restaurant & Lounge*)
- St. Michael's Harbor Shuttle, 101 N. Harbor Road, 410-745-2198
- St. Michael's Marina, 305 Mulberry Street, 410-745-2400

◼ LODGING

- Aida's Victoriana Inn, 205 Cherry Street, 410-745-3368
- Best Western St. Michael's Motor Inn, 1228 S. Talbot Street, 410-745-3333
- Cherry Street Inn, 103 Cherry Street, 410-745-6300
- Dr. Dodson House Bed & Breakfast, 200 Cherry Street, 410-745-3691
- Five Gables Inn & Spa, 209 N. Talbot Street, 410-745-0100
- Fleet's Inn, 20 E. Chew Avenue, 410-745-9678
- Hambleton Inn, 223 Cherry Street, 410-745-3350
- The Inn at Perry Cabin, 308 Watkins Lane, 410-745-2200
- Kemp House Inn, 412 Talbot Street, 410-745-2243
- Old Brick Inn, 401 Talbot Street, 410-745-3323
- The Parsonage Inn, 210 N. Talbot Street, 410-745-5519
- The Snuggery Bed & Breakfast, 203 Cherry Street, 410-745-2800
- Tar House Bed & Breakfast, 109 Green Street, 410-745-2175
- Two Swan Inn, 208 Carpenter Street, 410-745-2929

◻ RESTAURANTS

- Acapulco Cuisine of Mexico, 201 Marlboro Avenue, 410-763-9060
- Applebee's, 8999 Ocean Gateway, 410-770-9882
- Ava's Pizzeria and Wine Bar, 409 Talbot Street, 410-745-3081
- Big Al's Seafood Market, 302 N. Talbot Street, 410-745-3151
- Bistro St. Michaels, 403 S. Talbot Street, 410-745-9111
- Blue Crab Coffee, 102 Fremont Street, 410-745-4155
- Carpenter Street Saloon, 113 S. Talbot Street, 410-745-5111
- Characters, 200 S. Talbot Street, 410-745-6206
- Chesapeake Landing Restaurant & Market, 23713 St. Michaels Road, 410-745-9600
- Crab Claw Restaurant, 33 West Street, Navy Point, 410-745-2900
- Destiny's, 1216 Talbot Street, 410-745-5555
- Foxy's Marina Bar, 125 Mulberry Street, 410-745-4340
- Key Lime Café, 201 N. Talbot Street, 410-745-3158
- Market House, 415 S. Talbot Street, 410-745-6626
- Pascal's Tavern & Lounge, 101 N. Harbor Road, 410-924-4769
- Rise Up Coffee, 1216 S. Talbot Street, 410-430-8144
- Rupert's London Bar & Tea Room, 407 S. Talbot Street, 410-745-9090
- Rusticana Pizza & Restaurant, 1110 S. Talbot Street, 410-745-5955
- St. Michael's Crab & Steak House, 305 Mulberry Street, 410-745-3737
- St. Michael's Perk–Talbot Street Coffee House, 401 S. Talbot Street, 410-745-8150
- St. Somewhere, 101 N. Harbor Road, 410-924-4769
- Sherwood's Landing & Purser's Pub, 308 Watkins Lane (Inn at Perry Cabin), 410-745-2200
- Talbot Restaurant & Wine Bar, 208 Talbot Street, 410-745-3838
- Taste Gourmet Café, 105 N. Talbot Street, 410-745-4100
- Town Dock Restaurant, 125 Mulberry Street, 410-745-5577

SPECIAL EVENTS AND ACTIVITIES

Please check the Internet or call ahead, as dates, times, and locations may change.

January–April: St. Michael's Freshfarm Market, Church Cove, 8:30 a.m. to noon

June-September: Summer Concert Series, Thursday evenings, 6:30 to 8 p.m.,
sponsored by St. Michaels Community Center, Hollis Park, 410-745-6073
Moonlight Mixer, Chesapeake Bay Maritime Museum, 410-745-2916
Antique & Classic Boat Festival, Chesapeake Bay Maritime Museum, 410-745-2916
Big Band Night, Chesapeake Bay Maritime Museum, 410-745-2916

July: Independence Day Ceremony, St. Mary's Square, 410-745-9561
Fireworks!, St. Michaels Harbor, 410-745-9511
Moonlight Mixer, Chesapeake Bay Maritime Museum, 410-745-2916
Anniversary of Crab Days, Chesapeake Bay Maritime Museum, 410-745-2916

August: Moonlight Mixer, Chesapeake Bay Maritime Museum, 410-7435-2916

September: Labor Day Weekend Art Show, "Under the Tent," St. Luke's Church, 410-745-3095
Anniversary Boat Auction, Chesapeake Bay Maritime Museum 410-745-2916

October: Last Weekend, Fall into St. Michaels, throughout the town, 800-808-7622
Small Craft Festival, Chesapeake Bay Maritime Museum, 410-745-2916
5K Race through the town, 800-808-7622
Oysterfest, Chesapeake Bay Maritime Museum, 410-745-2916

December: Holiday Art Show, St. Mary's Square, 410-745-3095
First Saturday, shops, open until midnight, 800-808-7622
Christmas in St. Michael's, throughout the town, 410-745-0745
The Sweeter Side, celebrate the holidays with Christmas and music,
Chesapeake Bay Maritime Museum, 410-745-2916

TALBOT COUNTY

St. Michaels, MD

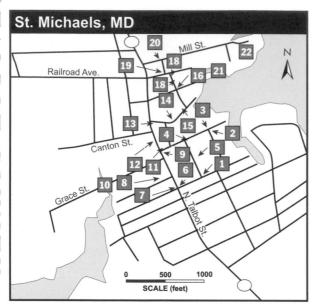

Railroad Ave.

Mill St.

Canton St.

Grace St.

N. Talbot St.

0   500   1000
SCALE (feet)

POINTS OF INTEREST

1 ST. MICHAEL'S MUSEUM, St. Mary's Square between East Chestnut and Mulberry Streets

2 THE COTTAGE, Water Street at Mulberry Street; original home of shipbuilder Robert Lamdin

3 AMELIA WELBY HOUSE, Mulberry Street at Water Street; home of the first Poet Laureate of Maryland

4 CANNONBALL HOUSE, Mulberry Street at St. Mary's Square
   In 1812, a British cannonball penetrated the roof and rolled down the stairs, frightening Mrs. Merchant, who was descending with her infant daughter in her arms.

5 ST. MARY'S SQUARE, between East Chestnut and Mulberry Streets

6 DR. MILLER'S FARMHOUSE, 1840, East Chestnut and South Talbot Streets

7 COL. JOSEPH KEMP HOUSE, Chestnut Street; home of a former Revolutionary soldier and patriot

8 THE BRUFF HOUSE, 1791, Grace Street at South Talbot Street

9 THE OLD INN, 1816, Mulberry Street at South Talbot Street; home of shipbuilder Wrightson Jones, it was later the Bank of St. Michaels.

10 San Domingo Creek, end of W. Chew Street,
rear entrance to St. Michaels

11 Mount Pleasant, 1806, Mulberry Street at
South Talbot Street; now the Maryland National Bank

12 St. Luke's Methodist Church, 1871,
South Talbot Street between Grace and Canton Streets

13 Christ Episcopal Church, 1878,
Willow Street at South Talbot Street

14 The Tarr House, 1667, Willow Street between
Talbot and Locust Streets; built by Edward Elliott,
founder and builder of Christ Episcopal Church

15 The Bruff-Mansfield House, 1778,
Locust Street at Green Street

16 Hell's Crossing, Locust and Carpenter Streets
Known to many sailors from ships that visited the wharf
in front of the building. The wharf once served the
St. Michaels ferry Olive.

17 Small Early-1700s Frame House,
corner of Carpenter and Locust Streets

18 Dr. Dodson's House, 1878, Locust Street at Cherry Street

19 The Snuggery, early 1700s, Cherry Street at end of Locust Street; originally a log house, now covered by siding

20 The Log House, late 1600s, 107 Mill Street; now covered with shingles

21 The Footbridge, Cherry Street; affectionately called the "Sweetheart Bridge."

22 The Chesapeake Bay Maritime Museum, Mill Street at the Harbor

Tilghman Island
2010 Census Population: 784

N. 38 451' W 76 20'

Included as part of Talbot County in 1707, Tilghman Island was originally called Great Choptank Island, then Foster's Island for Seth Foster who owned it in 1659, and later Ward's Island for another owner. Its last owners were the Tilghmans, beginning with Matthew Tilghman who bought it in 1752. Though Tench Tilghman is probably the most famous Tilghman, it is known only that he was born in that area of Talbot County.

The island has been connected to the mainland by bridges from the earliest days. The first bridge was followed by a drawbridge, which was moved to the Chesapeake Bay Maritime Museum at St. Michaels when it was replaced in the early twenty-first century. Crabbing, fishing, oystering, and seafood packing and canning were principal occupations of the community of watermen who make the island their home. The community of watermen once worked the Bay in the famed skipjacks. Only a few survive of the large fleet that once sailed the Bay. Those in the water go out on sailing charters rather than to dredge for oysters. Steamboats made regular stops at the island in the late nineteenth and early twentieth centuries.

Landmark buildings on the island include the Methodist Church, established in 1784 and rebuilt in 1879; and the restored St. John's Chapel, that dates from 1891. In the 1890s, a distinctive style of house style appeared on the island. The classic Tilghman Island house has a "V" shape with three front gables. Of the many built, only a few survive.

The island is also known as a yearly rest stop for thousands of monarch butterflies as they migrate to their winter stay in Mexico. It is similarly visited by great numbers of human visitors drawn to the island by its offerings of fine dining, skipjack charters, sport fishing, bicycling, and bird watching.

ACTIVITIES
Please check the internet or call ahead, as dates, times, and locations may change.

⛴ MARINAS
• Knapp's Narrows Marina, 6176 Tilghman Island Road, 410-322-5181

🛏 LODGING
• Black Walnut Point Inn, 417 Black Walnut Point Road, 410-886-2452
• Crosswinds, Inc., 21642 Jackson Point Road, 410-886-2826
• Harrison's Country Inn & Sportfishing, 21551 Chesapeake House Drive, 410-886-2121
• The Inn at Knapp's Narrows, 6176 Tilghman Island Road, 1-800-322-5181
• Island Home, 5918 Tilghman Island Road, 410-886-2454
• The Jackson House on Tilghman Island, 21483 Mission Road, 410-745-6772
• Tilghman Island Inn, 21384 Coopertown Road, 410-880-2141 (*Also includes a restaurant*)
• Watermark Bed and Breakfast, 8956 Tilghman Island Road, 410-745-2892

🍽 RESTAURANTS
• Bay Hundred Restaurant, 6176 Tilghman Island Road, 410-886-2126
• Bridge Restaurant, 6136 Tilghman Island Road, 410-886-2330
• Harrison's Chesapeake House Restaurant, 21551 Chesapeake House Drive, 410-886-2121
• Two if by Sea, 5776 Tilghman Island Road, 410-886-2447

Tilghman Island, MD

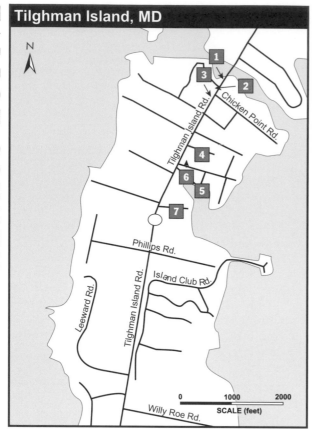

N

Chicken Point Rd.

Tilghman Island Rd.

Phillips Rd.

Island Club Rd.

Leeward Rd.

Tilghman Island Rd.

Willy Roe Rd.

0   1000   2000

SCALE (feet)

POINTS OF INTEREST

1 BAY HUNDRED RESTAURANT, 6178 Tilghman Island Road, 410-886-2126
2 CROSSWINDS, INC., 21642 Jackson Point Road, 410-886-2826
3 TILGHMAN ISLAND REALTY COMPANY, 6091 Tilghman Road, 410-886-2400
4 THE JACKSON HOUSE ON TILGHMAN ISLAND; vacation rentals, 410-745-6772
5 CHESAPEAKE BAY SKIPJACK *REBECCA T. RUARK*, Dogwood Harbor, 21308 Tilghman Island Road, 410-886-2176
6 ISLAND HOME, 5918 Tilghman Island Road; vacation rentals, 410-886-2454
7 HARRISON'S COUNTRY INN & SPORTFISHING, 21551 Chesapeake House Drive, 410-886-2121

Trappe
2010 Census Population: 1,077   N. 38 39' W. 76 04'

Some believe the name Trappe came from an order of Trappist monks, from an order that originated in an abbey in Normandy, France, called La Grande Trappe. It is said that off Main Street, not far from the center of the village, is a farm house that contains the remains of a monastery. There is another candidate for the origin of the name. As the story goes, there was an early tavern called The Partridge Trap and that patrons were said to be "visiting the Trap."

Whatever the origins of its name, the small village of Trappe developed in the 1750s around a crossroads. It was recognized and incorporated by Maryland's General Assembly in 1856. Its population supported several stores and kept doctors and men engaged in a variety of trades busy. There was a hotel and by 1858 it had four protestant churches, including white and African-American Methodist churches and St. Paul's Episcopal.

The new town's commissioners got right to work, voting for construction of wooden sidewalks, limiting speed through the town to eight miles an hour, and setting a 9:30 curfew for week nights and 10:00 on Saturdays. The peace and quiet of the town were further assured by a ban on wrestling, dancing, gaming, and banjo playing. Though there are fewer restrictions today, Trappe is still a peaceful country village.

Town folk were nonetheless adventurous. One, Captain Haddaway, carried Baltimore-built "knockdown" houses aboard his brig, the *Bloomfield*, around the Horn to San Francisco. There, he made a profit among the forty-niners desperate for a place to live.

ACTIVITIES
Please check the internet or call ahead, as dates, times, and locations may change.

⌖ MARINAS
• Gateway Marina, 1606 Marina Drive, 410-478-3304

⌖ RESTAURANTS
• Mitchum's Steak House, 4021 Main Street, 410-476-3902

Trappe, MD

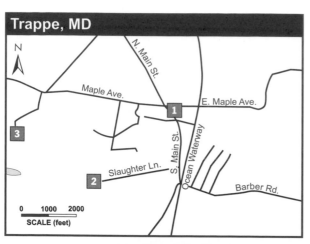

N

N. Main St.

Maple Ave.

E. Maple Ave.

1

3

S. Main St.

Ocean Waterway

Slaughter Ln.

2

Barber Rd.

0   1000   2000

SCALE (feet)

POINTS OF INTEREST

1 DICKINSON HOUSE, MAPLE STREET
Frame house once owned by the family of John Dickinson, whose pre-Revolutionary War letters from a Pennsylvania Farmer helped to inflame anti-British feelings among his fellow colonists.

2 MONASTERY SITE;
believed to have been located in the first house off Main Street going south.

3 TRAPPE LANDING
A principal steamboat landing for shipping Talbot County grain to Baltimore; was put out of business by trains and trucks.

Wye Landing
2010 Census Population: Not available

The name "Wye" identifies not only a river, but also a village — the home of an early Maryland governor, the state tree, and a popular boat landing and crabbing site. The name is believed to have come from a river by that name in England. There is a theory that the name was brought from Wales, along with "Severn" and "Tred Avon," names of other Maryland rivers. Welsh records tell us that a King Evan Lloyd "ruled the lands between the Severn and the Wye." A more likely theory is that the Eastern Shore connection comes from a Reverend William Wye, who lived nearby until his death in 1744.

The Wye River was at one time deep enough to serve packet sloops and schooners carrying freight and passengers to and from the Western Shore. They stopped at Wye Landing, as well as St. Michaels and Oxford. It is said that ocean-going sailing ships could dock at the landing, but today it is primarily a scenic place to visit and a good place to catch crabs.

POINTS OF INTEREST

1 CRABBING DOCK, very end of Wye Landing Road – sweetest crabs on the bay; boats can be rented at Schnaitman's Boat Rental.

Wye Landing, MD

Aspen Ln.

Wye Landing Ln.

Millcreek Ln.

1

Wye Hall Dr.

1

Wicomico County

Bivalve
2010 Census Population: 201

N. 38 18' W. 75 53'

Bivalve is a quiet country village lying within the original seventeenth-century grant known as the Nanticoke Hundred in then Somerset County. The first settlers undoubtedly chose this for its location on the Nanticoke River, which provided them with a plentiful seafood source and a major artery of communication. There seems to be no recorded documentation of the original settlement of the village. Wicomico County, incorporated in 1867, was part of old Somerset County. In 1883, the village was called Waltersville, named for the boat landing serving the Walter family plantation. In 1887, a post office was installed and Elrick Willing was appointed the first postmaster. Because Mr. Willing knew there was already a Waltersville in Frederick County, he renamed his charge Bivalve, referring to the two valves of the shell of an oyster, the mainstay of the local watermen's livelihood.

Among the leading citizens at that time were Larmores, Insleys, Messicks, Harringtons, Willings, Dunns, Horners, among others, almost all of whom worked the water. Some sailed schooners, bugeyes, and batteaus between the Nanticoke and Baltimore, Seaford, Delaware, and Norfolk. The largest group tonged oysters on the river from the first of September to the last of April. Their catch typically sold for thirty to forty cents a bushel. The prevailing wage was seventy-five cents for an eleven-hour day. There was very little money in circulation. A few families only lived in the village in the summertime.

⬛ MARINAS
• Cedar Hill Marina, 410-873-2993

▣ RESTAURANTS
• Sarge's Westside Grocery & Deli, 20835 Nanticoke Road, 410-873-2401

SPECIAL EVENTS
Please check the internet or call ahead, as dates, times, and locations may change.
May: Eastern Shore Lawn Tractor Racing Championship, www.lawntractorracing.org

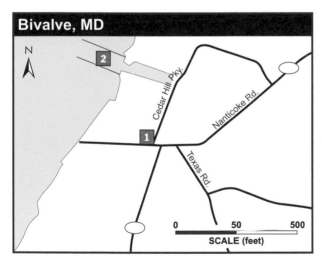

Bivalve, MD

N

Cedar Hill Pky.

Nanticoke Rd.

Texas Rd.

1

2

0   50   500
SCALE (feet)

POINTS OF INTEREST
1 BIVALVE UNITED METHODIST CHURCH, Nanticoke Road at Bivalve Wharf Road.
2 CEDAR HILL DOCK, MARINA, AND COMMUNITY PARK

WICOMICO COUNTY

Jesterville
2010 Census Population: 188

N. 38 17' W. 75 53'

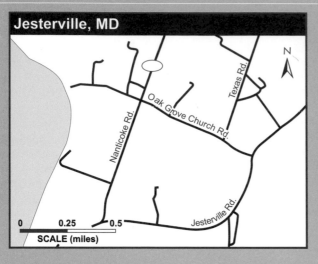

There is nothing funny about the name of this once-thriving community. It was named after John F. Jester, a prominent businessman at the turn of the century. The Jesters were among the first settlers in the area in the early 1700s.

Nanticoke
2010 Census Population: 225

N. 38 16' W. 75 54'

Nanticoke is situated on the river for which it is named. The original Algonquian word was "Nentego," by which the local Indians identified themselves as the "tidewater people" or "they who ply the tidewater stream." In 1676, the earliest English spelling was "Nanticok," which, at some later date, was changed to Nanticoke, perhaps to correspond with the way it had come to be pronounced. Little is known of the community's early history. Like its neighbor Bivalve, Nanticoke is a quaint little village where generations of residents have made their living by crabbing, oystering, fishing, and muskrat trapping.

ACTIVITIES

Please check the internet or call ahead, as dates, times, and locations may change.

⚓ MARINAS

None, there is a dredged harbor, used by watermen, but a visitor may shelter from a storm here.

🏨 LODGING

• Serene Acres, 20614 Nanticoke Road, 410-873-2593

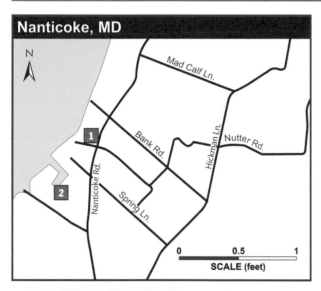

Nanticoke, MD

N

Mad Calf Ln.

Bank Rd.

Hickman Ln.

Nutter Rd.

Nanticoke Rd.

Spring Ln.

1

2

0   0.5   1
SCALE (feet)

POINTS OF INTEREST

1 NANTICOKE METHODIST CHURCH, Nanticoke Road
2 OLD NANTICOKE OYSTER PACKING HOUSE, as seen from the main dock

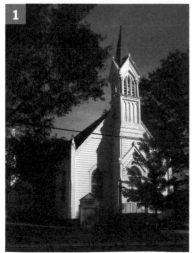

Salisbury
2010 Census Population: 30,343

N. 38 22' W. 75 36'

Salisbury is the County Seat of Wicomico County. The commercial hub of the Delmarva Peninsula, it is sometimes called the "Crossroads of Delmarva." Salisbury's location at the head of the Wicomico River was a major factor in its growth that began with its settlement as a small colonial outpost in Lord Baltimore's Maryland colony. The Wicomico River was the only navigable waterway to the Chesapeake Bay for the area's early settlers. In 1732, Salisbury became an official port and it grew to be second only to Baltimore.

The city has several remarkable nineteenth century buildings. The oldest is Poplar Hill Mansion, built c. 1805. General Humphrey Humphrey's House, built c. 1856, is typical of the Eastern Shore prior to the Civil War. Mrs. Herold's School, dating from 1860, was a private elementary school from 1920 to 1953. The most recent of the buildings is Little Eden, an L-shaped Victorian cottage dating from 1895. Its simplified style has been a popular design in the area.

Today, Salisbury is the headquarters of the multi-national corporation, Purdue Farms, and the large regional corporation, Piedmont Airlines. The city's primary industries are electronic components, pharmaceuticals, shipbuilding, and agriculture. It is the home of Powerwave Technologies, K&L Microwave, Lorch Microwave, Toroid Corporation, Harvard Custom Manufacturing, Navtrack Inc., MaTech Inc., Americahem, Spartech Policom FCD, Plymouth Tube, Silverton Marine, Chesapeake Shipbuilding, Tisheon Corporation, Trinity Sterile, Sharp Water, Salisbury University, Verizon, Peninsula Regional Medical Center, and Pepsi.

Wicomico County's public school system includes three high schools and numerous elementary and middle schools. There are three post-secondary institutions: Salisbury University, Wor-Wic Community College, and Sojourner Douglas College. The community is served by three newspapers, eleven radio stations, and six television stations, baseball and football teams, and various community organizations.

⬛ MARINAS
- Port of Salisbury Marina, 506 W. Main Street, 410-548-3176

⬛ LODGING
- Best Budget Inn, 1804 N. Salisbury Boulevard, 410-546-2238
- Best Value Inn, 2625 N. Salisbury Boulevard, 410-742-7194
- Best Western Salisbury Plaza, 1735 N. Salisbury Boulevard, 410-546-1300
- Chesapeake Inn, 712 N. Salisbury Boulevard, 410-219-3399
- Comfort Inn, 2701 N. Salisbury Boulevard, 410-543-4666
- Country Inn & Suites, 1804 Sweetbay Drive, 410-742-2688
- Courtyard/Marriott, 1289 Troopers Way, 410-742-4405
- Days Inn of Salisbury, 2525 N. Salisbury Boulevard, 410-749-6200
- Economy Inn, 1500 N. Salisbury Boulevard, 410-749-6178
- Hampton Inn, 121 E. Naylor Mill Road, 410-334-3080
- Microtel Inn & Suites, 3050 Merrit Mill Road, 410-742-2626
- Ramada Conference Center, 300 S. Salisbury Boulevard, 410-546-4400
- Residence Inn by Marriot-Salisbury, 2323 N. Zion Road, 410-543-0033
- Sleep Inn, 406 Punkin Court, 410-572-5516
- Temple Hill, 1510 S. Salisbury Boulevard, 410-742-3284
- Thrift Travel Inn, 603 N. Salisbury Boulevard, 410-742-5135

☐ RESTAURANTS

- Break Time, 1009 S. Salisbury Boulevard, 410-742-7665
- Brew River Restaurant, 502 W. Main Street, 410-677-6757
- Cactus Club, 200 Columbia Road, 410-546-3599
- English's Family Restaurants, 604 S. Schumaker Drive, 410-742-9511
- Lombardi's, 515 Civic Avenue-Twilley Plaza, 410-749-0522
- Market Street Inn, 130 W. Market Street, 410-742-4145
- Waterman's Cove Seafood Restaurant, 925 Snow Hill Road, 410-546-1400
- Zia's Italian Grill, 2408 N. Salisbury Boulevard, 410-543-9188

SPECIAL EVENTS AND ACTIVITIES

Please check the internet or call ahead, as dates, times, and locations may change.

February: Salisbury Optimist Club Home, Garden, Family and Craft Show, Civic Center, www.wicomicociviccenter.org

March: Annual Outdoor & Sportfishing EXPO, Civic Center, www.keepersofthebeach.com

April: Annual Pork in the Park Barbecue festival, Winterplace Park, www.porkinthepark.org
Annual Salisbury festival, downtown & Riverwalk Park, www.salisburyarea.com

June: International Poodle Club of America, Civic Center, www.poodleclubofamerica.org.

October: Seagull Century, bicycle racing, Salisbury University, www.seagullcentury.org
Chesapeake Wildfowl Expo, Ward Museum of Wildfowl Art, www.wardmuseum.org
Annual Wicomico County Autumn Wine Festival, Pemberton Historical Park, www.autumnwinefestival.org
Quota Club Christmas Craft Fair, Civic Center, www.wicomicociviccenter.org.

November: Salisbury Kennel Club Dog Show, Civic Center, www.salisburykennelclub.org
Delmarva Crafts Festival, Ward Museum of Wildfowl Art, www.wardmuseum.org

December: Salisbury Lions Club Holiday Classic, Civic Center, www.salisburychristmasshops.org

Salisbury, MD

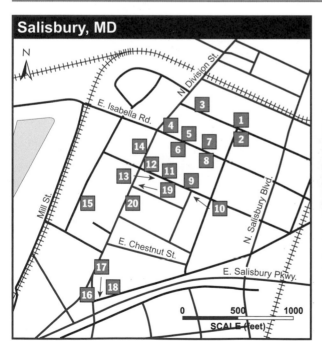

POINTS OF INTEREST

1 POPLAR HILL MANSION, c. 1805, 117 E. Elizabeth Street; Salisbury's oldest house
2 HOLLOWAY HOUSE, 1901, 511 N. Poplar Hill Avenue; Victorian Cape Cod cottage

3 B. Frank Kennerly House, 1904; Queen Anne style
4 Fred A. Grier House, 1896;
Victorian Queen Anne style with decorative windows
5 Alex Toadvine House, c. 1854,
105 E. Isabella Street; Greek Revival
6 Mitchell-Langeler House, c. 1908,
112 E. Isabella Street; Colonial Revival
7 Johnson-Morris House, c. 1892; Queen Anne style
8 "Little Eden," 1895; L-shaped Victorian cottage,
the Simplified style is a popular design here
9 Perry-Cooper House, c. 1880,
200 E. William Street; Second Empire style
10 Agnes D. Perry House, c. 1870, 313 Gay Street
Victorian shuttered cottage, was built on the south side
of the Perry-Cooper House and moved about 1915.
11 Jay Williams House, 1887, 201 E. William Street;
Greek Revival style
12 Ruark House, 1893, 107 E. William Street;
clapboard cottage
13 George Humphries House, c. 1850, 104 E. William Street;
Colonial Revival, moved from N. Division Street in 1920.

14 GILIS-GREER HOUSE, 1887, 401 N. Division Street; high-roofed Queen Anne style

15 OLD PRESBYTERIAN MANSE, c. 1850, 314 Park Avenue; Colonial style composite

16 ASBURY METHODIST CHURCH PARSONAGE, c. 1890, 201 N. Division Street; Queen Anne windows

17 GENERAL HUMPHREY HUMPHREYS' HOUSE, c. 1856, 115 Broad Street; typical of the Eastern Shore prior to the Civil War

18 WICOMICO PRESBYTERIAN CHURCH, 1859, 129 Broad Street; plain brick with two bays added in 1910

19 MRS. HEROLD'S SCHOOL, c. 1860, 325 N. Division Street; this Greek Revival was a private elementary school, 1920-1953

20 ROBERT GRIER HOUSE, 1879, 315 N. Division Street; newer front section incorporates a three-story tower

* A central plaza walking tour is also available.
  Check at the Chamber of Commerce or the Center at Salisbury,
  2300 N. Salisbury Boulevard, 410-548-1694.

WICOMICO COUNTY

Sharptown
2010 Census Population: 651

N. 38 32' W. 75 43'

When America declared its independence from Great Britain in 1776, Sharptown was little more than a hamlet on the south bank of the Nanticoke River. Although thirty-two miles from the river's mouth, it was the first high and dry spot on the south bank. It was an identifiable settlement as early as 1769, known first as Twiford's Wharf, then Slabtown, and finally Sharptown, for Maryland's Governor Horatio Sharp. The town was first incorporated in 1874, but that was repealed in 1880. It was incorporated again in 1888, repealed again in 1912, and then reincorporated that same year.

One of the earliest residents to leave his mark was Matthew Marine. He and his family arrived in Sharptown in 1818. As the founder of the Sharptown Marine Railway Company, Matthew owned the largest fleet of schooners of any one person on the Nanticoke. Shipbuilding

was another thriving industry in the town and, by the end of the nineteenth century, eighteen sailing vessels registered as U.S. merchant ships had been built in Sharptown. By 1877, the community had four dry good stores, a crate and basket manufacturing plant, a blacksmith/shipsmith shop, carpenter shops, and a sailmaker's shop.

The Methodist Protestant Church was established in Sharptown in 1845; forty years later they built a church on the corner of Railway and Church Streets. The present Asbury United Methodist Church was built in 1876. Since 1937, residents have enjoyed community get-togethers on a fourteen-acre property purchased by the fire department that year. Cherry Beach is another popular gathering place. My Lady Sewell's Manor was built in 1661 for the bride of Henry Sewell, Maryland's provincial treasurer. The manor has been restored and now is private home.

SPECIAL EVENTS AND ACTIVITIES
Please check the internet or call ahead, as dates, times, and locations may change.
Every Summer: Sharptown Fireman's Carnival

Sharptown, MD

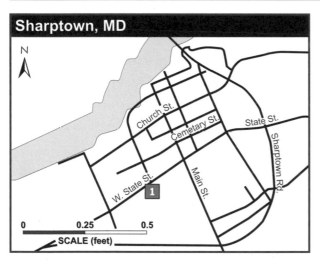

POINT OF INTEREST

1 SHARPTOWN CARNIVAL SITE;
   oysters were eaten by the ton here.

Tyaskin

2010 Census Population: 236

N. 38.20' W. 75 52'

The name Tyaskin is from the Tawachquan Indian word taiachquoan, meaning "bridge." They identified themselves as "the Indians at the bridge." The original bridge was built of logs made into rafts that were most often used for trapping. During the early 1900s, steamboats plied the river, making regular stops at Tyaskin Wharf. In 1982, the old wharf was still in existence, but the channel in Wetipquin Creek was badly shoaled.

🍽 RESTAURANTS

• Boonie's Restaurant and Bar, 21438 Nanticoke Road, 410-548-7879

SPECIAL EVENTS AND ACTIVITIES

Please check the internet or call ahead, as dates, times, and locations may change.
Fishing tournaments are held throughout the summer.

Tyaskin, MD

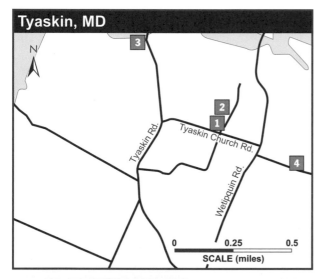

POINTS OF INTEREST

1. TYASKIN UNITED METHODIST CHURCH, 21424 Tyaskin Church Road
2. TYASKIN UNITED METHODIST CHURCH SIGN; rotating schedules are typical of many small villages on the Eastern Shore.
3. TYASKIN WATERFRONT PARK
4. ST. MARY'S EPISCOPAL CHURCH, 1845, on the right side of Tyaskin Road (MD Route 349)

> This structure was originally built in 1798 as a "chapel of ease" to accommodate parishioners in bad weather when roads became a more important means of transportation than water. They would have traveled by water in the past to Old Green Hill (St. Bartholomew Church on the Water).

Waterview

2010 Census Population: 40

N. 38 15' W. 75 54'

A *Wall Street Journal* article of August 18, 1967, described Waterview as a "faded resort town near the Chesapeake Bay." The village drew the magazine's attention because families from the Russian Embassy in Washington, D.C., chose to spend the summer with their children in the old resort's hotel — an example of how circumstances can give sudden prominence to an obscure village and name.

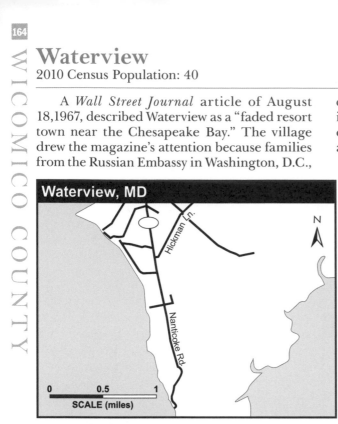

Waterview, MD

Hickman Ln.

Nanticoke Rd

N

0   0.5   1
SCALE (miles)

POINT OF INTEREST

1 TODAY WATERVIEW IS A SLEEPY HAMLET WITH FEW HOUSES.

Whitehaven

2010 Census Population: 43   N. 38 27' W. 75 47'

Whitehaven was established and named in 1700 by Colonel George Hale, who came to Maryland's Eastern Shore from Whitehaven, Cumberlandshire, England. He married Mildred Warner Washington, wife of Lawrence Washington and grandmother of George. The village was part of a 1663 grant originally called Noble Quarter, then later Ignoble Quarter, and might have had more. Bolton, built between 1730 and 1745, survived a fire in 1948 and stands today as a tribute to Whitehaven's earliest days.

The town has had many past lives, serving as a colonial port, shipbuilding center, steamboat port, and even a rumrunner's landing in the 1920s. Today Whitehaven is still the site of a free ferry across the Wicomico River that has operated for 250 years. The present ferry can carry three cars and runs from 6 a.m. to 7:30 p.m. in summer; 7 a.m. to 6 p.m. in spring; and 7 a.m. to 5:30 p.m. in winter.

Today, Whitehaven is far off the beaten path, but is still one of the Shore's most delightful waterfront villages. Most of its residents have working lives elsewhere; some as far away as Washington, but they have, nonetheless, created a very special sense of place and community. The entire town is on the National Historic Register. The Whitehaven Heritage Society, headquartered in the town's well-maintained, late nineteenth century, two-room schoolhouse, keeps a collection of Whitehaven documents and art, as well as holds community events. In 1946, an article in the *Baltimore Sun* called it "Utopia on the Wicomico." This sleepy little town saw its post office close in 1983, has no traffic lights, and is surrounded on three sides by a marsh that has spared it from development. As a result, it is one of the few places on the Bay to enjoy looking up into a star-filled sky.

▣ LODGING
• Whitehaven Hotel, 101 Whitehaven Road

▣ RESTAURANTS
• Red Roost, 2670 Clara Road, 410-546-5443

SPECIAL EVENTS AND ACTIVITIES
Please check the internet or call ahead, as dates, times, and locations may change.
October: Homecoming, when former townsfolk and their descendants return
December: Christmas Service at the Methodist Church

Whitehaven, MD

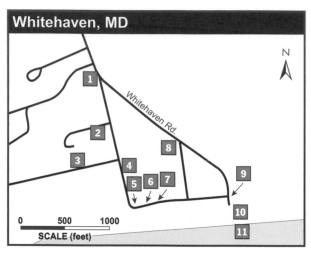

N

0   500   1000
SCALE (feet)

POINTS OF INTEREST

1 WHITEHAVEN SCHOOLHOUSE,
100 Church Street
> Typical one-room schoolhouse for grades
> one through seven. Now the headquarters
> of the Whitehaven Heritage Association.

2 THE WHITEHAVEN CHURCH, 1892,
108 Church Street;
rebuilt after Hurricane Hazel in 1955

3 BOLTON (Might Have Been More),
Locust Lane
> Oldest house, built between
> 1730 and 1745; the interior was
> rebuilt after a fire in 1948.

4 HARMON HOUSE, 115 Church Street;
two-story building, of frame
construction, with Carpenter Gothic trim

5 DORZ HOUSE, 105 River Street;
Federal style, Victorian door with
etched glass and raised panels

6 RUSSELL HOUSE, 1890S, 109 River Street

7 WILSON HOUSE, 111 River Street
> The gable end faces the street;
> it's pedimented, shingled and
> with a cutwork bargeboard.

8 WILLIAMS HOUSE, 100 Cinder Lane
> The entrance has stained glass with small
> raised panels with bulls-eye decorations.

9 THE WHITEHAVEN HOTEL B&B, 101 Whitehaven Road
Three stories with a mansard roof. The west and south facades
have the greatest detail: the west side contains the main
entrance and the south side faces the river and the ferry.

10 WHITEHAVEN FERRY HOUSE, Whitehaven Road;
a small frame house for the use of the ferry operator

11 WHITEHAVEN FERRY
A three-vehicle, six-passenger cable ferry that is free to the
public and runs in daylight hours twelve months a year between
Somerset County (Whitehaven Ferry Road) and Whitehaven;
for information and schedule, call 410-543-2765.

Worcester County

Furnace Town

2010 Census Population: Unavailable

N. 38 12' W. 75 38'

Furnace Town, about four miles south of Snow Hill, is the site of a nineteenth century village on Nassawango Creek in the heart of the Pocomoke State Forest. Its story is told through programs at the Furnace Town Living Heritage Museum, which is an outdoor museum that presents live demonstrations to re-create a vanished nineteenth century community. The museum contains various historic buildings, most notable of which is the Nassawango Iron Furnace. From 1828 to 1850, the Furnace employed hundreds of people, from miners to colliers and bargemen, all engaged in one way or another in mining bog iron ore, smelting it in the furnace, and loading the resulting pig iron bars onto barges to send down Nassawango Creek and the Pocomoke River to the Chesapeake Bay. Several other buildings have been moved to the site. One serves as the Furnace Town information center, which should be a first on any visit.

Another important building is the R. Frank Jones Museum, built in 1869 and moved to the Furnace Town Village in 1977. It contains exhibits on the history of the local area and on processing pig iron. The Mt. Zion One-Room School Museum was originally located in Snow Hill. The one-room school was used by the community until 1931 and moved in 1959 to its current location. The school museum offers displays of things that would typically be found in an early twentieth-century classroom. The forest preserve is open year-round for nature walks, bird watching, and canoeing.

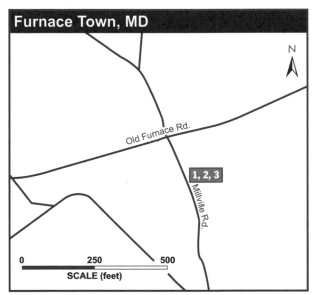

Furnace Town, MD

Old Furnace Rd.

Millville Rd.

1, 2, 3

N

0   250   500

SCALE (feet)

POINTS OF INTEREST

1 FURNACE TOWN LIVING HERITAGE MUSEUM, Snow Hill, Maryland

The musuem's website states, "Stroll beneath towering pines through the village of artisan shops including a broomhouse, blacksmith shop, printshop, weaving house and woodworkers shop. Linger in the Old Nazareth Church and the Museum for a glimpse into the past. Enjoy the scents, sounds, and sights of the nineteenth century Kitchen Garden. A number of activities featuring art, music, and living history are presented each season. The tranquil 25-acre grounds have picnic and walking areas for quiet solitude and peaceful afternoons."

2 FURNACE, 3816 Old Furnace Road; fueled by wood

3 REPRODUCTION CARTS; carry fuel to the furnace

Pocomoke City

2000 Census Population: 4,098   N. 38 04' W. 75 34'

Pocomoke City was first called Stevens Landing, then Meeting House Landing, then New Town until the present name was adopted in 1878. Today's wide main street is lined by few older buildings because most of the original ones were destroyed by fire in 1922. In its early years, the town prospered from shipbuilding. The Tull Shipyards built ocean-going schooners and steamers. Other businesses included the shipping of tobacco and lumber, brick manufacturing, processing fertilizer, and smelting the iron ore found nearby.

John Wennersten's book on the Eastern Shore describes it in the 1820s and 1830s as a riotous waterfront town, legendary for its gambling, cockfighting, drinking, and swearing. By some accounts, it was an ungodly place. In modern times, however, it has been called "the friendliest town on the Eastern Shore" and is "30 minutes from anywhere on the Eastern Shore" including Ocean City. Whether traveling by bicycle, boat, or auto, visitors will find a healthy sampling of traditional Eastern Shore hospitality in Pocomoke City.

⊠ MARINAS
• Pocomoke City Municipal Dock; call City Hall, 410-957-1333, for two nights free docking.

⊡ LODGING
• Day's Inn, 1540 Ocean Highway, 410-957-3000
• Friendship Farm Bed & Breakfast, 410-957-1094
• Holiday Inn Express, 125 Newtown Boulevard, 410-957-6444
• Littleton's Bed & Breakfast, Second Street, 410-957-1645
• Pocomoke Inn, 912 Ocean Highway, 410-957-1030
• Quality Inn, US 13 South, 410-957-1300

▣ RESTAURANTS
• Bonanza, US Route 13 South, 410-957-4292
• Don's Seafood & Lounge, US 13 South, 410-957-0177
• Downtown Coffee Shop, Market Street, 410-957-4700
• Friendly's, 2112 Old Snow Hill Road, 410-956-6500
• Golden Garden Chinese Restaurant, 146 Main Street, 410-957-2966
• Market Street Deli, 1206 Market Street, 410-957-1012
• Traders Chicken, Ribs and Barbecue, US Route 13 South, Ames Plaza, 410-957-1682
• Upper Deck Restaurant & Lounge, US Route 13 South, 410-957-3166
• Young Chow Chinese Buffet, Union Avenue, Pocomoke Plaza, 410-957-9927

SPECIAL EVENTS AND ACTIVITIES
Please check the internet or call ahead, as dates, times, and locations may change. For information on events, call 410-957-1919.

June: Cypress Festival, Father's Day Weekend, Cypress Park
    Annual Triathalon, YMCA,
Late August: Great Pocomoke Fair, Fairgrounds
Mid September: Downtown Block Party, Market Street downtown.
November: First Monday night after Thanksgiving, downtown
Early December: Christmas at Cosden House. Victorian Christmas, Cosden House.

Pocomoke City, MD

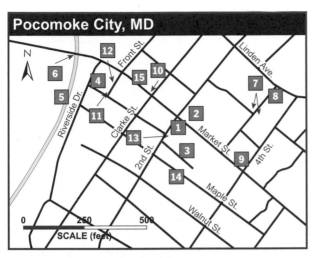

N

SCALE (feet)
0   250   500

1 COSTEN HOUSE, 206 Market Street;
   built after the Civil War, now a museum.
2 BETHANY UNITED METHODIST CHURCH,
   2nd Street
3 PITTS CREEK PRESBYTERIAN CHURCH,
   208 Market Street
4 DELMARVA DISCOVERY CENTER,
   2 Market Street, 410-957-9933
5 SCENIC RIVER CRUISE, Wednesday-Sunday,
   1 p.m., Market Street at the river,
   410-642-1415
6 THE OLD BRIDGE,
   Market Street at the river;
   a new one can be seen in the distance
7 ST. MARY THE VIRGIN EPISCOPAL CHURCH,
   18 3rd Street; first service in 1845

8 St. Mary's Old Vestry, 18 3rd Street
9 First Baptist Church, 4th and Market Streets
10 Marva Theater, 103 Market Street, 410-951-4320
11 Sturgis One Room Museum,
   Front Street, 209 Willow Street, 410-957-3110
12 Heritage House, 209 Willow Street
13 Salem Methodist Church, 504 2nd Street
14 Littleton T. Clark House B&B, 1860, 407 2nd Street
15 Pocomoke City Police Station, 300 2nd Street

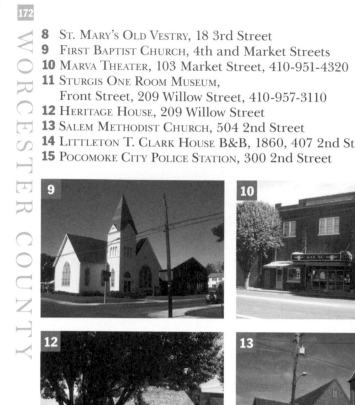

Snow Hill

2010 Census Population: 2,103

N. 38 11' W. 75 24'

Today's Snow Hill was for thousands of years the home of Native Americans. Europeans arrived in 1642 and their settlement grew and prospered as a farming and business community. In 1686, the town was chartered and soon declared a Royal Port. When Somerset County was divided into two counties, Snow Hill was designated the Worcester County seat.

Through the years, Snow Hill residents were involved in the American Revolution, hid official records during the War of 1812, and were divided by Northern and Southern sympathies during the Civil War. Although Maryland was a Union State, slavery was still legally practiced in Snow Hill. The Pocomoke River served as an escape route to freedom for runaway slaves on the Underground Railroad. Shipping, ship-building, agriculture, and commercial enterprise made Snow Hill a thriving town. The river carried goods and passengers bound for the Western Shore. Prosperous businessmen and ship captains built homes along the town's shaded streets. Much of the early downtown was destroyed by fire in 1834 and again in 1893, destroying not only buildings but many early records. Following the last fire, the downtown was rebuilt in brick, reflecting the architectural trends of the later nineteenth century. The charm of Snow Hill's past continues in today's thriving community.

That charm can be found in the Julia A. Purnell Museum, c. 1891, which was established to honor needle artist Julia Purnell and preserve items from Worcester County history. Among the many notable homes and buildings are the Alfred Pinchin House, c. 1882, that once was the Presbyterian manse; the former home of Ephraim King Wilson, a member of the Maryland House of Delegates and Senate; and the home of Richard Howard, captain of the last two steamers on the Pocomoke. Chanceford, dating from 1792, is the earliest known example of a gabled house in the county and the home of Governor John Walter Smith is one of the most elaborately detailed Queen Anne style houses on the Eastern Shore. All Hallows Episcopal Church, c. 1748-56, is one of the oldest and most elaborate mid-eighteenth century structures remaining on the Shore. The Samuel Gunn House, c. 1780, is an eighteenth century Georgian townhouse and one of the oldest in Worcester County. The nineteenth-century Makemie Memorial Presbyterian Church commemorates the original church built in 1683 when Francis Makemie established the first Presbyterian congregation in the America. The Dr. John Aydelotte House, c. 1835, was once used for the sale of slaves; it's the third building on the site.

Visitors to Snow Hill will find a side trip to Furnace Town, about four miles to the south, worth it. It is the site of a nineteenth century village in the heart of the Pocomoke State Forest. While there, it is possible to visit the Nassawango Iron Furnace, Maryland's only bog-ore furnace, the Furnace Town Living Heritage Museum. Information about annual festivals featuring art, music, and living history is available through the Worcester County Tourism Office in Snow Hill.

■ LODGING
- Chanceford Hall Inn B&B, 209 W. Federal Street, 410-632-2231
- River House Inn, 201 E. Market Street, 410-632-2722; best waffles ever!
- Snow Hill Inn, 104 E. Market Street, 410-632-2102 *(*Also includes a restaurant)*

■ RESTAURANTS
- Evelyn's Village Inn, 104 W. Green Street, 410-632-1282
- Shockley's Sub Shop, 112 Pearl Street, 410-632-0608

SPECIAL EVENTS AND ACTIVITIES
Please check the internet or call ahead, as dates, times, and locations may change.
January: Eastern Shore Architecture, Library
  Eastern Shore Wildlife Library
February: 17th Century Decorative Art, Library
February to December: First Friday, downtown, 5-8 p.m.
March: Card Party Fundraiser, Purnell Museum
  Doll Making Workshop by Fibers Guild, Library
  Rotary Gala, dinner & entertainment, Center for Arts & Entertainment
April: Variety of Vices, Purnell Museum
  Percussive Dance Ensemble, Library
  Knitting Workshop, by Fibers Guild, Library
  Yard Sale, Purnell Museum
May: Fiber Fest! Purnell Museum
  International Museum Day, Purnell Museum
  Ballet Performance, Library
June: Weaving Workshop, by Fibers Guild, Library
  Children's Discovery Day, Purnell Museum
July: Independence Day Celebration & fireworks
  Kid's Fiber Art Workshop, by Fibers Guild, Library
  Heritage Arts For Kids, Purnell Museum
August: Blessing of the Combines, downtown, "ag fest"
  Heritage Art For the Kids, Purnell Museum
  Kid's Fiber Art Workshop, by Fibers Guild, Library
September: Delmarva Needle Art Show & Competition, Purnell Museum, regional art exhibit
  End of Summer Sidewalk Sale
  Knitting Class, by Fiber Guild Library
October: Fiber Art Fashion Show and luncheon fund-raiser,
  Nassawango Country Club; call Purnell Museum for reservations
  Julia Purnell's Birthday Party, Purnell Museum
November: Card Party Fundraiser, Purnell Museum
December: Victorian Christmas Celebration, Purnell Museum
  Rotary Cruise in Germany
  Tree Lighting, downtown
  Holiday Dinner Tour, reservations needed
  All About Trees Auction
  Breakfast with Santa, Tavern on Green Street
  Santa's Workshop for Kids

Snow Hill, MD

0   250   500
SCALE (feet)

N

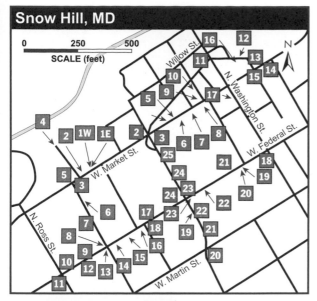

1 JULIA A. PURNELL MUSEUM, 1891

2 SAMUEL GUNN HOUSE,
200 W. Market Street, c. 1780 and c. 1825
> 18th century Georgian style, one of oldest townhouse dwellings in Worcester County.

3 ALL HALLOWS EPISCOPAL CHURCH, 1748-56,
corner of Church and Market Streets
> One of the oldest and most elaborate mid-18th century structures to remain on the Eastern Shore.

4 CAPTAIN GEORGE W. TRUITT HOUSE,
c. 1890, 118 W. Market Street; with three different periods of construction

5 MCKIMMEY-PORTER HOUSE,
c. 1805, 116 W. Market Street
> Pedimented Federal entrance, now partially hidden by a Victorian front porch that was added in the 1890s.

6 ADIAL P. BARNES HOUSE, 1899-1900, 107
W. Market Street; a mixture of Victorian, Queen Anne, and Colonial Revival

7 CHARLES W. CORDDRY HOUSE, 1924, 114 W. Market Street; home of a former mayor

8 MAKEMIE MEMORIAL PRESBYTERIAN CHURCH, 1888-89, 103 W. Market Street

> The original church was built in 1683 when Francis Makemie established the first Presbyterian congregation in the America. The new church features a High Gothic Revival style.

9 FIRST NATIONAL BANK, 1887, 110 W. Federal Street; longest-operating financial institution, Romanesque Revival

10 SNOW HILL MUNICIPAL BUILDING, 1908, 103 Bank Street; once housed the fire department and the mayor's office

11 GOODMAN'S CLOTHING STORE, c. 1893, 110 Green Street

> At the time of its closing in the 1990s, it was the longest-running business in Snow Hill.

12 JOHN BLAIR HOUSE, c. 1835, 201-A E. Market Street; one of oldest in Snow Hill

13 GEORGE WASHINGTON PURNELL HOUSE, c. 1860; now the River House Inn, elaborate Gothic Revival

14 JOHN PURNELL ROBINS HOUSE, c. 1938, 106 E. Market Street; distinctive Federal style

15 DR. JOHN AYDELOTTE HOUSE, c. 1835, 104 E. Market Street

> Now the Snow Hill Inn, the structure contains interesting Victorian features. Slaves were bought and sold here. The first two buildings were destroyed by fire.

16 OSCAR M. PURNELL HOUSE, c. 1900, 100 E. Market Street; example of high Victorian with Greco-Roman flourish

17 WORCESTER COUNTY COURT HOUSE, 1894, 1 W. Market Street
This site was the functional court from the mid-18th century.
The first two courthouses were destroyed by fire.

18 HENRY WHITE HOUSE, c. 1826, 101 W. Federal Street

19 WALTER P. SNOW HOUSE, c. 1850;
late Federal and Greek Revival, has nine fireplaces

20 ALL HALLOWS EPISCOPAL CHURCH RECTORY, c. 1820,
109 W. Federal Street; enlarged at the time of the Civil War

21 BRATTON-JONES HOUSE; combination frame
from two distinct periods: c. 1825 and c. 1880

22 NORMAN SHOCKLEY HOUSE, 1917, 111 W. Federal Street;
classic Colonial Revival

23 P. D. COTTINGHAM HOUSE, c. 1873;
erected for the town druggist

24 COATES HOUSE, c. 1857, 103 N. Church Street
One of the oldest houses on Church Street,
it features Federal and Greek Revival details.

25 MARY B. VINCENT HOUSE, c. 1860, 105 N. Church Street;
combination of mid-century finishes

POINTS OF INTEREST – WALKING TOUR WEST

1 JULIA A. PURNELL MUSEUM, 1891, 208 W, Market Street
   Housed in the former St. Agnes Catholic Church, the museum
   was established to honor needle artist Julia A. Purnell. It also
   contains items from Worcester County's history.

2 COLLINS-VINCENT HOUSE, c. 1890, 210 Market Street;
   Queen Anne style, once the home of Dr. John Riley

3 HARTMAN-SHOCKLEY HOUSE, c. 1840, 209 W. Market Street;
   additions were made to the original

4 SHIPYARD ALLEY; site of a ship-building company
   active in the 19th century

5 BENSON-MORRIS HOUSE, c. 1830, 302 W. Market Street;
   one of the oldest remaining dwellings along Market Street

6 J. EDWARD WHITE HOUSE, c. 1877, 106 N. Morris Street; once
   served as a Home Economics classroom and a lunchroom

7 THE JUDGE WALTER PRICE HOUSE, c. 1877,
   103 N. Morris Street; the style is eclectic
   with mixed Federal and Queen Anne styles

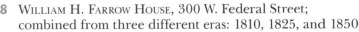

8 William H. Farrow House, 300 W. Federal Street; combined from three different eras: 1810, 1825, and 1850

9 Alfred Pinchin House, c. 1882, 302 W. Federal Street
This New Bedford-style house served as the Presbyterian manse until 1950. It has five fireplaces.

10 Ephraim King Wilson House, c. 1860, 304 W. Federal Street
Wilson was elected to the Maryland state house of delegates and also served as a Senator.

11 John J. Collins House, c. 1885, 401 W. Federal Street; one of the few examples of a Second Empire-style house

12 Selby-Tatterson House, c. 1890, 305 W. Federal Street; a Victorian classic

13 George T. Payne House, 1881, 301 W. Federal Street; Gothic Revival

14 Captain Richard Howard House, c. 1895, 211 W. Federal Street; captain of the last two steamers on the Pocomoke

15 Chanceford, 1792-93, 209 W. Federal Street
This structure has been known by various names over the past two hundred years: Ingleside, Tingle Place, and Boxhall. It's the earliest known example of a gabled house in the county.

16 William J. Wilson House, c. 1881, 207 W. Federal Street; Italianate style, suffered extensive fire damage in 2005

17 CHERRYSTONE, 208 W. Federal Street, 1790, c. 1820;
its gable-front elevation highlights the entrance
off Church Street.

18 GEORGE C. TOWNSEND HOUSE, 205 W. Federal Street,
c. 1840, 1870; was significantly rebuilt after the Civil War

19 GOVERNOR JOHN WALTER SMITH HOUSE,
1899-90, 104 S. Church Street
This structure is one of the most elaborately-detailed
Queen Anne style on the Eastern Shore.

20 GEORGE W. COVINGTON HOUSE, 1878, 119 W. Martin Street
Italianate style, Covington was a member of the
House of Representatives in 1898.

21 CLAYTON J. PURNELL HOUSE, 1894, 107 S. Church Street; he helped to organize the First National Bank of Snow Hill

22 DR. GEORGE WILSON BISHOP HOUSE, c. 1872, 103 S. Church Street; Victorian Style, distinctive arched porch

23 HARGIS-SHOCKLEY HOUSE, c. 1887; distinctive gabled roofs

24 WILLIAM R. SPURRIER HOUSE, c. 1875, 102 N. Church Street; middle-class Victorian domestic style

25 PURNELL SHOCKLEY HOUSE, c. 1905, 112 N. Church Street; originally on Market Square

Western Shore
of the Chesapeake

WESTERN SHORE PLANNERS
list for special occasions

Please check the Internet or call ahead, as dates, locations, and events may change over time.

ONGOING EVENTS

BALTIMORE CITY: There are many festivals, museums, Oriole baseball team, Ravens Football, etc. Call 877-BALTIMORE or check www.Baltimore.org for information.

HAVRE DE GRACE: Lighthouse Tours, April to October, 410-939-9040
    Farmers Market, Saturdays to May to October, Pennington Avenue, 410-939-3303
    Friday Concert in the Park, every Friday, June and July, Tydings Park, 410-939-5425

ANNAPOLIS: April to October, First Sundays, Art and Entertainment, 410-222-7949
    May to June, Annapolis Art Works, 410-263-7940
    June to August, US Naval Academy Band Concerts, 410-263-0263
    June to September, Wednesday Night Sailboat Races, 410-263-9279
    July and August, Quiet Waters Park Summer Concert Series, 410-222-1777
    August to October, Maryland Renaissance Festival, 410-266-7304

SHADYSIDE: Captain Salem Avery House Museum, 1418 Shadyside Road, 410-867-4486

ST. MARY'S CITY: June and July, St. Mary's College of Maryland River Concert Series, 240-895-4107

ST. CLEMENTS ISLAND: Memorial Day through October, St. Clements Island Museum, 301-769-2222
    Tide of Tolerance, One Act Play, outdoor drama;
    call for performance dates and times, 301-769-2222

UPPER MARLBORO: March to May, Chesapeake Tide Indoor Football, Show Place Arena, 301-952-7999

JANUARY

NORTH BEACH: Polar Bear Swim, Beach at 5th Street and Bay Avenue, 410-257-9618

ST. MICHAEL'S: Behind the Scenes at the Museum, Chesapeake Maritime Museum, 410-326-2042

ANNAPOLIS: Historic Annapolis Antiques Show, 410-267-8146
    Polar Beach Plunge, Sandy Point Park, 410-242-1515

FEBRUARY

SOLOMONS ISLAND: Made by Hand – Inspired by the Bay, Calvert Marine Museum, 410-326-2042, ext. 41

ANNAPOLIS: Black History Month, 410-280-0445

UPPER MARLBORO: Southern Maryland Spring Arts Show, Equestrian Center, 301-952-7999
    The 70's Soul Jam, Show Place Arena, 14900 Pennsylvania Avenue, 301-952-7999
    Greenburg Train & Toy Show, Show Place and Arena, 302-952-7999

MARCH

SOLOMONS ISLAND: Spring Break with the Otters, Calvert Marine Museum, 410-326-2042, ext. 41

UPPER MARLBORO: Mistresses & Murderers, Darnall's Chance House Museum, 14800 Gov. Bowie Drive, 301-952-8010
    Crab and Mallet All Breed Cat Show, Show Place Arena, 301-952-7999
    Colonial Tavern Dinner, Darnall's Chance House Museum, 14800 Gov. Bowie Drive, 301-952-8010
    Capital Blues Festival, Show Place Arena, 301-952-7999
    Step it Out – The Ultimate Challenge Step Show, Show Place Arena, 301-952-7999

ST. MARY'S CITY: Maryland Day Celebration

ST. CLEMENTS ISLAND: Maryland Day, St. Clements Island Museum, 301-769-2222

APRIL

ANNAPOLIS: Annual Bay Bridge Boat Show,
410-268-8828
Annual St. Johns College versus USNA
Croquet Match, 410-626-2539
UPPER MARLBORO: Evangel Cathedral, Easter
Production, Evangel Cathedral, 13901
Central Avenue, 301-249-9400
LEONARDTOWN: Easter Egg Hunt & Festival,
301-475-4200, ext. 1800
Run & Fun Walk For Hospice, 301-475-3610
March of Dimes Walk, 301-924-2235
Earth Day Celebration, 301 -994 -9791
Spring Fling Classic Car Show,
301-994-9666

MAY

HAVRE DE GRACE: Annual Decoy and Art
Festival, various locations
ESSEX: Baltimore County Waterfront Festival,
Lockheed Martin at Dark Head Cove,
410-682-6122
BLADENSBURG: A-May-Zing Animal Fest,
Waterfront Park, 301-779-0371
SOLOMONS ISLAND: Solomons Maritime Festival,
Calvert Marine Museum,
410-326-2042 ext.41
Mother's Day Brunch Cruise or Mother's
Day Evening Cruise, Calvert Marine
Museum, 410-326-2042 ext. 41
International Museum Day, Calvert Marine
Museum, 410-326-2042 ext. 41
COBB ISLAND: Cobb Island Day
ANNAPOLIS: May Day, 410-263-1360
Annual Maryland Maritime Heritage
Festival, www.MDHF.org
USNA Commissioning Week, 410-293-8687
The Navy Way Boot Camp, 410-263-811
UPPER MARLBORO: Annual Marlborough Day,
Main Street & Gov. Bowie Road,
301-952-9575
Wildlife '83, Maryland Wildlife Artists
Show, St. Barnabas Church, Leeland, Upper
Marlboro, 301-249-9671
Garden Fair& Bullroast, St. Barnabas
Church, Leeland, 301-249-9621
"FAIRlE" Festival, Patuxent 4H Center,
18405 Queen Annes Road, 888-607-9134
PINEY POINT: Piney Point Lighthouse Festival,
301-994-1471
LEONARDTOWN: Southern Maryland Spring
Festival, 301-994-0525
Downtown Tunes, 4th Saturday,
301-994-3052

JUNE

HAVRE DE GRACE: Guided Nature Historical
Walk, Lock House, 410-939-5780
LEONARDTOWN: St. Mary's Crab Festival,
fairgrounds
Flag Day Celebration, Governmental
Center, 301-875-8184, ext. 1341
Scotland – Blue & Grey Days, Point Lookout
State Park, 301-572-5688
NORTH BEACH: House and Garden Tour,
St. Anthony's parking lot, 301-855-6681
Art Show, 89016 Chesapeake Avenue,
301 -655-6681
Free Summer Concert, 5th Street and Bay
Avenue, 301-855-6681
SOLOMONS ISLAND: Fathers Day Brunch Cruise
or Evening Cruise, Calvert Marine Museum,
410-326-4042 ext. 41
UPPER MARLBORO: Pirate Fest, Darnall's
Chance House Museum,
14800 Gov. Bowie Drive, 301-952-8010

JULY

ANNAPOLIS: Fourth of July Celebration
410-263-1183
John Paul Jones Day, 410-293-8687
Fireworks on the Beach, Chesapeake Beach,
410-257-2230
COLTONS POINT: Potomac Jazz & Seafood
Festival, St. Clements Island Museum,
301-769-2222
HAVRE DE GRACE: Independence Celebration,
Tydings Park, 410-939-4362
Fireworks Cruise, reservations required,
410-939-4078
LEONARDTOWN: Freedomfest, Fairgrounds,
301-475-4200 ext. 1849
College of Southern Maryland Twilight
Performance Series, Leonardtown Campus,
301-934-7681
St. Mary's River Concert on location in
Leonardtown, 301-475-9791
NORTH BEACH: Free Summer Concert
& Fireworks Show, 301 -257-9618
Fireworks on the Beach, Chesapeake Beach,
410-257-2230
SOLOMONS ISLAND: Fireworks Cruise, Calvert
Marine Museum, 410-326-4042, ext, 41
Solomons Fireworks, 410-326-1950
Calvert Artists Guild Works Outdoor Show,
Boardwalk Pavilion, 410-326-2604
Sunset in the Tropics Cruise, Calvert
Marine Museum, 410-326-2042 ext. 41
ST. CLEMENTS ISLAND: Black Eyed Susan Day,
301-769-2222
ST. MARY'S CITY: Tide Water Archeology
Weekend, 240-895-4440

AUGUST

HAVRE DE GRACE: Annual Seafood Festival, 410-939-1525
Havre de Grace Art Show, Tydings Park, 410-939-9342
Juried Art Exhibition, Havre de Grace Visitor Center, 450 Pennington Avenue, 410-939-2068
Reenactment – Living History Program, Lock House, 410-903-5780
Guided Nature Historical Walk, Lock House, 410-939-5780

NORTH BEACH: Free Summer Concert, 5th and Bay Avenue, 855-6681
Bayfest, Bay Avenue from 1st to 7th, 410-576-9618

SOLOMONS ISLAND: USO Reenactment of WWII, Pavilion on the Boardwalk, 410-257-8488
Lighthouse Challenge, Calvert Marine Museum, www.cheslights.org

COBB ISLAND: Firemen's Parade

ANNAPOLIS: Annual Rotary Club of Annapolis Crab Feast, 410-327-1982
Kunta Kinte Celebration 410-339-0338
Annapolis Art Walk, 410-267-7077

UPPER MARLBORO: 1814 British Invasion, Prince Georges Bus Tour, Darnall's Chance House Museum, reservation and fee, 301-952-8010

ST. MARY'S CITY: Governors Cup Yacht Race, 240-895-3039

LEONARDTOWN: Beach Party on the Square, Leonardtown Square, 301-475-9791
Wharf Waterfront Celebration, 301-475-9791
Taste of St. Mary's, 301-737-3001

SEPTEMBER

ANNAPOLIS: Annual Seafood Festival, 410-266-3113
Annual Sailboat Show, 410-268-8828
Annual US Powerboat Show, 410-268-8828

DEALE: Annual Pro-Am Fishing Tournament, 410-807-0973

ESSEX: Essex Day, 400-500 blocks, Eastern Boulevard

HAVRE DE GRACE: Guided Nature Historical Walk, Lock House, 410-939-5780

HERRINGTON HARBOR NORTH: Deal Bluegrass Festival & Car Show

SOLOMONS ISLAND: Chesapeake Appreciation Days, Calvert Marine Museum, 410-326-4042, ext. 41
Annual Monster Mash Cruise, Calvert Marine Museum, 410-326-410, ext. 41
Haunted Lighthouse Tour, Calvert Marine Museum, 410-326-4042, ext. 41

ST. MARY'S CITY: Woodland Indian Discovery Day 240-899-4990
Riverfest, 240-899-4990

SCOTLAND: Lighthouse Challenge, 301-872-5688

OCTOBER

COLTONS POINT and ST. CLEMENT'S ISLAND: Blessing of the Fleet, St. Clement's Island Museum, 301-769-2222

HAVRE DE GRACE: Halloween Happenings, Maritime Museum, 100 Lafayette Street, 410-939-4800

LEONARDTOWN: US National Oyster Shucking Contest and the National Cook-off, County Fairgrounds, 301-863-5014
Trick or Treat on the Square, Leonardtown Square, 301-975-9791

LEXINGTON PARK: Oyster Festival, 301-863-5015

UPPER MARLBORO: Mayhem in Marlborough Ghost Walk, Darnall's Chance House Museum, 301-952-8010
Southern Maryland and Fall Home Show, Equestrian Center, 14900 Pennsylvania Avenue, 301-952-7999

NOVEMBER

HAVRE DE GRACE: The Four Bay Winds,
Native American Indian Gathering,
Lock House Grounds, 410-939-5780

SOLOMONS ISLAND: Salute to the Military,
Calvert Marine Museum,
410-326-4042 ext 41

ANNAPOLIS: Annual Annapolis by Candlelight,
410-867-7304

ESSEX: Cedar Point Mansion, Christmas Holly
Tour, 410-887-8217

UPPER MARLBORO: Annual Gingerbread House
Contest and Show, Darnell's Chance House
Museum, 301-952-8010
Annual Winter Festival of Lights, Watkins
Regional Park, 301 Watkins Park Drive,
301-699-2456
Evangel Cathedral Christmas Celebration,
Evangel Cathedral, 13901 Central Avenue,
301-249-4990

ST. MARY'S CITY: Hearth and Home in Early
Maryland, 301-249-4990

LEONARDTOWN: Antique Show & Sale, Leonard
Hall Jr. Naval Academy, 301-475-8029

DECEMBER

HAVRE DE GRACE: Mari-time Xmas, Maritime
Museum, 100 Lafayette Street
410-939-4800
Candlelight Tour, Susquehanna Museum,
Lock House, 410-939-5780
Candlelight Tour and Carver's Celebration,
Decoy Museum, 410-939-3739

ESSEX: Cedar Point Mansion, Christmas Holly
Tour, 410-887-0217.

NORTH BEACH: Christmas on the Beach,
5th & Bay Avenue, 410-257-9618

SOLOMONS ISLAND: Annual Christmas Walk,
410-326- 1950

ANNAPOLIS: Benson–Hammond Holiday Open
House, 410-798-9518
Midnight Madness Holiday Shopping,
410-349-4745
Eastport Yacht Club Lights Parade,
410-263-0415

UPPER MARLBORO: Hansel & Gretel Tea Party,
Darnall's Chance House Museum,
14800 Gov. Bowie Drive, 301-952-8010

LEONARDTOWN: Santa & Mrs. Clause on the
Square, 301-475-9791

COLTONS POINT: Annual Christmas Doll and
Train Exhibit, St. Clements Island Museum,
301-769-2222

Baltimore City

2010 Census Population: 620,961   N. 39 18' W. 76 37'

Baltimore City is the largest city in Maryland. Named in honor of the Lords Baltimore, the first proprietors and founders of Maryland, it was settled in 1729 as a tobacco port. The city's central location on the mid-Atlantic coast contributed to its rapid growth in coastal and trans-Atlantic trade and immigration. In time, the National Road (US Route 40) and the B&O railroad greatly increased its importance as a shipping and manufacturing center. Baltimore also played a significant role in events leading up to the American Revolution and the War of 1812. During the latter conflict, the bombs bursting over Fort McHenry in Baltimore's harbor inspired Francis Scott Key to write America's national anthem.

By the early nineteenth century, Jonestown and Fells Point had been incorporated into the city. With the passage of time, another important change took place as Baltimore's steel processing plants, transportation and shipping industries, and manufacturers gave way to a service-sector-oriented economy. Today, Johns Hopkins University and the Johns Hopkins Hospital are the city's largest employers. The Port of Baltimore is still busy, but the focus of the waterfront is now Harborplace, a premier shopping, entertainment, and tourist center and home of the National Aquarium and Maryland Science Center. The Metropolitan Area, which includes the city's surrounding suburbs, has approximately 2.6 million residents and is the twentieth largest in the United States. Today, Baltimore's city-wide economic revitalization efforts continue to deal with the persistent urban problems of poverty, crime, and inadequate public education.

The progress toward today's modern city center began on February 7, 1904, when the Great Baltimore Fire destroyed more than 1,500 buildings. It took two years for the city to recover. The next transforming event took place when concern for the neglected Inner Harbor led to construction of the Convention Center in 1979, which was followed by Harborplace, the National Aquarium, and the Baltimore Museum of Industry. In 1992, the Baltimore Orioles moved to Oriole Park at Camden Yards and, six years later, the Ravens moved into the M&T Bank Stadium next door.

They were followed by the Baltimore Basilica, the Municipal Museum, the McKim Free School, the Phoenix Shot Tower, the Sun Iron Building, the Johns Hopkins Hospital, and the World Trade Center that contributed to a distinctive and widely recognized skyline. Future plans call for the addition of "10 Inner Harbor," a tower of fifty to sixty floors at 300 Pratt Street. Two new towers at the Inner Harbor East are also planned.

The city has nine geographical regions, three hundred identified districts, and a distinctive Washington Monument that predates, by several decades, the better-known monument in Washington, D.C. Local residents proudly speak what has come to be known as "Baltimorese" and welcome visitors to the home town they call "Balmer."

There is much to see on a visit and the best place to start is the Baltimore Visitors Center, 401 Light Street, Inner Harbor West Shore, or visit on-line at www.baltimore.org. You'll find a variety of walking tours listed in *Baltimore's Star Spangled Trails* pamphlets, including the Heritage Walk; Mount Vernon Cultural Walk; Baltimore Waterfront Promenade; Baltimore Riot Trail; National Historic Seaport Scenic Byway; Gwynns Falls Trail; Charles Street Scenic Byway; Historic National Road; Jones Falls Trail; Falls Road Scenic Byway; Bolton Hill Blue Plaques; Pennsylvania Avenue Heritage Trail; Chesapeake Bay Gateways Network; and The Underground Railroad, Maryland's Network Freedom Star-Spangled Banner Trail. Fort McHenry has a wonderful ongoing War of 1812 exhibit, and Fort McHenry boat tours can be taken in the harbor. For additional activities and up-to-date event information, visit www.baltimore.org or call 877-Baltimore. You can also contact the Baltimore Office of Promotion & The Arts at 410-752-8632. Their website is www.bop.org.

◪ MARINAS
- Chesapeake Yachting Center, 114 Carroll Island Road, 410-335-4900
- Maryland Marina & Yacht Sales, 3501 Red Rose Farm Road, 410-335-8722
- Porter's Seneca Park Marina, 918 Seneca Park Road, 410-335-6563
- Sunset Harbor Marina, Inc., 1651 Browns Road, 410-687-7290

◪ LODGING – Bed & Breakfasts
- 1840s Carrollton Inn, 50 Albemarle Street, 410-385-1840
- 4 East Madison Inn, 4 E. Madison Street, 410-576-9352
- Aunt Rebecca's Bed & Breakfast, 106 E. Preston Street, 410-625-1007
- Blue Door on Baltimore, 2023 E. Baltimore Street, 410-732-0191
- Celie's Waterfront Bed & Breakfast, 410-522-2323
- Glenda's Bed & Breakfast, 2028 Park Avenue, 410-383-8535
- Inn at 2920, 2920 Elliott Street, 410-342-4450
- Scarborough Fair B&B, 1 E. Montgomery Street, 410-832-0010

◪ LODGING – Downtown Hotels and Conference Centers
- Admiral Fell Inn, Historic Fells Point, 888 S. Broadway, 410-522-7377
- Baltimore Marriott Inner Harbor at Camden Yards, 700 Aliceanna Street, 410-962-0202
- Baltimore Suites Hotel, 205 W. Madison Street, 410-728-6550
- Baltimore's Tremont Suite Hotels (EBC Marriott), 8 E. Pleasant Street, 410-576-1200
- Baltimore's Tremont Suite Hotels (Tremont Plaza Hotel), 222 St. Paul Place, 410-727-2222
- Brookshire Suites, 120 E. Lombard Street, 410-625-1300
- Clarion Collection A Peabody Court Hotel, 612 Cathedral Street, 410-727-7101
- Courtyard By Marriott Downtown Inner Harbor, 1000 Aliceanna Street, 410-923-4000
- Days Inn Inner Harbor Hotel, 100 Hopkins Place, 410-576-5000
- Hampton Inn & Suites Baltimore Inner Harbor, 131 E. Redwood Street, 410-539-7888
- Hilton Baltimore Convention Center Hotel, 401 W. Pratt Street, 410-573-8700
- Hilton Garden Inn, Baltimore Inner Harbor, 625 S. President Street, 410-234-0065
- Holiday Inn Express Baltimore at the Stadium, 1701 Russell Street, 410-727-1818
- Holiday Inn, Inner Harbor, 301 W. Lombard Street, 410-685-3500
- Hyatt Regency Baltimore, 300 Light Street, 410-528-1234
- Inn At Henderson's Wharf, 1000 Fell Street, 410-522-7777
- Intercontinental Harbor Court Baltimore, 410-234-0550
- Mount Vernon Hotel, 24 W. Franklin Street, 410-727-2000
- Pier's Hotel, 711 Eastern Avenue, 410-539-2000
- Quality Inn Harbor South, 1402 Bloomfield Avenue, 410-646-1700
- Radisson Plaza Lord Baltimore, 30 W. Baltimore Street, 410-539-8400
- Renaissance Harborplace Hotel, 202 E. Pratt Street, 410-747-1200
- Residence Inn Baltimore Downtown Inner Harbor, 17 Light Street, 410-962-1220
- Sheraton Baltimore City Center Hotel, 101 W. Fayette Street, 410-752-1100
- Sheraton Inner Harbor Hotel, 300 S. Charles Street, 410-962-8300
- Springhill Suites Baltimore Inner Harbor, 16 S. Calvert Street, 410-685-1095

◻ RESTAURANTS

AFGHANI
- Helmand Restaurant, 806 N. Charles Street, 410-752-0311

AMERICAN
- Bistro 300, 300 Light Street, 410-605-2839
- Brighton's, 530 Light Street, 410-234-0550
- Café Hon, 1002 W. 36th Street, 410-243-1133
- Café Promenade, 110 S. Eutaw Street, 410-962-0202
- Claddagh Pub & Restaurant, 2918 O'Donnell Street, 410-522-4220
- Crossroads Restaurant, 100 Village Square, Radisson Hotel at Cross Keys, 410-532-6900
- Eden West, 301 W. Lombard Street, 410-685-3500
- Eight East, 8 E. Pleasant Street, 410-576-1200
- ESPN Zone, 601 E. Pratt Street, 410-685-3776
- Five Guys Burgers & Fries, 201 E. Pratt Street, 410-224-7175
- Georges' on Mount Vernon Square, 101 W. Monument Street, 410-727-1314
- Gertrude's, 10 Art Museum Drive, 410-889-3399
- Hard Rock Café, The Power Plant, Inner Harbor, 601 E. Pratt Street, 410-347-7625
- Hooters of Baltimore, 301 Light Street, 410-244-0367
- Houlihan's Restaurant, 601 E. Pratt Street, 410-872-0058
- J. Paul's Dining Salon, 301 Light Street, 410-659-1889
- John Steven Ltd., 1800 Thames Street, 410-327-5561
- Kooper's Tavern, 1702 Thames Street, 410-563-5423
- Lord Baltimore Grill, Radisson Plaza Hotel Baltimore, 20 W. Baltimore Street, 410-539-8400
- M&S Grill, 201 E. Pratt Street, 410-547-9333
- Milton's Grill, 336 N. Charles Street, 410-547-9333
- Miss Shirley's Café, 513 Cold Spring Lane, 410-889-5272
- Mt. Vernon Stable & Saloon, 909 N. Charles Street, 410-685-7427
- Power Plant/The Cordish Company, 601 E. Pratt Street, 6th Floor, 410-752-5444
- The Prime Rib Inc., 1101 N. Calvert Street, 410-539-1804
- Ram's Head Live!, 20 Market Place, 410-244-8854
- Ryleigh's Oyster, 36 Cross Street, 410-539-2093
- Tradewinds Restaurant and Lounge, Best Western Hotel & Conference Center, 5625 O'Donnell Street, 410-633-9500
- Tug's Restaurant, Tremont Plaza Hotel, 222 St. Paul Place, 410-244-7300
- Werner's, 231 E. Redwood Street, 410-752-3335
- The Wine Market, 921 E. Fort Avenue, Suite 135, 410-244-6166
- The Women's Industrial Exchange, 533 N. Charles Street, 410-685-4388

ASIAN FUSION
- Red Maple, 930 N. Charles Street, 410-547-0149
- Tsunami–Baltimore, 1300 Bank Street, Suite 120, 410-327-1370

CHINESE
- Ding How Restaurant, 631 S. Broadway, 410-327-8888
- P. F. Chang's China Bistro, 600 E. Pratt Street, Suite 101, 410-649-2750

COFFEE BAR
- Dottie's, 3091 W. Lombard Street, 410-685-3500

CONTINENTAL
- Spice Company, 4 W. University Parkway, 410-235-8200
- Xandu, 10 N. Calvert Street, 410-528-5110

CUBAN
- Babalu Grill, 32 Market Place, 410-234-9898

DELIS
- Attman's Authentic New York Delicatessen, 1019 E. Lombard Street, 410-563-2666
- Boheme Café, 400 E. Pratt Street, 410-347-9898
- Plaza Deli, Tremont Plaza Hotel, 222 St. Paul Place, 410-528-8800

DESSERT CAFÉS
- Dangerously Delicious Pie, 1036 Light Street, 410-522-7437

ECLECTIC
- b Bolton Bistro, 1501 Bolton Street, 410-383-8600
- The Bicycle, 1444 Light Street, 410-234-1900
- The Brewer's Art, 1106 N. Charles Street, 410-547-6925
- Corks, 1026 S. Charles Street, 410-752-3810
- Illusions: Magic Bar & Lounge, 1025-27 S. Charles Street, 410-727-5811
- Jack's Bistro, 3123 Elliott Street, 410-878-6542

FOOD COURT/COUNTER
- Expresso, Inc., 550 Light Street, 410-234-0550

FRENCH
- Brasserie Tatin, 105 W. 39th Street, 443-278-9110
- Crepe Du Jour, 1609 Sulgrave Avenue, 410-542-9000
- Petit Louis Bistro, 4800 Roland Avenue, 410-366-9393

GREEK
- The Black Olive, 814 S. Bond Street, 410-276-7141
- Ikaros Restaurant, 4805 Eastern Avenue, 410-633-3750

ICE CREAM SHOPS
- The Marble Slab Creamery, 201 E. Pratt Street, 410-685-7522
- The Olde Malt Shop, 635 Fort Avenue, 410-727-5769

INDIAN
- Akbar, 823 N. Charles Street, 410-539-0944
- India Rasoi Restaurant, 411 High, 410-385-4949
- Indigma, 802 N. Charles Street, 410-605-1212
- Mehek, 811 S. Broadway, 410-522-9191
- Memsahib Indian Cuisine, 400 W. Lexington Street, 410-576-7777
- Mughal Garden Restaurant, 920 N. Charles Street, 410-547-00012

INTERNATIONAL
- Big Kahuna Cantina, 301 Light Street, 410-539-7060
- Edens Lounge The Garden of Soul, 15 W. Eager Street, 410-244-0405
- Ixia Restaurant Bar Lounge, 518 N. Charles Street, 410-727-1800

IRISH
- James Joyce Irish Pub & Restaurant, 616 S. President Street, 410-727-5107
- Lucy's Irish Pub & Restaurant, 21 N. Eutaw Street, 410-837-2100
- Slainte Irish Pub & Restaurant

ITALIAN
- A Germano's Trattoria, 300 S. High Street, 410-752-0709
- Aldo's Ristorante Italiano, 306 High Street, 410-727-0700
- Amissi's, 231 High Street, 410-528-1096
- b Bolton Hill Bistro, 1501 Bolton Street, 410-383-8600
- Boccaccio Restaurant, 925 Eastern Avenue, 410-234-1322
- Caesar's Den, 223 S. High Street, 410-547-0820
- Chiapparelli's Restaurant, 237 S. High Street, 410-837-0309
- Ciao Bella Restaurant, 236 S. High Street, 410-685-7733
- Cinghiale, 822 Lancaster Street, 410-547-8282
- Da Mimmo Finest Italian Cuisine, 217 S. High Street, 410-727-6876
- Della Notte Ristorante, 801 Eastern Avenue, 410-837-5500
- La Scala Ristorante Italiano, 1812 Eastern Avenue, 410-783-9200
- La Tavola Ristorante Italiano, 248 Albemarle Street, 410-685-1859
- Sabatino's Italian Restorant, 901 Fawn Street, 410-727-2667
- Sotto Sopra, 405 N. Charles Street, 410-625-0534
- Tiburzi's Italian Grill & Café, 900 S. Kenwood Avenue, 410-327-8100
- Velleggia's Italian Seafood Restaurant, 829 Pratt Street, 410-685-2620

JAPANESE
- Edo Sushi Inner Harbor, Inc., 201 E. Pratt Street, 410-843-9804
- Giesha Sushi Bar, 201 N. Charles Street, 41-685-2099
- Matsuri Restaurant, 1105 S. Charles Street, 410-752-8561
- Minato Japanese Restaurant, 1013 N. Charles Street, 410-332-0332
- Ra Sushi Bar Restaurant, 1300 Lancaster Street, 410-522-3200

MEDITERRANEAN
- Lebanese Taverna, 719 S. President Street, 410-244-5533
- Mezze, 1606 Thames Street, 410-563-7600
- Pazo Restaurant, 1425 Aliceanna Street, 410-534-7296
- Tabrizi's, 500 Harborview Drive, 410-727-3663

MEXICAN
- Blue Agave Restaurante Y Tequileria, 1052 Light Street, 410-576-3938
- California Tortilla-Baltimore, 300 W. Pratt Street, 410-605-0991
- Gecko's, 2318 Fleet Street, 410-732-1961
- Mex Tequila Bar, 26 Marketplace, 410-528-0128

NEPALESE
- Kumari, 911 N. Charles Street, 410-547-1600
  847 E. Fort Avenue, 410-757-2222
- Lumbini Restaurant, 322 N. Charles Street, 410-244-5556

NEW AMERICAN
- Charleston Restaurant, 1000 Lancaster Street, 410-332-7373
- Juniors, 1111 S. Charles Street, 410-727-1212
- Sascha's 527 Restaurant, 527 N. Charles Street, 410-539-8880
- Timothy Dean Bistro, 1717 Eastern Avenue, 410-534-5650

ORGANIC
- Woodberry Kitchen, 2010 Clipper Park Road, #126, 410-464-8000

SEAFOOD
- Bertha's, 734 S. Broadway, 410-327-5795
- Blue Sea Grill, 614 Water Street, 410-837-7300
- Bo Brooks at Lighthouse Point, 2780-A Lighthouse Point, 410-558-0202
- Burke's Café & Comedy Factory, 36 Light Street, 410-752-4189
- Captain James Landing Restaurant, 2127 Boston Street, 410-327-8600
- Kali's Court, 1606 Thames Street, 410-276-4700
- L.P. Steamers, 1100 E. Fort Avenue, 410-576-9293
- McCormick & Schmick's Seafood Restaurant, 711 Eastern Avenue, 410-234-1300
- Mo's Crab & Pasta Factory, 502 Albemarle Street, 410-837-8600
- Mo's Fisherman's Wharf Restaurant, 219 S. President Street, 410-837-8600
- Mother's Federal Hill Grill, 1113 S. Charles Street, 410-244-8686
- John Steven Ltd., 1800 Thames Street, 410-327-5561
- The Oceanaire Seafood Room, 801 Aliceanna Street, 410-872-0000
- Phillips Harborplace Restaurant, Inner Harbor-Light Street Pavilion, 301 Light Street, 410-685-6600
- Pisces, Hyatt Regency Baltimore, 300 Light Street, 410-605-2835
- Roy's of Baltimore, 720-B Aliceanna Street, 410-639-0099
- Rusty Scupper Restaurant, 402 Key Highway, 410-727-3678
- Ruth's Cris Steak House, Pier 5, 711 Eastern Avenue, 410-230-0033 Water Street, 600 Water Street, 410-783-0033
- Ryleigh's Oyster, 36 E. Cross Street, 410-539-2093
- Shuckers of Fells Point, 1629 Thames Street, 410-522-5820
- Watertable, Renaissance Harborplace Hotel, 202 E Pratt Street, 410-685-VIEW

SOUTHERN
- Night of the Cookers, 885 N. Howard Street, 410-383-2095
- Rub Authentic Texas Barbecue, 1843 Light Street, 410-244-5667

SPANISH
- Babalu Grill, 52 Marketplace, 410-234-9898
- La Taska Spanish Tapas Bar & Restaurant, 201 E. Pratt Street, 410-209-2563
- Restaurante Tio Pepe, 10 E. Franklin Street, 410-539-45675
- Tapas Teatro, 1711 N. Charles Street, 410-332-0110

STEAKHOUSES
- The Capital Grill, 500 E. Pratt Street, 410-703-4064
- Fleming's Prime Steakhouse and Wine Bar, 720 Aliceanna Street, 410-332-1666
- Fogo de Chao, 600 E. Pratt Street, 410-528-9292
- Morton's The Steakhouse, 300 S. Charles Street, 410-547-8255
- Ruth's Cris Steakhouse, Pier 5 at the Inner Harbor, 711 Eastern Avenue, 410-230-0033 Water Street, 600 Water Street, 410-783-0033
- Shula's Steakhouse (Sheraton Baltimore City Center Hotel), 101 W. Fayette Street, 410-385-6601

THAI
- Lemongrass-Baltimore, 1300 Bank Street, Suite 100, 410-327-7835
- Ten-O-Six, 1006 Light Street, 410-528-2146

TURKISH
- Cazbar, 316 N. Charles Street, 410-528-1222

VEGETARIAN
- One World Café, 10 W. University Parkway, 410-235-5777

SPECIAL EVENTS AND ACTIVITIES

For up-to-date information on many ethnic festivals and their admissions fees, visit www.baltimore.org, call 877-BALTIMORE, or visit Baltimore Office of Promotion & The Arts website, www.bop.org, or call 410-752-8632.

American Visionary Art Museum, 410-244-1900
Artscape, visit www.artscape.org
Baltimore Convention Center Antique Show, www.baltimoresummerantiques.com
Baltimore Farmer's Market, www.bop.org
Baltimore Museum of Art, 410-573-1700
Baltimore Museum of Industry, 410-727-4808
Baltimore Orioles Baseball Team, 410-685-9800
Baltimore Ravens, M&T Bank Stadium, 410-261-RAVE
Centerstage, 410-332-0033
Fire Museum of Maryland, 410-321-7500
Fort McHenry National Monument and Historical Shrine, www.nps.org
France-Merrick Performing Arts Center and Hippodrome Theater, 410-547-SEAT
Jewish Museum of Maryland, 410-732-6400
Little Italy, www.littleitalymd.com
Maryland Science Center, 410-685-5225
Maryland Zoo, 410-366-LION
Myerhoff Symphony Hall, 410-783-8000
Patterson Park music events, www.bop.org
Pier 6 Concert Pavilion, 410-783-4189
Pimlico Race Course and The Preakness, 410-542-9400
Port Discovery Children's Museum, 410-727-8120
Port of Baltimore Cruise Season, www.cruisemaryland.com
Reginald F. Lewis Museum of African American History & Culture, 410-263-1800
S.S. John Brown, Liberty Ship, Inner Harbor West Wall, www.sailbaltimore.org
U.S.S. Constellation, Inner Harbor, www.baltimore.org/Constellation
Walters Art Museum, 410-547-9000

Baltimore, MD

SCALE (miles)
0   2.5   5

POINTS OF INTEREST

1 BALTIMORE ORIOLES BASEBALL TEAM,
   410-685-9800
2 JEWISH MUSEUM OF MARYLAND, 410-732-6400
3 AMERICAN VISIONARY ART MUSEUM,
   410-244-1900
4 BALTIMORE MUSEUM OF ART, 410-573-1700
5 PIER 6 CONCERT PAVILION, 410-783-4189
6 ARTSCAPE, visit www.artscape.org
7 BALTIMORE SYMPHONY ORCHESTRA CONCERTS,
   410-783-8000
8 MARYLAND ZOO, 410-366-LION
9 WALTERS ART MUSEUM, 410-547-9000
10 S.S. JOHN BROWN, LIBERTY SHIP, INNER
   HARBOR WEST WALL, www.sailbaltimore.org
11 LITTLE ITALY, www.littleitalymd.com
12 MARYLAND SCIENCE CENTER, 410-685-5225
13 REGINALD F. LEWIS MUSEUM OF AFRICAN
   AMERICAN HISTORY & CULTURE, 410-263-1800
14 PORT DISCOVERY CHILDREN'S MUSEUM,
   410-727-8120

15 PORT OF BALTIMORE CRUISE SEASON,
   www.cruisemaryland.com
16 BALTIMORE FARMER'S MARKET, www.bop.org
17 BALTIMORE MUSEUM OF INDUSTRY,
   410-727-4808
18 MYERHOFF SYMPHONY HALL, 410-783-8000
19 PIMLICO RACE COURSE AND THE PREAKNESS,
   410-542-9400
20 BALTIMORE RAVENS, M&T BANK STADIUM,
   410-261-RAVE
21 PATTERSON PARK, visit www.bop.org
   for a listing of their musical events
22 BALTIMORE CONVENTION CENTER,
   www.baltimoresummerantiques.com
23 FRANCE-MERRICK PERFORMING ARTS CENTER
   AND HIPPODROME THEATER, 410-547-SEAT
24 CENTERSTAGE, 410-332-0033
25 FORT MCHENRY NATIONAL MONUMENT AND
   HISTORICAL SHRINE, www.nps.org
26 FIRE MUSEUM OF MARYLAND, 410-321-7500

Anne Arundel County

Annapolis
2010 Census Population: 38,394   N. 38 50' W. 76 30'

Annapolis is widely known for its rich colonial heritage and waterfront location at the confluence of the Severn River and Chesapeake Bay. The city occupies three peninsulas and surrounds four tidewater creeks for a total of sixteen miles of waterfront. The city's historic district has numerous splendid eighteenth-century homes, a dock, and marketplace that attract thousands of visitors as well as residents. Designated a National Historic District in 1965, the center city has an ordinance that protects its homes, buildings, and atmosphere.

The first settlers arrived in the area as early as 1649 and called the subsequent area of widely scattered farms Providence, in the county later called Anne Arundel for the wife of Cecelius Calvert, Second Lord Baltimore. To advance trade in his colony, Calvert called for the creation of towns and the town of Arundelton appeared on a 1671 survey map. By 1684, it was called Ann Arundell Town, and in 1695, the General Assembly moved from St. Mary's City to the more-centrally located Severn River town. They changed its name to Annapolis, honoring Princess Anne, who later became the Queen of England. It also became the capital of Maryland.

The city enjoyed its Golden Age between 1750 and 1780 when it was the political, commercial, and cultural center of Maryland. On the eve of the American Revolution, Marylanders held their own "Tea Party" in Annapolis when the owner of the brig *Peggy Stewart* was forced to burn his ship as a protest against his payment of the hated British tax on its cargo of tea. Today, the homes of four Maryland Signers of the Declaration of Independence still stand in Annapolis. For a short time, from late 1783 to early 1784, the new U.S. Congress met in the State House to ratify the Treaty of Paris, ending the Revolutionary War, and to accept the resignation of General George Washington as Commander-in-Chief of the Continental Army.

On its hill overlooking the town, Maryland's State House calls attention to the presence of Maryland government in Annapolis, which swells the city population when the legislature is in session. Similarly familiar is the U.S. Naval Academy that occupies a sizable portion of the Annapolis waterfront and is an integral part of the life of the town. The city's harbor attracts local boaters and yachtsmen from around the world and the Annapolis City Dock is the scene of a host of special events for residents and visitors. Foremost among them are the U.S. Sailboat and Powerboat Shows every fall. At the head of the Dock is the historic Market House, which has been a traditional stop for almost anyone wanting a locally made quick meal or carry-out while downtown.

One of the best ways to enjoy what downtown has to offer is afoot, exploring its circles, narrow winding streets, and wider townhouse-lined boulevards. Guided walking tours are available from the Visitors Center on West Street. It is also possible to take Segway tours (410-280-1577); water tours (410-268-7601 ext. 104); and sailing cruises (410-263-7847). The Naval Academy's Visitor's Center also offers guided tours of the grounds from the Armel-Leftwich Center inside Gate 1.

⛵ MARINAS
- Annapolis Powerboat School, 7001 Bembe Beach Road, 410-267-7205
- Annapolis Sailing School, 701 Bembe Beach Road, 800-368-1594
- Chesapeake Sailing School & Charters, 7074 Bembe Beach Road, 410-269-1594
- Sarles Boatyard & Marina, 808 Boucher Avenue, 410-263-3661
- Springriver Annapolis Canoe & Kayak, 311 Third Street, 419-263-2303
- Watermark Tours, Charters, Cruises, 410-268-7601 ext. 100
- Womanship, Inc., 137 Conduit Street, 800-342-9295
- World Performance Sailing School, 213 Eastern Avenue, 410-280-2040
- Yacht Basin Company, 2 Compromise Street, 410-263-7171

LODGING: B&Bs – Annapolis Historic District
- 1908 – William Page Inn Bed & Breakfast, 8 Martin Street, 410-626-1506
- The Annapolis Inn, 144 Prince George Street, 410-295-5200
- Annapolis Royal Folly, 65 College Avenue, 410-263-3999
- Annapolitan Bed & Breakfast, 1313 West Street, 410-990-1234
- Ark & Dove Bed & Breakfast, 149 Prince George Street, 410-268-6277
- Barn on Howard's Cove Bed & Breakfast, 500 Wilson Road, 410-266-6843
- Charles Inn Bed & Breakfast, 74 Charles Street, 410-268-1451
- Chez Amis Bed & Breakfast, 85 East Street, 410-263-6631
- Flag House Inn Bed & Breakfast, 26 Randall Street, 410-2180-2721
- Gatehouse Bed & Breakfast, 249 Hanover Street, 410-280-0024
- Inn at Horn Point, 100 Chesapeake Avenue, 410-268-1126
- Inn at Spa Creek, 417 Severn Avenue, 410-263-8866
- Laurel Grove Inn, 28891 Southhaven Drive, 410-224-4228
- Peninsula House, 11 Chester Avenue, 410-267-8796
- State House Inn, 25 State Circle, 410-990-0024
- Taylor House, 936 Arbutus Road, 410-991-6704
- Two-O-One Bed & Breakfast, 201 Prince George Street, 410-268-8053

LODGING: Hotels – Annapolis Historic District
- Annapolis Marriott Waterfront Hotel, 80 Compromise Street, 410-268-7555
- Country Inn & Suites by Carlson Annapolis, 2600 Housley Road, 410-571-6700
- Hampton Inn & Suites, 124 Womack Drive, 410-571-0200
- Historic Inns of Annapolis, 58 State Circle, 410-263-2641
- Loews Annapolis Hotel, 126 West Street, 410-263-7777
- O'Callagan Hotel Annapolis, 174 West Street, 410-263-7700
- Westin Annapolis, 100 Westgate Circle, 410-972-4300

RESTAURANTS – Annapolis Downtown
- Rams Head Tavern & Fordham Brewing Company, 33 West Street, 410-268-4545
- Reynold's Tavern, 7 Church Circle, 410-295-5555
- Ristaurante Piccola Roma, 200 Main Street, 410-268-7898
- Subway, 228 Main Street, 410-990-0095
- Tsunami, 51 West Street, 410-990-9868
- Yin Yankee Café, 105 Main Street, 410-268-8703

RESTAURANTS – Eastport
- Boatyard Bar & Grill, 400 Fourth Street, 410-216-6206
- Carroll's Creek Café, 410 Severn Avenue, 410-263-8102
- Chart House, 300 Second Street, 410-268-7166
- Lewnes' Steak House, 401 Fourth Street, 410-263-1617
- The Main Ingredient Café & Catering, 914 Bay Ridge Road, 410-626-0388
- O'Learys Seafood & Restaurant, 310 Third Street, 410-263-0084
- The Rockfish, 400 Sixth Street, 410-267-1800
- Ruth's Cris Steak House, 301 Severn Avenue, 420-990-0033
- Wild Orchid Restaurant, 200 Westgate Circle, 410-268-0800

SPECIAL EVENTS AND ACTIVITIES

Please check the internet or call ahead, as dates, times, and locations may change.

January: Historic Annapolis Antiques Show, 410-267-8146

February: Black History Month, 410-280-0445

April: Annual Bay Bridge Boat Show, 410-268-8828
  Annual St. John's College vs. USNA Croquet Match, 410-626-2539

April–October: First Sundays, art and entertainment, 410-222-7949

May: May Day, 410-263-1360
  Charterfest, www.annapolisalive.org/calendar
  Annual Maryland Maritime Heritage Festival, www.MDMHF,org
  Bay Bridge Walk, 1-777-BAY-SPAN *(Note: this was cancelled recently so be sure to confirm.)*
  USNA Commissioning Week, 410-293-8687

May–June: Annapolis Art Works, 2009, 410-263-7940

June–August: US Naval Academy Band Concerts, 410-263-0263
  The Navy Way Boot Camp, 410-263-8111

June–September: Wednesday Night Sailboat Races, 410-263-9279

July: Fourth of July Celebration, 410-263-1183
  John Paul Jones Day, 410-293-8687

July–August: Quiet Waters Park Summer Concert Series, Saturdays, 410-222-1777

August: Annual Rotary Club of Annapolis Crab Feast, 410-327-1982
  Kunta Kinte Celebration, 410-349-0338
  Annapolis Art Walk, 410-267-7077

August–October: Maryland Renaissance Festival, 410-266-7304

September: Annual Sea Food Festival, 410-266-3113
  Anne Arundel County Fair, 410-923-3400

October: Annual US Sailboat Show, 410-268-8828
  Annual US Powerboat Show, 410-268-8828

November: Annual Annapolis by Candlelight, 410-867-7304

December: Benson-Hammond Holiday Open House, 410-798-9518
  Midnight Madness Holiday Shopping, 410-349-4745
  Eastport Yacht Club Lights Parade, 410-263-0415

Annapolis, MD

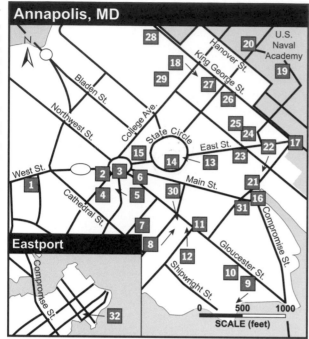

Eastport

SCALE (feet)
0   500   1000

POINTS OF INTEREST

1 ASBURY METHODIST CHURCH, 1888,
87 West Street
> This Gothic Revival housed one of the earliest African-American congregations in Annapolis.

2 REYNOLDS TAVERN, 1747-55, Church Circle
> This structure has served as a tavern, a residence, and was the former site of the Anne Arundel County library. It's now a tearoom and inn.

3 ST. ANNE'S EPISCOPAL CHURCH, 1859, Church Circle; the third structure on this site is a Romanesque Revival, the St. Anne's window was designed by Tiffany.

4 BANNEKER-DOUGLAS MUSEUM, 1874, 84 Franklin Street
> This Gothic Revival was once the African Methodist Church. It's now an African-American Museum of Life and History.

5 ANNE ARUNDEL COUNTY COURTHOUSE, 1834, 6 Church Circle; third oldest courthouse in Maryland

6 MARYLAND INN, 16 Church Circle; built as an inn before the American Revolution

7 JONAS GREEN HOUSE, 1740s, 124 Charles Street; site of Jonas and Anna Green's print shop, printers of the *Maryland Gazette*.

8 Zimmerman House, 138 Conduit Street; Queen Anne style, Zimmerman authored *Anchors a' Weigh*

9-10 Charles Carroll House, 1680-1710, 107 Duke of Gloucester Street, and St. Mary's Catholic Church, 1860, 109 Duke of Gloucester Street

> Home of Charles Carroll of Carrollton, one of four Maryland signers of the Declaration of Independence in Annapolis. The house is seen below St. Mary's Church on Weems Creek. St. Mary's Church is a Gothic Revival structure.

11 City Hall/Ballroom, 1760s, 160 Duke of Gloucester Street

> After the building was burned during the Civil War, the three surviving walls were incorporated in the present building.

12 Maynard-Burgess House, 1847, 163 Duke of Gloucester Street; owned for 150 years by members of two African-American families

13 Old Treasury Building, 1735-37, State Circle; oldest public building in Maryland

14 State House, 1772, State Circle

> Oldest State House in continuous legislative use and the only State Capital to have been Capital of the U.S. It has the largest wooden dome in the country built without nails. In the Old Senate Chamber, George Washington resigned his commission as Commander-in-Chief of the Continental Army and the U.S. Congress ratified the Treaty of Paris, which ended the Revolutionary War.

15 Government House, 1868, State Circle; French Empire mansion and home of the Governor

16 City Dock

> This has been the center of Annapolis's maritime life for over three hundred years. Site of the Alex Haley Memorial, commemorated by a plaque and a statute of Alex Haley, author of novel Roots. The site is also popularly known as Ego Alley because of the many yachts that tie up there.

17 U.S. NAVAL ACADEMY, C. 1749, VISITOR'S ENTRANCE, GATE 1, Randall and King George Streets
> Photo ID Required. The USNA Armel-Leftwich Field House, just inside the gate, is the starting point for tours.

18 OGLE HALL, C. 1749, 24 King George Street; former home of Maryland governor and present site of the Naval Academy Alumni Association.

19 NAVAL ACADEMY CHAPEL, 1904
> Several of its stained glass windows were designed by Tiffany; beneath the chapel is the crypt of Revolutionary War hero John Paul Jones.

20 UNITED STATES NAVAL ACADEMY MUSEUM, 1939
> This state-of-the-art museum houses ship models, portraits, uniforms, and naval and marine corps memorabilia.

21 MARKET HOUSE, Market Space; this has been the site of city markets since 1784.

22 MIDDLETON TAVERN, 1754, 2 Market Space; Samuel Middleton's colonial tavern is still popular today

23 SHIPLAP HOUSE, 1715, 18 Pinkney Street
> Once a tavern, it's now the home of the Historic Annapolis Foundation's Administrative offices.

24 BRICE HOUSE, 1767-73, 42 East Street
This impressive Georgian mansion is now owned
by the International Masonry Institute.

25 WILLIAM PACA HOUSE AND GARDEN,
1763-65, 186 Prince George Street
This five-part Georgian mansion includes a two-acre,
walled garden. Tours are available.

26 HAMMOND–HARWOOD HOUSE, 1774, 19 Maryland Avenue;
colonial architect William Buckland's masterpiece

27 CHASE–LLOYD HOUSE, 1769-74, 22 Maryland Avenue
Edward Lloyd IV bought the unfinished house from Samuel
Chase, a signer of the Declaration of Independence. Lloyd's
daughter, Mary, wed Francis Scott Key in the parlor in 1802.

28 CHARLES CARROLL, THE BARRISTER HOUSE, 1724-27,
St. John's College and King George Streets
This structure was saved from destruction by
Historic Annapolis and moved to St. John's campus,
where it serves as the college's Admissions Office.

29 MCDOWELL HALL, 1742, St. John's Campus
Begun by a colonial governor, it later housed the entire college;
the hall is named for the first president of the college.

30 FIRST PRESBYTERIAN CHURCH, 1828,
Duke of Gloucester at Conduit Street
Completely remodeled in 1948, the lower level
was the site of an early public school for girls.

31 HISTORIC ANNAPOLIS FOUNDATION HISTORY QUEST,
99 Main Street
This former colonial warehouse is now a museum with several
multimedia presentations and exhibits, plus a gift shop; used
for events and as a starting point for tours.

32 ANNAPOLIS MARITIME MUSEUM, 723 Second Street, Eastport
(cross Spa Creek Bridge, first left on Severn, right on Second to end)
Exhibits on Bay marine life, area waterways,
and Annapolis watermen and their work.
Ask for a walking tour map of Eastport.

Deale

2010 Census Population: 4,945   N. 38 47' W. 76 32'

Deale is named for James Deale who settled in the area and bought three tracts of land in 1736. A waterfront village developed there along the shores of Rockhold, Parkers, and Carrs Creeks that flow into the Bay. One of the earliest homes built in Deale is Sudley, which dates between 1720 and 1730. It is typical of the Medieval Transitional style of architecture, and has undergone three significant renovations. One in the eighteenth century adopted Georgian-style features; more changes were made in 1800. Finally, it was restored in 1945. The home's owners include a number of notable citizens from Maryland, Virginia, and Delaware and is associated with the county's Quaker heritage. It is on the National Register of Historic Places.

Most of the community's commercial activity takes place along Rockhold Creek, which is the address of Happy Harbor Restaurant, a famous Deale landmark. The community is the site of three marinas and a charter fishing boat fleet of more than forty boats. Sport fishing is a driving force here; the Deale Pro-Am Fishing Tournament is held here every year.

MARINAS
- Shipwright Harbor, 6047-57 Herring Bay Road, 410-867-7686
- Rockhold Creek Marina, 453 Deale Road, 410-867-7919

There are also several small marinas throughout Deale.

LODGING
- Happy Harbor Inn B&B, 533 Deale Road, 410-867-0949 (*Also includes a restaurant*)
- Inn at Deale B&B, 410-867-1202

RESTAURANTS
- Bay Harbor Marina, 6031 Herrington Bay, 410-867-2392
- Calypso Bay Restaurant & Dock Bar, Tracy's Landing, 410-867-9787
- Jake's Steaks, 5720 Deale-Churchton Road, 410-867-8368
- Skipper's Pier, Drum Point Road, 410-867-7110

SPECIAL EVENTS AND ACTIVITIES
Please check the internet or call ahead, as dates, times, and locations may change.

September: Annual Deale Pro-Am Fishing Tournament
   Deale Bluegrass Festival & Car Show, Herrington Harbor North

Deale, MD

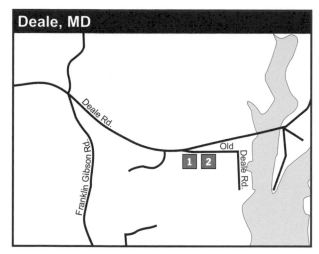

POINTS OF INTEREST

1 ST. MARK'S CEMETERY, Deale Road (Route 256) at Herring Bay Road
> St. Mark's Chapel, built in 1924, is located at 5757 Solomons Island Road, Lothian.

2 HERRINGTON HARBOR NORTH HISTORIC VILLAGE, 389 Deale Road (at Old Deale Road), 410-867-4343

2a HOLLAND UNITED BROTHERS AND SISTERS MEETING HOUSE

2b NUTWELL SCHOOL, 1885
> One-room schoolhouse, first for whites and then African-American children

2c WILLIAM PARRAN HOUSE, 1880s; moved from Prince Frederick

2d SMALL DAIRY BUILDING, 1880s; moved from Lothian

2e SMOKE HOUSE, 1820

2f CORN CRIB FROM LOTHIAN, 1910

2g HOOPER'S ISLAND DRAKETAIL, THE *MARY E*

Galesville
2010 Census Population: 684

The area that is today's Galesville was originally a large grant of land owned by early John and Mary Brown in 1652. Hence, it was originally named Brownton, or simply Brown's. In 1684, the settlement was identified as West River Landing and was designated a port of entry. The village of a few buildings clustered around the busy landing grew rapidly.

In 1672, a group of Quakers settled in the area and established the West River Quaker Meeting, which is considered the birthplace of organized Quakerism in Maryland. Over the ensuing years large numbers of Quakers attended annual Meetings of the West River Friends. They put up tents or other shelters, which led to Brown's being called as "Tenthouse Creek," a name that's still heard today.

The village grew beyond the gathering of tents, and eventually had more substantial buildings, including a general store and the shops of a blacksmith and carpenter. The most important business was the large colonial shipyard established by Stephan Steward, a shipwright and delegate to the first Continental Congress. In 1781, because Steward was known for building fast ships, had a nearly complete twenty-gun ship on the ways, and was a member of the Continental Congress, the British sent two warships to destroy his shipyard. They burned the ship and badly damaged the shipyard in the only military action in Anne Arundel County during that war. Some two hundred years later, the site of Steward's shipyard was discovered. In 1995, archaeologists began extensive excavations to study, document, and preserve the site.

The community's first post office, established in 1789, resulted in its name being changed to Galloway. The village continued to be a busy port served by a steamship line connecting Annapolis and Baltimore. In 1924, the name of the town was changed to Galesville in honor of Richard Gale, a prominent Quaker planter in the area. The name Hartge has been associated with the village from its beginning. Today the Hartge Yacht Yard is famous for their yachts, bateaux, log canoes, bugeyes, and other classic Chesapeake Bay boats. In 1934, the yard built replicas of the *Ark* and the *Dove*, the ships that carried Maryland's first colonists to the New World. The scenic village and its waterfront, plus antique and other unique shops and well-known seafood restaurants, attract a steady flow of visitors, many of whom have returned to make it their home.

A collection of historical records and memorabilia are maintained at the Galesville Heritage Society's Museum. Nearby historic sites include Tulip Hill, owned by the Quaker Samuel Galloway who often entertained George Washington and owned the famed racehorse Selim; the West River Quaker Burial Ground on the site of the 1672 West River Meeting House; the Steward Colonial Shipyard; the 1879 Hartge/Homestead Museum; and Heritage House, office of the Galesville Heritage Society.

ACTIVITIES
Please check the internet or call ahead, as dates, times, and locations may change.

⚓ MARINAS
- Hartge Yacht Yard, 4880 Church Lane, 410-867-2188
- Herrington Harbor North, 389 Deale Road, 410-867-4343
- Pirates Cove Marina, 4817 Riverside Drive, 410-867-1321

🍽 RESTAURANTS
- The Inn at Pirate's Cove, 4817 Riverside Drive, 410-867-2300
- Topside Inn, 1004 Galesville Road, 410-867-1321
- Wagner's Steamboat Landing Restaurant, 4851 Riverside Drive, 410-867-7200
- West River Market & Deli, Located in the heart of town, 410-867-4844

Galesville, MD

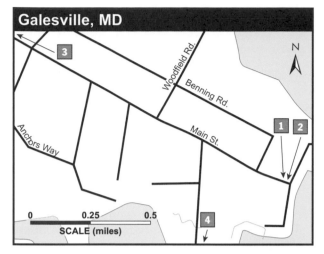

Woodfield Rd.

Benning Rd.

Main St.

Anchors Way

N

3

1 2

4

| 0 | 0.25 | 0.5 |

SCALE (miles)

POINTS OF INTEREST

1 HERITAGE HOUSE AND GALESVILLE HERITAGE SOCIETY, 988 Main Street, behind the West River Market

This is the place to start for information on places to see and visit. It also houses a collection of historical records and memorabilia.

2 WILLIAM PENN MARKER, Route 255, near Heritage House

3 WEST RIVER QUAKER BURIAL GROUND, on site of the 1672 West River Meeting House, Route 255

This property overlooks the sites of two magnificent estates. Tulip Hill, c. 1756; named for the many tulip poplars, it was the home of Quaker Samuel Galloway, who owned Selim, a great racehorse. George Washington was a frequent dinner guest there. Cedar Park, on Cumberstone Road, was recorded by Richard Ewen in 1666 as "Ewen upon Ewenton," a brick house built over an original frame structure possibly dating to 1656.

4 HARTGE/HOMESTEAD MUSEUM, 1879, Church Lane at White Stake Point

Traces the Hartge family's woodworking history from pianos to boats, 1832-2000; 410-268-1837

London Town

2010 Census Population: 0

ANNE ARUNDEL COUNTY

Historic London Town and Gardens is a twenty-three-acre park on the South River in Edgewater. The park is owned by Anne Arundel County and managed by the London Town Foundation, a non-profit organization. It has within its boundaries part of the late seventeenth- and early eighteenth century town of London, which is currently being excavated by archaeologists.

London Town was founded in 1683 and, in its early years, contended with Annapolis as the leading port in Anne Arundel County. It was the chief port for the annual tobacco fleet to load its cargo bound for England. London Town was also the main ferry crossing on the route between Williamsburg and points north. By the early 1700s, the town was flourishing. The ferry, as well as the tobacco trade, gave rise to a number of businesses, including the shops of ship carpenters and other craftsmen, a ropewalk, and taverns.

The only eighteenth century house that survived the demise of the town in the 1800s was built by carpenter and ferryman William Brown. He operated the large Georgian brick house overlooking the river and ferry landing as an inn. By 1800, the ferry, the house, and the town were in decline. By 1828, all that remained was the Brown house, which was used as the Anne Arundel County almshouse until 1965.

Anne Arundel County residents, interested in history, persuaded the county government to begin work on preserving the Brown house and creating a public park and garden on the site. The Brown House is now a National Historic Landmark surrounded by gardens and overlooking the ongoing recreation of the original town and archaeological excavations. In 2007, an impressive new Visitor Center opened, and, in 2012 a state-of-the-art multi-media exhibit featuring London Town's many-faceted story was installed and ready to educate and enthrall visitors. The site is available for public and private events.

POINTS OF INTEREST

1 VISITOR CENTER, HISTORIC LONDON TOWN & GARDENS, 1683; 839 Londontown Road, Edgewater, Maryland, 410-222-1919, www.historiclondontown.org
Discover London Town's multimedia exhibit and museum. Includes:
- WILLIAM BROWN HOUSE, c. 1740s; Georgian brick house overlooking ferry landing
- LORD MAYOR'S TENEMENT, 2002; first building reconstructed in the historic area, it was the home of David Mackelfresh, Lord Mayor of London Town.
- CARPENTER SHOP, 2007; this was the second reconstructed building in the historic area.
- Archaeological rediscovery of London Town by the Anne Arundel County Lost Towns Project, begun in 1995

Londontown, MD

Solomons Island Rd.

Maryland Ave.

Oakwood Rd.

Londontown Rd.

1

1

Shadyside
2010 Census Population: 5,803

N. 38 50' W. 76 52'

The Swamp was how early maps identified the peninsula occupied by the village that became Shadyside in the 1880s when resort towns began to boom. It was also known for reasons lost in time as Parrishes's Choice and Rural Felicity. Early Shadyside was a popular resort with hotels and cottages and cruise ships arriving regularly from Baltimore. The Captain Salem Avery House Museum is a survivor of Shadyside's early days and preserves much of the area's history with boats, models, talks, and dinners. A part of Woods Wharf is operated by the county, and a private company builds and rents boats. Though a few oyster boats tie up at the wharf, most of those that operate out of Shadyside are pleasure boats. Many of today's watermen are Black and the village is the home of the Black Watermen of the Chesapeake Living History Museum.

RESTAURANTS
- Restaurant Peninsule, Cedarhurst Road, 410-867-8664
- Richard's Corner Grill, 301-261-5655
- Shannon's, 1468 Snug Harbor Road, 410-867-1502
- Snug Harbor Inn, 1484 Snug Harbor Road, 301-261-9771

SPECIAL EVENTS AND ACTIVITIES
Please check the internet or call ahead, as dates, times, and locations may change.

On-going: Black Watermen of the Chesapeake Living History Museum; in the Discovery Village on Parrish Creek; features environmental education programs, hands-on experiences; watermen's tools, memorabilia, and oral histories.

Fall: Shadyside Heritage Society Oyster Festival, Captain Salem Avery House, 410-867-4486

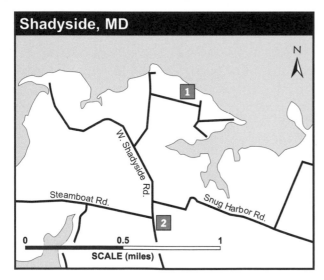

POINTS OF INTEREST
1 CAPTAIN SALEM AVERY HOUSE MUSEUM, 1418 East West Shadyside Road, 410-867-4486, www.shadysidemuseum.org
2 LULA SCOTT COMMUNITY CENTER, 6243 Shadyside Road

Baltimore County

Essex

2010 Census Population: 39,262

N. 39 18' W. 76 27'

Essex originally meant "East Saxon." In Maryland, it was once part of a colonial estate, known as Paradise Farm. Created in 1909 by the Taylor Land Company, the town was laid out in ten blocks, running from Mace Avenue to Marlyn Avenue. The idea was to give Baltimoreans a place to live beyond the city limits that would give them a taste of country life. One of the first residents was Henry Guttenburgher who built the first general store on the corner of Eastern Avenue and Mace Avenue. Between 1910 and 1912 the Taylor Land Company donated lots for the Essex Methodist and St. John's Lutheran churches and a volunteer fire department. The fire station was built in 1921 and an elementary school opened in 1925. Kenwood High School enabled the creation of Essex Community College, now CCBC-Essex, which moved to its present location in 1968.

Another important early business in Essex was the Eastern Rolling Mill which opened in 1919, and finally shut down operations in the 1990s. The real growth in the community was due to the establishment of the Glenn L. Martin Company, which reached its peak employment of 53,000 during World War II. Thereafter, it and Martin Airport were bought by the state and today are owned and operated by Lockheed Martin. A devastating fire in 1957 destroyed a block of original commercial buildings, which were unable to recover before new shopping centers drew business growth elsewhere.

A desire to revitalize the community has led to the development of a new single-family home community and a new commercial area on the site of the Middle River Station. The opening of MD-43 Extended has contributed to that revitalization by connecting the old waterfront community and Carroll Island with the booming White Marsh area.

MARINAS

- Essex Yacht Harbor Marina, 500 Sandalwood Road, 410-687-6634
- Key Yacht Club, 410-477-2578
- North Point Cove Marina, 410-477-3276
- Riley's Marina, 1901 Old Eastern Avenue, 410-686-1771
- Riverside Marina, 600 Riverside Drive, 410-686-1500
- Sunset Harbor Marina, 1651 Browns Road, 410-687-7290
- Weaver's Marine Service, 730 Riverside Drive, 410-686-4944
- West Shore Yacht Center, Muddy Gut, 410-686-6998

LODGING

- Baurenschmidt Manor B&B, 2316 Baurenschmidt Drive, 410-687-2223

RESTAURANTS

- A-1 Crab Haven, 1600 Old Eastern Avenue, 410-687-6000
- Al's Seafood, 1551 Eastern Boulevard, 410-687-3264
- Cactus Willie's, 7940 Eastern Avenue, 410-282-8268
- Carolina Gardens, 1110 Beech Drive, 410-391-5798
- Crew's Quarters, 534 Riverside Drive, 410-780-1960
- Island View Waterfront Café, 2548 Island View Road, 410-687-9799
- River Watch Restaurant & Marina, 207 Nanticoke Road, 410-687-1422

SPECIAL EVENTS AND ACTIVITIES

Please check the internet or call ahead, as dates, times, and locations may change.

May: Baltimore County Waterfront Festival,
   Lockheed-Martin at Dark Head Cove, 410-682-6122
September: Essex Day, 400-500 Blocks, Eastern Boulevard
November: Middle River Watershed Community Coalition
December: Cedar Point Mansion, Christmas Holly Tour, 410-887-0217

BALTIMORE COUNTY

Essex, MD

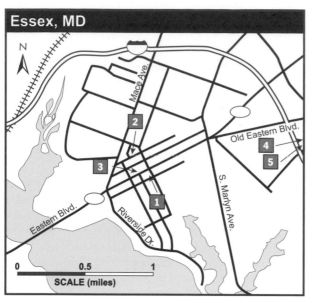

N

Mace Ave.

Old Eastern Blvd.

S. Marlyn Ave.

Eastern Blvd.

Riverside Dr.

2

3

1

4

5

0   0.5   1

SCALE (miles)

POINTS OF INTEREST

1 ESSEX UNITED METHODIST CHURCH, 524 Maryland Avenue

2 ST. JOHN'S LUTHERAN CHURCH, 518 Franklin Avenue

3 HERITAGE SOCIETY OF ESSEX & MIDDLE RIVER, 516 Eastern Boulevard, 410-574-6934

4 BALLESTONE MANOR HOUSE, 1780-1880, 1935 Back River Neck Road, 410-887-0218

5 CEDAR POINT MANSION/MUSEUM, adjacent to Ballestone Mansion, 410-887-0217

Middle River
2010 Census Population: 25,191

N. 39 20' W. 76 26'

Middle River is a densely populated area formerly dominated by the Glenn L. Martin Aircraft Company. It was a small rural town when Glenn L. Martin, a pioneer in the aircraft industry, purchased 1,260 acres there in 1929. Over the years, his plant was visited by Lindbergh, Orville Wright, Douglas Corrigan, and Amelia Earhart, among others. When the Martin factory turned to warplanes, it became the largest aircraft factory in the country and was visited by President Roosevelt and Vice-President Truman. Ultimately, the state of Maryland purchased the former Martin-Marietta Airport.

With the presence of Middle River and several navigable creeks, the community has a great number of marinas and waterfront restaurants.

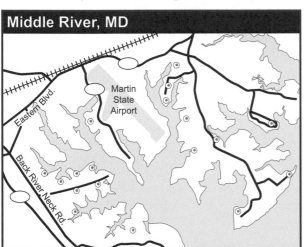

Middle River, MD

POINTS OF INTEREST

1 MIDDLE RIVER: Served by some two dozen marinas (represented by dots on the map; one is shown below) offering easy access to Baltimore City and the upper Chesapeake Bay.

Boat Sales & Brokerage · Full Service Marina
Homeport Marine Store · Trailer Sales
BALTIMORE BOATING CENTER.COM
Jim High · Brenda Wilmoth · Bill Cox

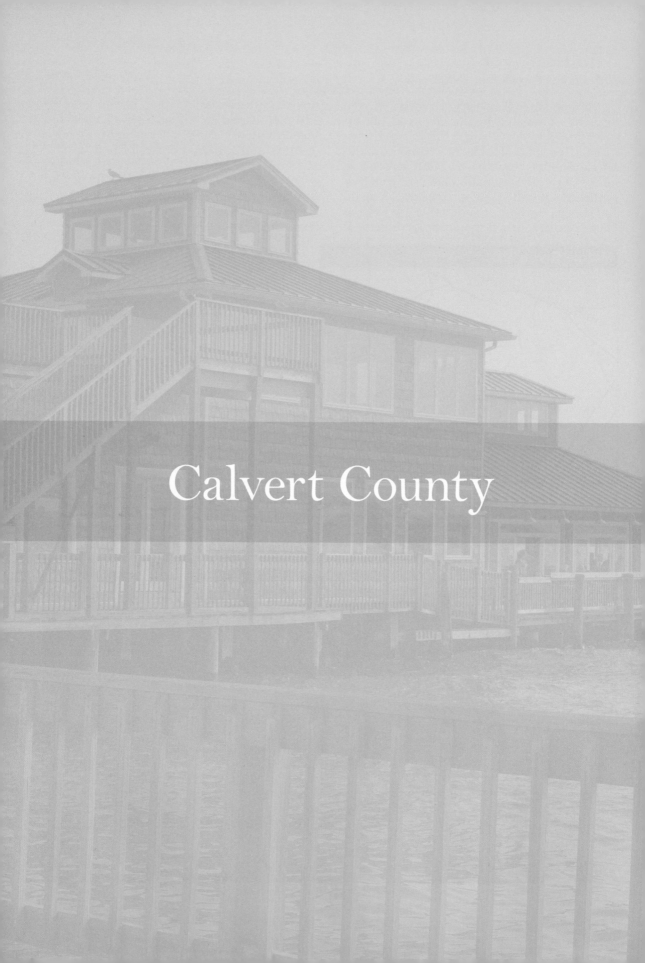

Calvert County

Broomes Island

2010 Census Population: 405

N. 38 25' W. 76 33'

Broomes Island is located near the mouth of St. Leonard Creek, the largest tributary entirely within Calvert County. It is not really an island, but a peninsula that extends halfway across the Patuxent River. In 1651, the peninsula was part of a large tract covering 2,750 acres that got its name when it was granted to John Broome. In the vicinity, several key naval battles were fought during the War of 1812. At least two aged buildings have survived the years since Broomes Island was settled. Though Christ Episcopal Church, built before 1692, had to be torn down, its bricks were used to build the present church in 1769. The second structure is Brooke Manor Place, built by and named for the first family to settle in Calvert County. Robert Brooke arrived in 1650 with his wife, ten children, and twenty-three servants. The house was badly damaged by the British in the War of 1812.

In the early- and mid-twentieth century, Broomes Island was the site of a substantial oyster canning industry. More recently, however, most residents of the island commute to other places for work. A fairly recent tradition initiated by former State Senator Bernie Fowler is a "wade-in" during which participants wade into the waters of the Patuxent River until their feet are no longer visible. The purpose is to make people aware of the river's levels of water clarity. Several notable politicians take part in the annual event. Residents and visitors in the know are sure to stop at Stoney's Restaurant for the best crab cakes in the Chesapeake region. In 2003, the island survived Hurricane Hazel but not without damage to many buildings.

LODGING

- Island Creek Bed & Breakfast, 9435 Riverview Road, 410-586-0576

RESTAURANTS

- Stoney's Seafood House, Oysterhouse Road, 410-586-1888 *(*Best crab cakes!!)*

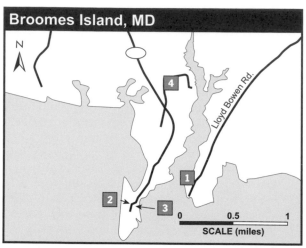

Broomes Island, MD

N

Lloyd Bowen Rd.

0   0.5   1

SCALE (miles)

POINTS OF INTEREST

1 BROOKE MANOR PLACE, across Island Creek; named for the Robert Brooke, head of the first family to settle in Calvert County.
2 WESLEYAN CHURCH, 8520 Church Road
3 STONEY'S SEAFOOD HOUSE, Oysterhouse Road, 410-586-1888; site of an early oyster house.
4 CHRIST EPISCOPAL CHURCH, 1672, Route 264 (outside of town); present church was constructed with bricks from earlier building.

Chesapeake Beach

2010 Census Population: 5,753

N. 38 41' W. 76 32'

Chesapeake Beach was established as a resort community at the end of the Chesapeake Beach Railway, a short-line railroad from Washington, D.C and the Bay. With steamers running regularly from Baltimore and trains from Washington, the weekend population reached more than ten thousand during the 1920s, but the economic depression in 1929 and a devastating hotel fire ended the need for the railroad. The construction of the Bay Bridge in the early 1950s further reduced the number of vacationers traveling to the resort by train. Visitors could just as easily drive to Ocean City instead.

Today, the old railroad station is an excellent museum with many resort and train photos and an old passenger car. In recent times, a new boardwalk and pier, as well as new condominium development, has stimulated growth and the addition of a new water park, a new resort spa, and an upscale seafood restaurant. The Herrington Harbor Marina, which was voted the best marina in the United States, is a few miles north. It also hosts the United States Naval Research Chesapeake Bay Detachment that experiments with various military radar systems and fire-suppression technology.

Residents here regularly face severe weather. Most recently, Hurricane Hazel, in 2003, was the worst, damaging many homes beyond repair and knocking out electrical services for a week. The city has continued to grow, spreading from the intersection of Fishing Creek and the Chesapeake Bay. The creek has been dredged to allow pleasure craft, commercial fishing vessels, and a few small U.S. Navy vessels to dock in the city. The southern end of town remains heavily wooded and is distinguished by the large sandstone Randall Cliffs. They tower 180 feet above the bay and are constantly being eaten away by freeze/thaw and wave action. They are famous as the best source of Miocene fossils in the world.

MARINAS
- Breezy Point Marina, 5320 Breezy Point Road, 410-414-9292
- Rod & Reel Dock, 4160 Mears Avenue, 301-855-8450
- Rod & Reel Marina West, 4055 Gordon Stinnett Avenue, 410-275-5218

LODGING
- Breezy Point Cabins, 5230 Breezy Point Road, 301-758-9981
- Chesapeake Beach Resort & Spa, 4165 Mears Avenue, 410-257-5596

RESTAURANTS
- Abner's Crab House, 3748 Harbor Road, 410-257-3689
- Beach Cove, 8416 Bayside Road, 301-855-0025
- Crooked I Sports Bar & Grill, 8323 Bayside Road, 410-257-7999
- Little Panda Restaurant, 7863 Bayside Road, 410-257-2545
- Peking, Inc., 3801 Chesapeake Beach Road, 410-257-3333
- Rod & Reel Restaurant, 4165 Mears Avenue, 410-257-2735
- Smokey Joe's Grill, 4165 Mears Avenue, 410-257-6126
- Traders Seafood Steak & Ale, 8132 Bayside Road, 410-257-6126

SPECIAL EVENTS AND ACTIVITIES
Please check the internet or call ahead, as dates, times, and locations may change.
July: Fireworks on the Beach, 410-257-2230

Chesapeake Beach, MD

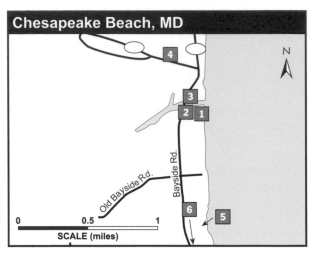

N

Old Bayside Rd.

Bayside Rd.

| 0 | 0.5 | 1 |
SCALE (miles)

POINTS OF INTEREST

1 CHESAPEAKE BEACH RAILWAY MUSEUM, 4155 Mears Avenue, 410-257-3892
2 ROD & REEL CHARTER, 4160 Mears Avenue, 301-855-8450
3 CHESAPEAKE BEACH WATER PARK, 4079 Gordon Stinnett Avenue, 410-257-1404
4 A-1 ANTIQUES AND COLLECTIBLES, 3736 Chesapeake Beach Road, 301-855-4500
5 BOARDWALK PARK, c/o Chesapeake Beach Town Hall, 410-257-2230
6 RANDALL CLIFF COMMUNITY CHURCH, Bayside Road, Route 261 near Randall Road (south of Chesapeake Beach)

Lower Marlboro

2010 Census Population: Not available

N. 38 39' W.76 41'

Back in 1965, when the Lower Marlboro post office closed its doors for the last time, the postmaster reminded those attending the ceremony that Lower Marlboro had once been a "great town." It was true. Apparently, Captain John Smith passed through the area and called it "Tauscus." Coxtown is said to be an early name for the village on the Patuxent River that was one of the first settlements in Calvert County. It developed as a port for the shipment of tobacco from surrounding farms.

In the nineteenth century, the town had a store, a blacksmith's shop, a cooperage, and Stephan Steward's shipyard. In 1777, the first galley built by Steward's yard was christened the *Conqueror*. The fifty-foot-long galley's first crew probably numbered fewer than eighty-eight. Relatively small galleys and crews were typical in the Maryland navy. Marlboro had no vessels defending it in 1781 during the American Revolution when a British ship raided the town, capturing all the stores they could carry and leaving the local inn on fire. With the constant threat of attack, the final years of the war were a disaster for the town, causing shipping to cease and many businesses to be abandoned.

During the War of 1812, frightened residents deserted the town when they received reports that Marlboro was in the path of a large British force on the way to burn Washington. The town was spared, however, when the British stopped at Benedict instead. Local shipping and commerce were interrupted again during the Civil War. Though Calvert County escaped conflict, its residents struggled to survive a lack of supplies from what little steamship traffic could reach Lower Marlboro. At the end of the war, new warehouses, a slaughterhouse, a blacksmith shop, and a gristmill opened and proved a good investment for their owners and the town. The new prosperity brought a tailor, a carpenter, a wheelwright, and a cobbler. In 1888, steamboat traffic had increased and was maintained until the steamboats stopped running entirely. In 1868, the first Methodist Church, called Largent's Chapel, was established and, in 1870, Marlboro resident Thomas Clagget became the rector of All Saint's Church, which had been consecrated as the first Episcopal Church in the United States in 1792.

Lower Marlboro was flooded frequently, which caused it to be dubbed "Swampoodle" by local folk. A more serious problem was fire. A devastating blaze in 1936 destroyed most of the downtown and it never recovered. In the early 1970s, a restoration effort got underway and, by 1985, nine houses had been moved from other parts of the county to Lower Marlboro, but to no avail. When the post office closed in 1965, the postmaster's eulogy was recorded for history. It was short and to the point: "Great town. Really a great town. Fifty years ago."

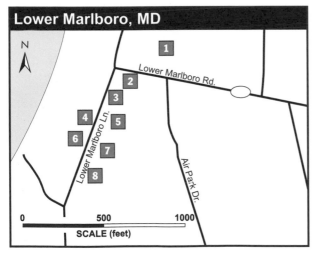

POINTS OF INTEREST

1 GRAHAM HOUSE, Patuxent Manor; best viewed from 4160 Lower Marlboro Road (former Varden Street)

CALVERT COUNTY

2 HINMAN HOUSE/HARBOR MASTER'S HOUSE,
Lower Marlboro Lane and Marlboro Road, 1835;
the builder used materials from a house built before 1835.

3 MILLS HOUSE, Lower Marlboro Lane;
built before 1830 with additions over the next 100 years

4 GRIFFITH-ARMIGER HOUSE, 6517 Lower Marlboro Lane;
19th century house containing some interior
18th-century moldings

5 FANNY GIBSON HOUSE, Lower Marlboro Lane, 19th century;
behind it is a classic, early 20th century Maryland tobacco
barn.

6 ELIJAH WELLS HOUSE/CARR-WELLS HOUSE, Lower Marlboro
Lane; built in the 19th century, it was moved to its present
location in the 1880s.

7 SPICKNALL HOUSE, Lower Marlboro Lane, 19th century

8 DALLAS-WARD TENANT HOUSE, Lower Marlboro Lane
(at the end of a small dirt lane)

North Beach
2010 Census Population: 1,978   N. 38 42' W. 76 32'

North Beach was platted in 1800 and was originally settled largely by residents for nearby Baltimore and Washington whose vacation cottages shared the waterfront community with working watermen. During the 1940s, it was a gambling mecca for summer visitors from Washington. When the Bay Bridge opened in 1955, it soon lost its summer vacationers to Ocean City; in the 1960s and 1970s, it became a destination for motorcycle gangs. However, when legalized gambling ended, the heyday of North Beach as a rollicking resort came to an end. Today's residents are mainly permanent residents.

Following years of decline, there's been a rebirth of civic pride and a strong sense of community. The Bayside History Museum was among the recent developments that included a senior citizens' apartment complex and a primary care medical facility. Every June brings visitors flocking to the North Beach House and Garden Tour, and in August, the town's annual Bayfest is a popular event. Year-round, local antique shops attract customers and beachcombers delight in searching for fossil shark's teeth. The key to finding the teeth is to explore the beach just south of the pier, following the debris line. There, in a few minutes, in the detritus that has washed ashore, diligent searchers will find a dozen or more small teeth, most only half-an-inch long or smaller. Larger teeth are found on the cliffside beaches nearby, most of which are on private property and require permission.

LODGING
• Chesapeake Bay Vacation Cottage, 4036 5th Street, 410-257-7330

RESTAURANTS
• Bilvil, A Beaches Café, 4114 7th Street, 410-286-7214
• Neptune's Seafood Pub, 8800 Chesapeake Avenue, 410-257-7899
• Thursday's Bar and Grill, 9200 Bay Avenue, 410-257-8695
• Westlawn Inn, 9200 Chesapeake Avenue, 410-257-0001

SPECIAL EVENTS AND ACTIVITIES
Please check the internet or call ahead, as dates, times, and locations may change.
January: Polar Beach Swim, beach at 5th Street and Bay Avenue, 410-257-9618
June: North Beach House and Garden Tour, St. Anthony's parking lot, 301-855-6681
   North Beach Art Show, 89016 Chesapeake Avenue, 301-855-6681
June–August: Free Summer Concert, 5th and Bay Avenue, 301-855-6681
July: Free Summer Concert/ Fireworks Show, 5th and Bay Avenue, 410-257-9618
August: Bayfest, Bay Avenue from 1st to 7th Streets, 410-257-9618
December: Christmas on the Beach, 5th and Bay Avenue, 410-257-9618

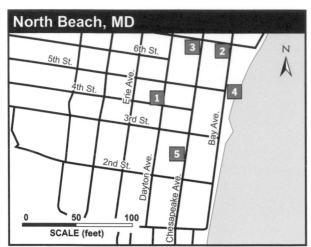

North Beach, MD

POINTS OF INTEREST

1 BAYSIDE HISTORY MUSEUM,
   9006 Dayton Avenue, 410-495-8386
2 ARTWORKS, 9128 Bay Avenue,
   410-286-5278
3 WILLETTA'S ANTIQUES, 301-855-3412,
   and NICE & FLEAZY ANTIQUES CENTER,
   7th & Bay Avenue, 310-855-5066
4 NORTH BEACH PUBLIC BEACH,
   5th & Bay Avenue, 410-257-9618
5 NORTH BEACH UNION CHURCH,
   8912 Chesapeake Avenue, 410-257-3555

Solomons Island
2010 Census Population: 2,368   N. 38 20' W. 76 28'

The waterfront community of Solomons on Solomons Island where the Patuxent River and Chesapeake Bay meet has been inhabited since colonial times. It offered a strategic location during the War of 1812 for Commodore Joshua Barney's flotilla to attack British vessels on the Bay. The deep, protected harbor has been a busy maritime center ever since. Nearly one hundred years later, it played a significant role in another war. Solomons was chosen by the Allied Command during World War II as a training site for amphibious invasion forces. As a result, three naval bases opened nearby on the Patuxent River. Between 1942 and 1945, the war brought jobs and new residents to swell the town's population from roughly 260 to more than 2,600. More than 60,000 troops were trained in the area and put their training to good use at Tarawa, Guadalcanal, and many other landings.

Peacetime brought development to the community as well. Shortly after the Civil War, businessman Isaac Solomon established a cannery at Solomons. Shipyards also developed in the nineteenth century as a result of Solomons' growing fishing fleet. The Marsh Shipyard built schooners and sloops and later became famous for its bugeyes and even later skipjacks.

In more recent times, Solomons became home of the University of Maryland's Chesapeake Biological Laboratory. It was fairly isolated until 1977 when the Governor Thomas Johnson Bridge was built to St. Mary's County and the Patuxent Naval Air Station. Solomons now attracts visitors and boaters with numerous marinas, seafood restaurants, gift shops, a boardwalk, a Sculpture Garden, and the Calvert Marine Museum. It has three major hotels, a U.S. Navy family-recreation center, and a church retirement home. A devastating fire destroyed Bowen's Inn, a condominium building, and other properties, causing five million dollars in damages, but Solomons is recovering, as it has from other disasters, including the Great Depression and a severe storm in 1933.

⌖ MARINAS
- Beacon Marina, 255 Lore Road, 410-326-9292
- Calvert Marina, 14485 Dowell Road, 410-326-4251
- Harbor Island Marina, 105 Charles Street, 410-326-3441
- Solomons Harbor Marina, 205 Holiday Drive, 410-326-1052
- Solomons Yachting Center, 255 Alexander Lane, 410-326-2401
- Spring Cove Marina, 455 Lore Road, 410-326-2161
- Zahnizer's Yachting Center, 245 C Street & Back Creek, 410-326-2166

⌖ LODGING
- Back Creek Inn Bed & Breakfast, Alexander and Calvert Streets, 410-326-2022
- Blue Heron Bad & Breakfast, 14614 Solomons Island Road, 410-326-2707
- Comfort Inn Solomons, Lore Road, 410-326-6303
- Holiday Inn Select Solomons Hotel, Conference Center & Marina, 155 Holiday Drive, 410-356-2009
- Locust Inn Rooms, 14478 Solomons Island Road, 410-326-9817
- Solomons Victorian Inn, 125 Charles Street, 410-326-4811

RESTAURANTS

- Boomerangs Original Ribs, 13820 H. G. Truman Road, 410-326-6050
- The C. D. Café, Inc., 14350 Solomons Island Road, 410-326-3877
- Calypso Bay Crab House, 120 Charles Street, 410-231-2275
- Captain's Table, 275 Lore Road, 410-326-2772
- Catamarans Seafood & Steaks, 14470 Solomons Island Road, 410-326-8399
- China Harbor Seafood Restaurant, 13958 H. G. Truman Road, 410-326-6888
- DiGovanni's Dock of the Bay, 14556 Solomons Island Road, 410-326-6400
- Dry Dock Restaurant, 245 C Street, Zahnizer's Yachting Center between C Street and Back Creek, 410-326-4817
- Dynasty Chinese Restaurant, 13322 H. G. Truman Road, 410-394-1185
- Harbor Island Restaurant, 120 Charles Street, 410-326-9522
- Isaac's at the Holiday Inn Select, 155 Holiday Street, 410-394-3618 ext. 2144
- Jethro's Restaurant & Annie's Ice Cream, 13880 N. Solomons Island Road, 394-6700
- The Naughty Gull Restaurant & Pub, 450 Lore Road, Spring Cove Marina, 410-326-4855
- Solomons Pier Restaurant & Lounge, Patuxent Avenue, 410-326-2424
- Stoney's Kingfishers, 14442 Solomons Island Road, 410-394-0236
- Stoney's Solomons Pier, 14575 Solomons Island Road, 410-326-2424

SPECIAL EVENTS AND ACTIVITIES

Please check the internet or call ahead, as dates, times, and locations may change.

February: Made by Hand – Inspired by the Bay,
Calvert Marine Museum, 410-326-2042 ext. 41

March: Spring Break with the Otters, Calvert Marine Museum, 410-326-2042 ext. 41

May: Solomons Maritime Festival, Calvert Marine Museum, 410-326-2042 ext. 41
Mothers Day Brunch Cruise and Evening Cruise,
Calvert Marine Museum, 410-326-2042 ext. 41
International Museum Day, Calvert Marine Museum, 410-326-2042 ext. 41

June: Fathers Day Brunch Cruise and Evening Cruise,
Calvert Marine Museum, 410-326-4042 ext. 41

July: Fireworks Cruise, Calvert Marine Museum, 410-326-4042 ext. 41
Solomons Fireworks, 410-326-1950
Calvert Artists Guild Works Outdoor Show, Boardwalk Pavilion, 410-326-2604

August: USO Reenactment of WWII, Pavilion on the Boardwalk, 410-257-8488

September: Chesapeake Appreciation Days, Calvert Marine Museum, 410-326-4042 ext. 41
Annual Monster Mash Cruise, Calvert Marine Museum, 410-326-410 ext. 41
Haunted Lighthouse Tour, Calvert Marine Museum, 410-326-4042 ext. 41

November: Solomons Island Salute to the Military,
Calvert Marine Museum, 410-326-4042 ext. 41

December: Solomons Island Annual Christmas Walk, 410-326-1950

Solomons, MD

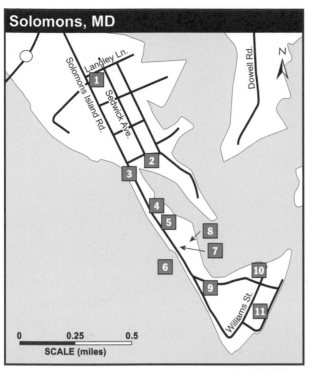

Langley Ln.

Solomons Island Rd.

Sedwick Ave.

Dowell Rd.

N

Williams St.

1

2

3

4

5

8

7

6

10

9

11

0   0.25   0.5

SCALE (miles)

POINTS OF INTEREST

1 CALVERT MARINE MUSEUM,
   14200 Solomons Island Road South
2 OUR LADY STAR OF THE SEA CATHOLIC
   CHURCH, 1888, 225 Alexander Street;
   410-326-3535
3 THE BRIDGE (1893, 1907, 1915, 1948-49,
   1957, 1985)
4 J. C. LORE OYSTER HOUSE, 1888-1978,
   14430 Solomons Island Road;
   exhibits in the Calvert Marine Museum
5 SOLOMONS UNITED METHODIST CHURCH,
   1870, 14454 Solomons Island Road

6

6 SOLOMONS PIER, 14757 Solomons Island Road South; formerly a movie theater, dance pavilion, hotel, and restaurant, only the restaurant survives

7 ST. PETER'S EPISCOPAL CHURCH, 1889, 14584-14600 Solomons Island Road

8 M. M. DAVIS SHIPYARD SITE, 14584-14600 Solomons Island Road

9 STEAMBOAT WHARF, 1866; approximate site shown on the map

10 CHESAPEAKE BIOLOGICAL LABORATORY VISITORS CENTER, 1 William Street

11 NORTHAMPTON SITE AND CHESAPEAKE BIOLOGICAL LABORATORY, 1922, 1 William Street and Farren Avenue

Charles County

Benedict

2010 Census Population: 261

Benedict is a village opposite Hallowing Point on the Patuxent River in Charles County. Settled in 1683 and named in honor of Benedict Leonard Calvert, the fourth Lord Baltimore, it was recorded in 1695 as Benedict-Leonard Town. The town served as a river port, shipping center, and ferry landing throughout the nineteenth century and into the twentieth. The present bridge was built in 1950.

The British anchored off the town during the War of 1812 while blockading the Patuxent River. Five thousand troops left Benedict to attack Washington and returned after burning that city. They sailed out of the river shortly thereafter. From 1813 to 1937, steamboats carrying freight and passengers regularly stopped at Benedict. During the Civil War, Camp Stanton, named for Edwin Stanton, then Secretary of War, was set up nearby to recruit and train Black troops for the Union Army. Now the town is home to a couple of small seafood restaurants and the church.

ACTIVITIES

Please check the internet or call ahead, as dates, times, and locations may change.

▣ MARINAS
- Benedict Marina, 19305 Wilmot Drive, 301-843-9306; 19311 Wilmot Street, 301-274-2882
- De Soto's Landing and Marina, 18163 De Soto Place, 301-870-8145
- De Soto's Landing Marina, 301 De Soto Lane, 301-870-8145
- Ray's Pier Marina, 18170 De Soto Place, 301-274-3733
- Seaside Marina, 19311 Wilmot Drive, 301-274-2882

▣ LODGING
- Benedict Marina, 19405 Wilmot Lane, 301-843-9306 *(*Also includes a restaurant)*
- De Soto's Landing Marina, 301 De Soto Lane, 301-870-3733 *(*Also includes a restaurant, 301-870-8145)*
- Ray's Pier Marina, 18170 De Soto Place, 301-274-3733 *(*Also includes a restaurant)*
- Seaside Marina, 19311Wilmot Drive, 301-274-2882 *(*Also includes a restaurant)*

▣ RESTAURANTS
- Mamma Lucia Italian Restaurant, 443-486-4701

Benedict, MD

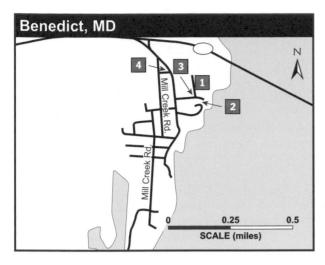

SCALE (miles)

POINTS OF INTEREST

1 RAY'S PIER AND MARINA,
18170 De Soto Place, 301-274-3733
2 DE SOTO'S LANDING MARINA,
301 De Soto Lane, 301-870-8145
3 ST. FRANCIS DE SALES CATHOLIC CHURCH,
7185 Benedict Avenue
4 BENEDICT LOCAL STORE, Benedict Avenue

Cobb Island

2010 Census Population: 1,166   N. 38 16' W. 76 51'

Cobb Island is lies in the Potomac at the mouth of the Wicomico River. The first record of it is dated 1642, when it was purchased by Captain James Neale, whose name graces the sound that separates the island from the mainland. Legend has it that he was a pirate who preyed upon Spanish treasure ships in the West Indies, which could have something to do with the island being named for the crudely-made Spanish coin known as a cob, to which the main body and shape of the island bears a strong resemblance.

No one lived on the island until 1889 when George Vickers built a house and farmed the surrounding land. The Cobb Island Bar figured in much of the violence of the nineteenth century's Oyster Wars, during which there were several killings. Of more lasting import was the construction by the federal government of a lighthouse on Cobb Island to steer heavy river traffic around, clear of hazards. The Cobb Island Bar forms a sheltered anchorage that sailors take advantage of during storms that regularly hit the Potomac. During hurricanes, however, islanders often must contend with flooding. The original lighthouse was completely destroyed by fire in 1939, but rebuilt soon thereafter.

Of wide significance and a source of community pride is an event that took place in December 1900. That month, a team of scientists led by Reginald Fessenden accomplished the first radio voice transmission from one fifty-foot mast to another a mile away across Neale Sound. The team met to plan their transmission out of the home of George Vickers, a Philadelphia newspaperman who undoubtedly gave the event full coverage. That first message was "Is it snowing where you are?" The answer was "Yes." The turreted Vickers House, a Victorian grande dame overlooking the sound, was one of the houses where the scientists stayed.

By 1927, the island had a post office and two years later was incorporated as a township. It got a reliable bridge to the mainland in 1932 and electricity in 1939.

The island lies close by the Dalgren Naval Warfare Center's firing range and residents have learned to heed the warnings when the navy plans to test-fire experimental naval weapons. During the firing, a navy patrol boat is stationed off Cobb Island to clear the area. An additional warning to boaters is broadcast on Channel 16. They may also call 877-845-5656.

Cobb Island was at first a resort area, but today is a year-round community of men who work the water for harvests of fish, crabs, and oysters. The lighthouse on the island is well-known to sailors as they navigate the Potomac to one of the island's four marinas or to stop for a meal at one of several crab houses.

▣ MARINAS
- Captain John's Crab House & Marina, 16215 Cobb Island Road, 301-259-2315 (*Great fried oysters!*)
- Pirates Den Marina and Crab House, 12364 Neale Sound Drive, 301-259-3879
- Saunder's Marina, Located on the mainland at the north end of Neale Sound, 301-259-2309
- Shymanski's River Marina, 16320 Cobb Island Road, 301-259-2221

▣ RESTAURANTS
- Cobb Island Gallery, 12133 Neale Sound Drive, 301-259-4900
- Fish Tales Bar and Grill, 17045 Cobb Island Road, 301-259-2600
- Pirates Den Marina & Crab House, 12364 Neale Sound Drive, 301-259-3879
- Shymanski's Dockside, 16320 Cobb Island Road (at the mainland end of the bridge), 301-259-2221

SPECIAL EVENTS AND ACTIVITIES
Please check the internet or call ahead, as dates, times, and locations may change.
May: Cobb Island Day, Old Fisherman's Cobb Island home page on Maryand.party.com.
August: Firemen's Parade, Cobb island Volunteer Fire Department, 301-259-4258

Cobb Island, MD

POINTS OF INTEREST

1 VICKERS HOUSE, 1889, Neale Sound Drive
Built by Philadelphia newspaperman
George Vickers; the first audio radio
transmissions were planned here.

2 SIGN, Potomac River Drive at Cobb
Island Road; marking the site of radio
transmissions

3 COBB ISLAND BAPTIST CHURCH,
17608 Cobb Island Road

4 COBB ISLAND LIGHTHOUSE;
can be seen offshore from
Potomac River Drive
near Wicomico Drive

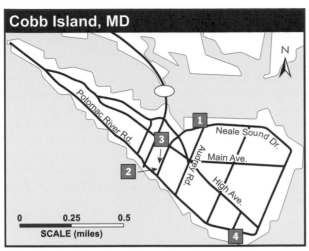

Marshall Hall

2010 Census Population: Not available

N. 38 40' W. 77 05'

The original inhabitants of the "ancient seat" of Marshall were Algonquin Indians. Recent archaeological excavations have yielded proof of their occupancy in primitive weapons, pottery, and mortars. Marshall Hall was a five hundred-acre tract surveyed for William Marshall in 1651. In the years leading to the American Revolution, Thomas Hanson Marshall represented Charles County in the provincial convention in Annapolis in 1775. In 1776, John Marshall was the First Major of the Maryland's Lower Battalion in the Continental Army.

In bygone days, Marshall Hall was well-known to Washingtonians for its amusement park built in 1888. In another era, between 1949 and 1968, the four-county area of Southern Maryland, including Marshall Hall, offered the only legal slot machines in the United States outside of Nevada. The National Park Service finally tore down all vestiges of the amusement park in 1980, which is now part of the Park Service's Piscataway Park.

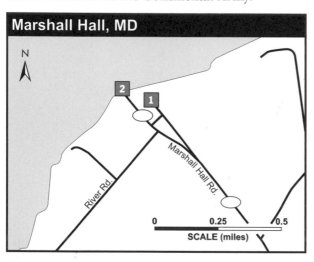

Marshall Hall, MD

N

0   0.25   0.5

SCALE (miles)

POINTS OF INTEREST

1 MARSHALL HALL, Old Marshall Hall Road (Route 227); the shell of the Hall is all that remains of the once grand mansion and out-buildings

2 MARSHALL HALL BOAT LAUNCH, end of Marshall Hall Road, town of Bryans Road, Maryland

Port Tobacco

2010 Census Population: 13

N. 38 31' W. 77 01'

The first Englishman to see what is now Port Tobacco was Captain John Smith when he explored the Potomac River in 1608. He found there an Indian village named Potopaco belonging to twenty warriors and their families who were part of the Powhatan Confederacy. In 1639, Father White, a Jesuit priest who had come to St. Mary's City with the first settlers, baptized the queen of the Potopaco Indians and 130 of her subjects. By 1650, the white settlers had stripped away most of the virgin forest, destroying the Indians' simple farms and driving them from the forests and waters where they had hunted and fished. Not only did the settlers displace them, but they also brought diseases unknown to the Indians. By the mid-seventeenth century, the Potopaco tribe had disappeared.

Before 1669, Port Tobacco was designated one of the first official ports of entry. It was first called Chandlerstown, then Charlestown, and then Port Tobacco, which was an English adaptation of the Indians "Portobaco." In its early days, it was one of Maryland's primary river ports. In 1807, it contained fifty houses, an Episcopal Church, a warehouse, and, as the county seat, a courthouse and a jail.

During the Civil War, almost all of its citizens were ardent Confederates and the community became a center of intrigue and espionage. Olivia Floyd of nearby Rose Hill was a Confederate spy who carried many messages to a signaling station across the Potomac. The area has a ghost. As the story goes, a large blue tick hound owned by an itinerant peddler was set to guard a large cache of gold hidden near Rose Hill. Negro slaves said that on the day the peddler was killed his dog came thundering over the hill in a cloud of smoke. The most significant event in the town's history occurred in 1865. When President Abraham Lincoln's assassin, John Wilkes Booth, was on the run with a $100,000 reward on his head, he was hidden near the town before he escaped across the Potomac River.

In the twentieth century, progress brought the railroad and steamboats to Port Tobacco, which became a busy port and landing for the Pennsylvania Railroad's thirty-five steamboats. Eventually, however, silting in the river ended the steamboat traffic and a new railroad station and removal of the county seat to La Plata doomed any remaining industry. Even the community's church was demolished and moved by ox cart to La Plata and rebuilt. The town slowly began to decay.

The population of present-day Port Tobacco is very different from its historical counterpart: for the most part, the farmers, merchants, dockworkers, legal functionaries, and even assorted craftsmen have been replaced by businessmen, government administrators, computer operators, car salesmen, and politicians.

CHARLES COUNTY

Port Tobacco, MD

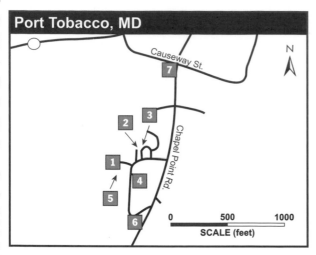

Causeway St.

Chapel Point Rd.

N

7

3

2

1

4

5

6

0   500   1000

SCALE (feet)

POINTS OF INTEREST

All locations are along Chapel Point Road,
off Route 6 West.

**1 CHARLES COUNTY COURTHOUSE
REPLICA AND MUSEUM**
> The Elijah Wells Print Shop for the *Port
> Tobacco Times* and museum is located on
> the second floor of the courthouse.

**2 BARNES-COMPTON HOUSE
(CHIMNEY HOUSE)**, mid- to late-18th
century; built on the site where
another house had stood since 1730.

3 PODGET HOUSE (STAGG HALL), 1740

4 QUENZEL ("QUINSWLL") HOUSE AND STORE,
19th century; the owner sold dry goods,
jewelry, and watches

5 CHRIST CHURCH SITE AND GRAVEYARD, 1692;
the church was moved to La Plata

6 SMITHY HOUSE, c. 19th century

7 ONE-ROOM SCHOOL HOUSE, 1876,
Chapel Point Road at Causeway Road

* Sites shown on old map include the Smoot Hotel,
St. Charles Hotel, Boswell Store, Smoot Warehouse,
Bowie House, Post Office, Baker House, Wade
Button House, and Centennial Hotel.

** See charming 1800s site drawing of the town at the
following website http://www.msa.md.gov/megafile/
msa/stagsere/se1/se5/008000/008000/008069/pdf/
msa_se5_8069.pdf

Harford County

Bush, Old Harford
No longer exists

N. 39 24' W. 76 14'

The town of Bush that once occupied this site was the Harford County seat for nine years. It had thirty or forty dwellings, a grist mill, tanyard, and several inns and stores. It was the scene of active rebellion against England on the eve of the Revolutionary War. In June 1774, the citizens gathered to air their concerns and created what came to be known as the Bush River Declaration, or simply the Bush Declaration. Thirty-four citizens signed it and sent it to the Convention meeting in Annapolis. The Bush Declaration was a resolution of the signatories to support the patriot cause — if not quite yet complete separation from England. Just as the towns of Old Baltimore and Joppa had served their purpose, so Bush slowly slipped into decay and disappeared. Of all the buildings that once existed, only the large coach house on Route 7 remains. The Bush Declaration Natural Resources Management Area is now located in this area.

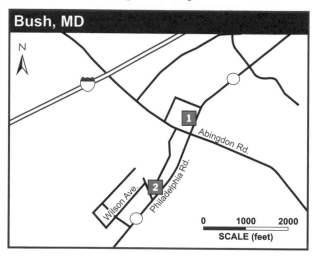

Bush, MD

N

Abingdon Rd.

Wilson Ave.

Philadelphia Rd.

0   1000   2000

SCALE (feet)

POINTS OF INTEREST

1 OLD COACH HOUSE, Philadelphia Road (Route 7) just east of Route 136
2 SIGN: "BUSH DECLARATION," Philadelphia Road (Route 7), 0.4 miles east of Route 136

"THE BUSH DECLARATION"
HARFORD TOWN
COUNTY SEAT OF HARFORD COUNTY
FROM ITS ORIGIN MARCH, 1774, UNTIL
MARCH, 1783. HERE THE FIRST
DECLARATION OF INDEPENDENCE
EVER ADOPTED BY AN ORGANIZED BODY
OF MEN DULY ELECTED BY THE PEOPLE
WAS PROCLAIMED ON MARCH 22, 1775.
MARYLAND HISTORICAL SOCIETY

Havre de Grace

2010 Census Population: 12,952   N. 39 33' W. 76 06'

The story of Havre de Grace actually begins with the arrival of Captain John Smith who explored the area in 1608. He passed what is now known as Palmer's Island where the early settlers built a fort as protection from the warlike Susquehannock Indians. After defeat by the Susquehannocks in the early 1640s, the Marylanders signed a treaty with them in 1652. More settlers arrived to claim land in the area, the first of whom was Godfrey Harmer who patented a two hundred-acre tract at the mouth of the Susquehanna River that he called Harmer's Town. Later owners began running the first ferry across the Bay in 1695. It remained in operation for the next 170 years.

On August 29, 1782, a soldier, Claude Blanchard, who was returning with Rochambeau's troops from the Battle of Yorktown, wrote in his diary, "It has been proposed to build a city here on the right bank near the ferry where we crossed. It should be called Havre de Grace." And so it began. A second story attributes the naming of the town to the Marquis de Lafayette, who visited often and was reminded of the French seaport of Le Havre, which had originally been named Le Havre-de-Grâce. Inspired by Lafayette's comment, it is said, the residents incorporated the town as Havre de Grace in 1785.

However it came by its name, a town grew around the ferry landing. With seven houses and a warehouse, it became a candidate for county seat in 1787 and by 1798 numbered forty houses. Real growth began with the opening of the Susquehanna Canal in 1802; by 1807, a steady stream of boats were traveling the canal from Columbia, Pennsylvania, to Havre de Grace and the Bay. The canal was a target of the British during the War of 1812 and, on May 3, 1813, the British attacked and burned Havre de Grace.

With the coming of peace, the port grew and profited from maritime traffic on the canal and arriving at the town wharf. That came to a halt in 1835, shortly after the arrival of the railroad, which replaced the canal. The Susquehanna and Tidewater Canal House is open to visitors and a former lock house has been converted to the Susquehanna Museum. The Concord Point Lighthouse near Havre de Grace is the oldest continuously lit lighthouse on the East Coast. It was automated in 1928.

After the Civil War, the Lower Susquehanna Ferry ended operation when the new Philadelphia, Wilmington, and Baltimore Railroad bridge was built. In 1923, a second railroad bridge, one with double tracks, was built. In the late 1880s, the waterfront was lined with several ice houses that stored winter ice, the large fish packing houses of Silver & Spencer, and flour and feed mills. With World War II, the town experienced tremendous growth when it became a bedroom community for the Aberdeen Proving Grounds and Bainbridge Training Center across the river.

A race track opened at Havre de Grace in 1912. There Man of War and War Admiral were among the famous horses that ran on the track until it closed in 1950. Besides racing fans and horsemen, hunters, fishermen, and waterfowl gunners were attracted to the Upper Bay town and all that the nearby Susquehanna had to offer. Havre de Grace became well-known for its decoy carvers whose craftsmanship is on display at a Decoy Museum. The town had a colorful social life in the 1920s. The Bayou Hotel was a hot spot with big-name bands playing for dancers on its terrace. With the twenty-first century, Havre de Grace's recreational opportunities, its historic buildings, and its magnificent location at the head of the Bay continue to be appreciated and developed.

⛴ MARINAS
- Havre de Grace City Yacht Basin, Tydings Park, 410-939-0015
- Havre de Grace Yacht Sales & Marina at Log Pond, 410-939-2221
- Tidewater Marina, 410-939-0950

🛏 LODGING
- Currier House Bed & Breakfast, 800 S. Market Street, 410-939-7886
- La Cle D'or Guesthouse, 226 N. Union Avenue, 410-939-6562
- Spencer Silver Mansion, 200 S. Union Avenue, 410-939-1485
- Vandiver Inn, 301 S. Union Avenue, 410-939-5200
- Water's Edge Guest Cottage, 433 St. John Street, 410-939-3334

▢ RESTAURANTS

- The Bayou, 927 Pulaski Highway, 410-939-3565
- Coakley's Pub, 406 St. John Street, 410-939-8888
- Havre de Grace Ritz Café, 100 N. Washington Street, 410-939-5858
- Java By the Bay, 118 N. Washington Street, 410-939-0227
- Ken's Steak and Rib House, 400 N. Union Avenue, 410-939-5440
- La Cucina Italian Restaurant, 103 N. Washington Street, 410-939-1401/1402
- Laurrapin Grille, 209 N. Washington Street, 410-939-3663
- MacGregor's Restaurant, 331 St. John Street, 410-939-3003
- Tidewater Grille, 300 Franklin Street, 410-939-3313

SPECIAL EVENTS AND ACTIVITIES

Please check the internet or call ahead, as dates, times, and locations may change.

Ongoing events: Lighthouse tours, April-October, foot of Lafayette Street.410-939-9040.
  Havre de Grace Farmer's Market, Saturdays, May to October, 9 a.m. to noon,
  Pennington Avenue between Washington Street and Union Avenue, 410-939-3303
  Friday Concert in the Park, every Friday, June & July, Tydings Park, 410-939-5425

May: Annual Decoy & Art Festival, various locations
  Guided Nature Historical Walk, North Park Trail, 410-939-5780
  Re-enactment – Living History Program, Lock House Grounds, 410-939-5780

June: Guided Nature Historical Walk, Lock House, 410-939-5780

July: Havre de Grace Independence Celebration, Tydings Park,
  concert and fireworks, 410-939-4362
  Firework's Cruise, two-hour cruise, reservations required, 410-939-4078

August: Annual Havre de Grace Seafood Festival, 410-939-1525
  Havre de Grace Art Show, Tydings Park, 410-939-9342
  Juried Art Exhibition, Havre de Grace Visitor Center,
  450 Pennington Avenue, 410-939-2068
  Re-enactment – Living History Program, Lock House, 410-939-5780
  Guided Nature – Historical Walk, Lock House, 410-939-5780

September: Guided Nature Historical Walk, Lock House, 410-939-5780

October: Halloween Happenings, Maritime Museum, 100 Lafayette Street, 410-939-4800

November: The Four Bay Winds – Native American Indian Gathering, Lock House Grounds

December: Mari-time Xmas, 100 Lafayette Street, 410-939-4800
  Annual Candlelight Tour, Susquehanna Museum, 410-939-5780
  Candlelight Tour and Carver's Celebration, Decoy Museum, 410-939-3739

Havre de Grace, MD

POINTS OF INTEREST

1 BAYOU HOTEL, Commerce Street
A hot spot in the 1920s with dancing on
the terrace to big name bands.

2 DECOY MUSEUM, 215 Giles Street,
410-939-3739

3 MARITIME MUSEUM, 100 Lafayette Street,
410-939-4800

4 CONCORD POINT LIGHTHOUSE, Concord
& Lafayette Streets, 410-939-3213
Oldest continually illuminated lighthouse
on the East Coast, automated in 1928.

5 JOHN O'NEILL HOUSE/LIGHTKEEPER'S
HOUSE, Concord & Lafayette Streets,
410-939-3213
John O'Neill was the hero of the War
of 1812; this house was occupied by the
O'Neill family for 158 years.

6 BECHTOLD HOUSE & BAKERY,
109 S. Washington Street;
Carpenter Gothic, characteristic
of the most common style when
it was built in the late 1880s

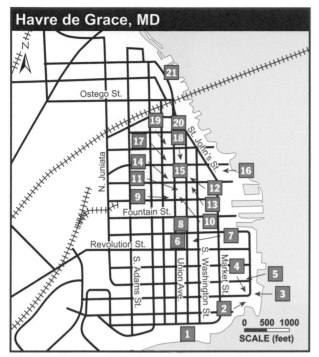

7 Vandiver Mansion, 301 S. Union Street, 1886; late 19th century Queen Anne

8 Spencer-Silver Mansion, 200 S. Union Avenue, 1896; only High Victorian in Havre de Grace

9 Vosbury House, 123 S. Union Avenue, 1888

10 Carver House, 1888, 115 S. Union Avenue, 1888; late 19th century Queen Anne

11 Havre de Grace United Methodist Church, southeast corner of Congress and Union Avenues, 1901; Gothic Revival style

12 Carver Craig House, 453 Congress Avenue, c. 1850; Greek Revival

13 Silverstein House, 414 Congress Avenue, 1865; the only house of brick built in the Italianate Style.

14 St. John's Episcopal Church, northwest corner of Congress and Union Avenues, 1809; oldest church in the city

15 City Hall, 1870, 121 N. Union Avenue.

16 The American Legion Hall
(Abraham Jarrett Thomas House), 501 St. John Street, 1834
John Rodgers, a ferry operator, was the proprietor
of a tavern there; it was later the Lafayette Hotel.

17 The Seneca Mansion, 220 N. Union Avenue, 1869

18 Thomas Hopkins House, 229 S. Union Avenue, 1838

19 Aveilhe-Goldsboro House, 300 S. Union Avenue, c. 1881

20 Statue of Lafayette, in traffic isle at W. Union Avenue and St. John's Street; built in 1976 to honor Lafayette, who is credited with naming the city.

21 Susquehanna and Tidewater Canal House, 817 Conesteo Street; a former lock house that also houses the Susquehanna Museum.

Joppa (Joppatowne)
2010 Census Population: 12,616   N. 39 26' W. 76 22'

Postal records catalogue a number of names for the town known today as Joppa or Joppatown. In the census report, it is listed as Joppatowne. It was known originally as Gunpowder, for the nearby Gunpowder River and Falls, then was changed to Joppa Cross Roads in 1819, and briefly to Little Gunpowder in 1829. In the eighteenth century, the town showed promise of becoming the largest city in Maryland. Between 1712 and 1768, it served as the Baltimore County. A center of the tobacco trade, the town was also the site of the Joppa Iron Works and a shipyard. At its peak, Joppa was a community of about fifty homes, a church, a prison, several inns and shops, schools, armament factories, and warehouses.

With the rise of Baltimore and Annapolis, Joppa declined and eventually closed as a port. By 1815, all that remained of the promising city were ruins and the historic Rumsey Mansion built by Benjamin Rumsey. The mansion has been restored and is now the home of the Harford County Executive. The town slept into the twentieth century, when, in 1962, a new generation of Planned Unit Developments (PUD) in the United States was launched by the Panitz Company. The resulting tide of dwellings that swept almost to the door of the old Rumsey Mansion was named Joppatown. A new church nearby protects the old gravestones of St. John's Parish Church and a small collection of artifacts from what are probably buried foundations of early buildings.

ACTIVITIES

Please check the internet or call ahead, as dates, times, and locations may change.

MARINAS
- Mariner Point Park; boat launching, no other facilities

LODGING
- Super 8 Motel, 1015 Pulaski Highway (Exit 74), 410-676-2700

RESTAURANTS
- Mountain Branch, 1827 Mountain Road, 410-836-9600

Joppa, MD

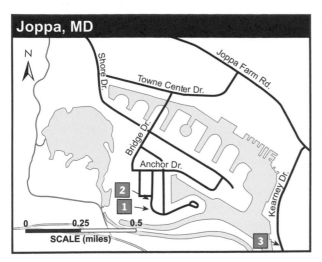

POINTS OF INTEREST

1 RUMSEY MANSION HOUSE, 700 Court Drive; an outstanding example of colonial Georgian architecture
2 EPISCOPAL CHURCH OF THE RESURRECTION, Old Church Drive at Court and Anchor Drives, 410-679-8700
3 MARINER POINT PARK AND MUSEUM, 100 Kearny Drive

Lapidum

2010 Census Population: Not available

N. 39 36' W. 76 08'

There was once a town known as Lapidum on the south bank of the Susquehanna River at the highest navigable spot across from Port Deposit. It grew from three land grants: Eightrapp in 1665; Faton in 1679; and Land of Promise in 1684. The last was appropriately named as settlers began transforming the land from forest to farmland. Corn and tobacco were the chief cash crops and the river fostered the development of a thriving fishing industry. The area grew as an important commercial center, owing to its location as the highest deepwater landing on the Chesapeake Bay and its proximity to the Susquehanna and Tidewater Canal.

In 1729, Thomas Cresap established a ferry from Lapidum near Smith's Falls, which was referred to as the Upper Ferry. A road from the ferry to Philadelphia was added in 1731. The ferry operated until 1818, when a bridge from Port Deposit to Rock Run Mill opened just upstream from Lapidum. Initially, the town profited from the ferry's financial success. Conrad Baker built the three-story, Victorian Susquehanna Hotel in 1868. Other buildings followed, including a church, a mill, a Masonic hall, a school, and numerous houses, stores, and warehouses, as well as wharves. By 1900, the railroad had put the ferry and canal out of business and, eventually, ice accumulations known as ice gorges destroyed the remaining warehouse and wharves. The hotel continued as a fishing lodge and men's club until 1960, when it was torn down. Today the site of the former town is part of the Susquehanna State Park. Gone are the marinas, restaurants, and lodgings, leaving only the sites of a canal lock and hotel.

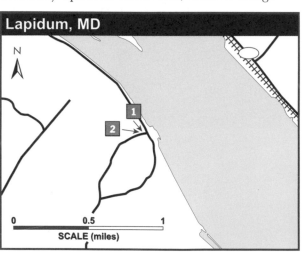

Lapidum, MD

N

0   0.5   1
SCALE (miles)

POINTS OF INTEREST

Today there are only the remains of (photos courtesy of Wikipedia.com):

1 LOCK 9
2 HOTEL SITE

Old Baltimore
No longer exists

N. 39 24' W. 76 14'

The town of Old Baltimore was situated on the east bank of the Bush River, a mile south of the present Pennsylvania Railroad. It was about a quarter of a mile wide, between the Bush River on the west and Romney Creek on the east. The site was chosen by the first settlers in 1661 because the location was a good one, protected on all but its north side from the Indians. By 1680, a crude fence enclosed two log houses with a well. A burial ground was in a nearby field in a grove of large walnut trees. It is said one of the graves holds the bones of William Osborn, a local ferryman who acquired land in 1667 and built one of the first houses. In 1674, it was designated the site for a courthouse and jail.

An ordinary, or inn, was built in 1676. In 1684, the Sheriff of Baltimore County summoned a jury to the house of James Phillips at Bush River to "appraise sixty acres to make the compliment of one hundred acres which is this day to be layed out for the Towne according to the recently passed 'Act for the advancement of Trade'." The town actually existed as the county seat only until 1693, when the government was moved to Joppa on the Gunpowder River. All that remains are a collection of artifacts now owned by the U.S. Army Garrison at Aberdeen Proving Ground and curated at the Maryland Archaeological Conservation Laboratory.

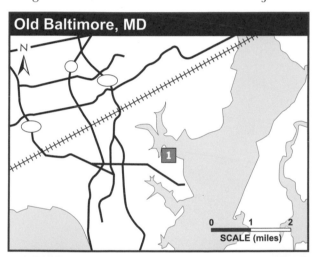

POINTS OF INTEREST

By contacting the authorities at the Aberdeen Proving Ground well in advance of a visit, it may be possible to visit the site.

1 SIGN AT EXCAVATION SITE AT OLD BALTIMORE

Prince George's County

Bladensburg
2010 Census Population: 9,148

N. 38 56' W. 76 56'

Originally called Garrison's Landing, Bladensburg was named in honor of Thomas Bladen, Governor of Maryland from 1742 to 1747. The town was established on the Anacostia River as a regional commercial center in 1742 with sixty acres laid out in one-acre lots. By 1746, only eighteen had been improved, but it was the Anacostia River, a mile wide and forty feet deep at its mouth, that made the difference. The town was further enhanced the following year, when it was designated a tobacco inspection station and grading port. In its heyday, Bladensburg was reportedly the second largest and fastest-growing seaport on the whole eastern seaboard. Only Yorktown, Virginia, handled a greater volume of tonnage.

The port is best remembered for the Battle of Bladensburg in 1814 during the War of 1812. The British victory there cleared the way for them to march on to Washington. Later in the 1800s, Bladensburg's role as a seaport diminished as silting of the Anacostia River prevented larger ships from reaching the port, which closed in 1840.

Among other notable events were the first balloon ascension in 1784 and a famous duel. Though dueling was outlawed in 1800, that didn't prevent the town from being the scene of an historic duel twenty years later when the U.S. Naval hero Steven Decater was mortally wounded by a fellow naval officer, Commodore James Barron. More pleasant memories were to come from the discovery of a natural spring said to have been noted for its medicinal properties. The popularity of the "Spa Springs" resulted in a road being built to accommodate the great number of visitors who flocked to its waters. Now, however, the spring is capped off and a filling station occupies the site. More recently, a large tooth found nearby was identified as an Astrodon Johnsoni dinosaur, which was subsequently named the state dinosaur.

⛴ MARINAS
• Mariner Point Park; boat launching, no other facilities

🛏 🍽 LODGING / RESTAURANTS
• Indian Queen Tavern, Baltimore and Upshur Streets

SPECIAL EVENTS AND ACTIVITIES
Please check the internet or call ahead, as dates, times, and locations may change.
May: A-May-Zing Animal Fest, Waterfront Park, 301-779-0371

Bladensburg, MD

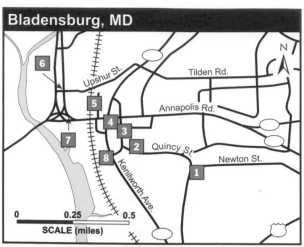

SCALE (miles)
0   0.25   0.5

POINTS OF INTEREST

1 1. MARKET MASTER'S HOUSE, 4001 48th Street, 1760; built by Christopher Lowndes, merchant shipbuilder and first Postmaster

2 2. BOSTWICK, 3901 48th Street, 1746; built by Christopher Lowndes, it was the home of Benjamin Stoddert, first Secretary of the Navy.

3 OLD EVERGREEN CEMETERY, 3642 52nd Avenue, c. 1730; known as the "Old Presbyterian Burying Grounds," it was actively used until the 1960s.

4 HILLEARY MCGRUDER HOUSE, 4703 Annapolis Road

> William Hilleary purchased the land from the Bladensburg Town Commissioners in 1742 for two pounds and ten shillings. His family descended from French Huguenots who first settled in New York in the 16th century.

5 INDIAN QUEEN TAVERN (GEORGE WASHINGTON HOUSE), 4302 Baltimore Avenue, c. 1752; became a major tavern and stagecoach stop run by Peter Carnes, the first US balloonist.

6 ST. PAUL'S (KINGDOM MISSIONARY) BAPTIST CHURCH, 4107 47th Street, 1818

> Originally built by Presbyterians, the church was founded by a freed slave and has served an African American Baptist congregation since shortly after the Civil War.

7 MEMORIAL CROSS, Baltimore Avenue at Bladensburg Road

8 OLD PORT OF BLADENSBURG SITE, now a community park on the Anacostia, just off Annapolis Road; features a visitor center, hiking paths along the river, and a small park for children.

Eagle Harbor
2010 Census Population: 63

N. 38 34' W. 76 41'

Eagle Harbor was originally a busy Patuxent River landing known as Trueman Point in the eighteenth, nineteenth, and early twentieth centuries. In its early years, it was used by area plantations for shipping tobacco and, by 1747, was an official tobacco inspection station. In 1817, George Weems, who owned a tobacco warehouse at Trueman Point Landing, established the Weems Steamboat Company, connecting the port to other points along the Patuxent River. Regular steamboat traffic continued until the 1930s. In 1925, developer Walter L. Bean purchased land adjacent to Trueman Point Landing with the vision of creating a resort community for middle-class African Americans from the area. Lots were offered at $50 or less and the community was advertised as "a high-class summer colony for the better people." After a number of summer cottages were constructed, the community incorporated as the town of Eagle Harbor in 1929, named for the Washington, D.C.'s Eagle newspaper. The town is "an enclave of summer cottages and year-round homes," governed by a Board of Commissioners. In recent years, the town hall was expanded to become a community center with a broad deck overlooking the Patuxent.

The Chalk Point Generating Station, which was owned by the Potomac Electric Power Company until it was sold to the Mirant Corporation in 2000, is located adjacent to the town.

POINTS OF INTEREST

1 EAGLE HARBOR ENTRANCE SIGN
2 EAGLE HARBOR COMMUNITY CENTER, Patuxent Boulevard

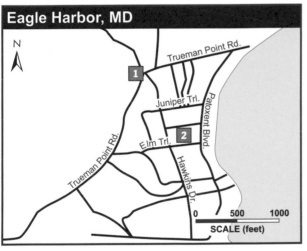

Upper Marlboro

2010 Census Population: 631

PRINCE GEORGE'S COUNTY

Upper Marlboro lies in an area of Prince Georges County that was settled sometime around 1695 and was designated by the General Assembly as a port of entry on the Western Branch of the Patuxent River in 1706. Laid out over one hundred acres, it encompassed three estates: Grove Landing, Meadows, and Darnall's Chance. The last, built sometime between 1694 and 1712, still stands across from today's county administration building. Darnall's Chance was restored as a house museum and has been open to the public since the 1980s. The area around the port was named for the Duke of Marlborough, John Churchill, an ancestor of Winston Churchill. At the time, the town was a busy river landing for the shipment of tobacco. It became the Prince George's County seat in 1721.

In 1744, residents had the town resurveyed and at that time it was officially designated Upper Marlborough as opposed to the port of Marlborough fifteen miles to the south in Calvert County. The latter is now known as Lower Marlboro. In the midst of tobacco country, the town became a social and civil center for the area's farmers and a number of prominent merchants and lawyers who were active in Maryland politics. Upper Marlborough was also the site of a major tobacco auction that lasted until farming tobacco all but disappeared in Maryland.

In the mid-1700s, Maryland's governors and landed gentry were avid fans of horse-racing. They imported many fine thoroughbreds from abroad and formed the Maryland Jockey Club that sponsored races at a track south of the town. Those races continued until 1972 when the Bowie Race Track opened. Today that track is part of the county-owned Equestrian Center.

The town was incorporated in 1870 and some twenty years later the spelling of the name was changed to Marlboro. Apparently, Marlborough was too long for the rubber stamps used by the local post office. A more significant change affected the life of the town. Farming of the surrounding land caused silting of the Western Branch of the Patuxent, which ended Upper Marlboro's viability as a tobacco port. Housing developments eventually spread over the surrounding farmland. The business of the town became centered around the Courthouse and county government offices.

Signs of the old port are gone. In fact, the waterfront is now more than two miles away. The Patuxent Rural Life Museum, Duvall Tool Museum, Merkle Wildlife Sanctuary, and Mount Calvert Historical and Archeology Park all tell parts of the story of the town and area once known as Marlborough. The Prince Georges Equestrian Center draws many people to Upper Marlboro to attend the county fair, a regional antiques show, and many local events held at the Show Place Arena on the former racetrack grounds.

LODGING
- Camelot by Martin's, 13901 Central Avenue, 301-390-1479
- Sleep Inn & Suites, 9400 Marlboro Pike, 301-599-9400

SPECIAL EVENTS AND ACTIVITIES

Please check the internet or call ahead, as dates, times, and locations may change.

February: Southern Maryland Spring Home Show, Equestrian Center, 301-952-7999
  The 70's Soul Jam, Show Place Arena, 14900 Pennsylvania Avenue, 301-952-7999
  Greenberg Train &Toy Show, Sahow Place Arena, 301-952-7999

March: Mistresses and Murderers, Darnall's Chance House Museum, 14800 Gov. Oden Bowie Drive, 301-952-8010
  Crab & Mallet All Breed Cat Show, Show Place Arena, 301-952-7999
  Colonial Tavern Dinner, Darnall's Chance House Museum, 14800 Gov. Oden Bowie Drive, 301-952-8010
  Chesapeake Tide Indoor Pro Football, Show Place Arena, 301-952 7999
  Capital Blues Festival, Show Place Arena, 301-952-7999
  Step it Out!, The Ultimate Challenge Step Show, Show Place Arena, 301 952-7999

April: Chesapeake Tide Indoor Pro Football, Show Place Arena, 301-952-7999
  Evangel Cathedral Easter Production, Evangel Cathedral, 13901 Central Avenue, 301-249-9400

May: Annual Marlborough Day, Main Street and Gov. Oden Bowie Road, 301-952-9575
  Wildlife '83, Maryland Wildlife Artists Show, St. Barnabas Church, Leeland, 301-249-9671
  Garden Fair & Bullroast, St. Barnabas' Church, Leeland, Upper Marlboro, 301-249-9621
  Chesapeake Tide Indoor Pro Football, Show Place Arena, 301-952-7999
  Maryland "FAERIE" Festival, Patuxent 4-H Center, 18405 Queen Anne Road, 888-607-9134

June: Pirate Fest, Darnall's Chance House Museum, 14800 Gov. Oden Bowie Drive, 301-952-8010

August: 1914 British Invasion, Prince Georges Bus Tour, Darnall's Chance House Museum, 301-952-8010

October: Mayhem in Marlborough's Ghost Walk, Darnall's Chance House Museum, 301-952-8010; reservations and admission's fee
  Southern Maryland and Fall Home Show, Equestrian Center, 14900 Pennsylvania Avenue, 301-952-7999

November: Annual Gingerbread House Contest & Show, Darnall's Chance House Museum, 14800 Gov. Oden Bowie Drive, 301-952-8010
  Annual Winter Festival of Lights, Watkins Regional Park, 301 Watkins Park Drive, 301-699-2456
  Evangel Cathedral Christmas Celebration, Evangel Cathedral, 13901 Central Avenue, 301-249-9400

December: Hansel & Gretel Tea Party, Darnall's Chance House Museum, 14800 Gov. Oden Bowie Drive, 301-952-8010

PRINCE GEORGE'S COUNTY

PRINCE GEORGE'S COUNTY

Upper Marlboro, MD

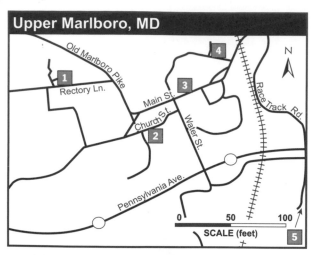

Old Marlboro Pike

Rectory Ln.

Main St.

Church St.

Water St.

Race Track Rd.

Pennsylvania Ave.

N

0   50   100

SCALE (feet)

1   2   3   4   5

POINTS OF INTEREST

1 TRINITY EPISCOPAL CHURCH, on the grounds of the old Presbyterian Church, 1848; the graveyard is older than the town.

2 UPPER MARLBORO BRANCH LIBRARY, 14730 Main Street

3 DR. WILLIAM BEANES' GRAVESITE
Dr. Beane was a well-respected local physician who was involved in the arrest of marauding British troops. He was then arrested by the British. Francis Scott Key attempted to negotiate Dr. Beane's release by substituting himself. This resulted in both men being held on the British ship, *Baltimore*, outside Fort McHenry, where Key wrote the words that became the Star Spangled Banner.

4 BILLINGSLEY MANOR HOUSE MUSEUM, 6900 Green Landing Road, 301-627-0730; as seen from Patuxent River Park

5 DARNALL'S CHANCE HOUSE MUSEUM, 14000 Gov. Oden Bowie Drive, 301-952-8010

6 PATUXENT RIVER PARK MUSEUM, 16000 Croom Airport Road, 301-627-6074

7 DUVALL TOOL SHOP AT THE PATUXENT RURAL LIFE MUSEUM, Patuxent River Park, 16000 Croom Airport Road, 301-627-6074

* Note: #'s 6 and 7 are south of Upper Marlboro, and do not appear on the map.

* Other places to visit include the Merkle Wildlife Sanctuary & Visitor Center, 11704 Fenna Road, 301-888-1410, and the Mount Calvert Historical & Archeology Park, 16302 Mount Calvert Road, 301-627-1286.

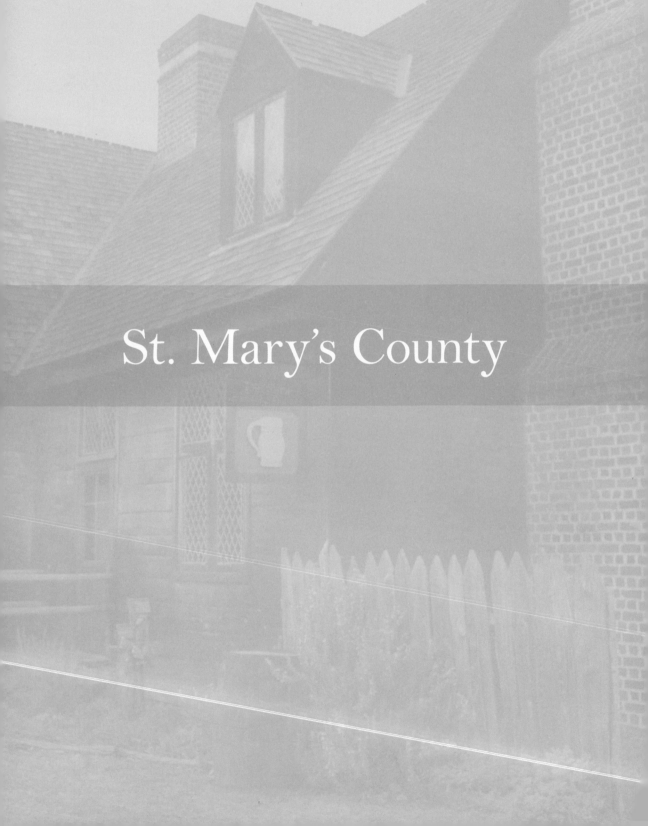

St. Mary's County

Coltons Point
2010 Census Population: Not Available

N. 38 13' W. 76 45'

Coltons Point is a small unincorporated town and summer resort. It is near St. Clements Island where, in 1634, the first European settlers landed and founded the colony of Maryland. There is water taxi service to St. Clements Island from Memorial Day through October and events celebrating the founding throughout the year. It was listed on the National Register of Historic Places in 1972. A lighthouse and marinas serve residents and visitors who arrive by water.

The St. Clements Island-Potomac River Museum, which was founded in 1975, traces Maryland's early history and that of the Potomac River and Chesapeake Bay through artifacts and information gleaned by archaeologists working in the area. The museum also sponsors a variety of cultural events, one of which is the annual October Blessing of the Fleet. Three flags fly over the site representing the United States, the State of Maryland, and St. Mary's County. On the grounds are the Little Red Schoolhouse, formerly the 1820 Charlotte Hall School, and two Potomac dory boats, the 1916 *Early Times* and the 1919 *Doris C.*

The Mother of Light Shrine, a devotional monument popularly called the Lady of St. Mary's County, was recently constructed of bricks and rocks collected around the world, including the Holy Land. The statue is a reminder that the settlers named the county for the Mother of Jesus and celebrated the first Catholic Mass in English-speaking North America.

⚓ MARINAS
- Cather Marine, 38270 Palmer Drive, 301-769-3335
- Coltons Point Marina, 38000 Kopel's Road, 301-769-3121

🛏 LODGING
- Coltons Point Artist Studio Retreat, 20259 Coltons Point Road, 301-769-3272
- Coltons Shipping Point Farm, 39244 Burch Road, 301-769-4359
- Nekadesh Farm Bed & Breakfast, 20250 Wellington Court, 301-769-4333

SPECIAL EVENTS AND ACTIVITIES
Please check the internet or call ahead, as dates, times, and locations may change.
Ongoing Events: Water Taxi Service to St. Clements Island, Memorial Day through October, 301-769-2222

Tide of Tolerance, One Act Play/Outdoor Drama, Call for performance 301-769-2222.

March 25: Maryland Day, St. Clements Island Museum, 301-769-2222

July: Potomac Jazz and Seafood Festival, St. Clements Island Museum, 301 769-2222

St. Clements Island History & Heritage Day, St. Clements Island Museum 301-769-2222

October: Blessing of the Fleet, St. Clements Island Museum, 301 769-2222

December: Annual Christmas Doll & Train Exhibit, St. Clements Island Museum, 301-769-2222

Coltons Point, MD

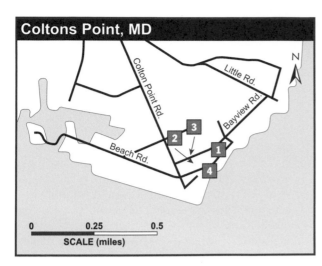

POINTS OF INTEREST

1 ST. CLEMENT'S ISLAND AND POTOMAC RIVER MUSEUM, 38370 Point Breeze Road, 301-769-2222
2 ST. MARY'S SHRINE FOR SEAFARERS, 38370 Point Breeze Road
3 COLTONS POINT SCHOOL, 38370 Point Breeze Road
4 FERRY TO ST. CLEMENTS ISLAND, dock at 38370 Point Breeze Road

Leonardtown

2010 Census Population: 2,930

Originally called Newtown, Leonardtown was established in 1654 as the seat of St. Mary's County. Meetings of the county court were held at the house of John Hammond. In 1708, the village, which was then called Seymour Town for Maryland's governor at the time, was officially declared a town of fifty acres divided into one hundred-acre lots with a courthouse that is still serving the county. Nearly twenty years later, Seymour was renamed Leonardtown in honor of Lord Baltimore's brother, Leonard Calvert, who was Maryland's governor at the time.

In its early days, Leonardtown served as a port for the shipment of produce from local farms. During the War of 1812, one thousand British marines, foraging in the area, raided the town. By 1860, there were approximately thirty-five dwellings, a county newspaper, two hotels, and several stores. It was now a busy port and a landing for steamboats carrying goods and passengers all over the Bay that functioned well into the twentieth century. It was also a stopping point for a floating theater that came each year.

A cannon from the Ark, the ship that carried the original colonists to Maryland guards the entrance to the Old Jail Museum, which is a repository of area history. Built in 1858, the jail also served as a home for the jailor's family who occupied the first story. The prisoners were kept on the floor above. Tudor Hall, a Georgian-style mansion, is the home of the local historical society.

An important addition to be enjoyed by residents and visitors alike was Leonardtown Public Park that opened in 2008. A winery opened the following year. In addition to being the seat of county government, Leonardtown serves as a bedroom for local industries.

⛴ MARINAS

- Combs Creek Marina, 21670 Joe Hazel Road, 301-475-2017

🛏 LODGING

- Executive Inn & Suites Park Avenue, 41655 Park Avenue, 301-475-3000

🍽 RESTAURANTS

- Arizona Pizza, 40874 Merchants Lane, 301-997-1700
- Brewing Grounds Coffee, 41658 Fenwick Street, 301-475-8040
- Buffalo Wings & Beer, 40845 Merchants Lane, 301-475-2711
- Café Des Artistes, 41655 Fenwick Street, 301-997-0500
- Carousels Ice Cream, Merchants Lane, 301-476-2388
- Cerro Grande Mexican Restaurant, 22695 Washington Street, 301-997-0808
- Chillin Time, 22745 Washington Street, 301-997-0091;
  On the Square, 22695 Washington Street, 301-997-0808
- The County Seat, 22696 Washington Street, 301-997-0097
- Crab Knockers Seafood, 40955 Merchants Lane, 301-475-7830
- Fitzie's Restaurant & Pub, 21540 Joe Hazel Road, 301-375-1913
- Four Star Pizza, 22725 Washington Street, 301-475-1600
- The Front Porch at the Sterling House, 22770 Washington Street, 301-997-1009
- Happy Dragon Chinese Restaurant, 40955 Merchants Lane, 301-474-9695
- Hong Kong Buffet, 40865 Merchants Lane, 301-475-8608
- Kevin Thompson's Corner Kafé, 41565 Lawrence Avenue, 301-373-8873
- Linds's Café, 22685 Washington Street, 301-475-5395
- Oga's Asian Cuisine, 22475 Washington Street, 301-475-0168
- Olde Town Cupboard, 22696 Washington Street, 301-997-0770
- Olde Town Pub, 22785 Washington Street, 301-475-8184
- Room with a Brew, 40890 Merchants Lane, 301-925-3043
- Tea N Scones Café & Wine Bar, 22697 Washington Street, 301-997-1110
- The Tea Room, 26005 Point Lookout Road, 301-475-1980
- Willow's Restaurant & Tavern, 24509 Point Lookout Road, 301-690-2019

SPECIAL EVENTS AND ACTIVITIES

Please check the internet or call ahead, as dates, times, and locations may change.

April: Easter Egg Hunt & Festival, 301-475-4200 ext. 1800
   Run and Fun Walk for Hospice, 301-475-3610
   March of Dimes Walk, 301-934-2235
   Earth Day Celebration, 301-994-9791
   Spring Fling Classic Car Show, 301-994-9666
May: So Maryland Annual Spring Festival, 301-994-0525
   Downtown Tunes, 4th Saturdays, 301-904-4452
June: St. Mary's Crab Festival, Fairgrounds
   Flag Day Celebration, Governmental Center, 301-904-5974
July: Freedomfest, Fairgrounds, 301-475-4200 ext. 1849
   College of Southern Maryland Twilight Performance Series, Leonardtown Campus,
   301-934-7861
   St. Mary's River Concert on Location in Leonardtown, 301-475-9791
August: Beach Party on the Square, Leonardtown Square, 301-475-9791
   Leonardtown Wharf Waterfront Celebration, 301-475-9791
   Taste of St. Mary's, 301-737-3001
October: U. S. National Oyster Shucking Championship Contest and the National Oyster
   Cook-off, County Fairgrounds, 301-863-5015
   Trick or Treat on the Square, Leonardtown Square, 301-475-9791
November: Antique Show & Sale, Leonard Hall Jr. Naval Academy, 301-475-8029
   Veteran's Day Parade & Ceremony, 301-475-9791
   Christmas on the Square & Annual Tree Lighting, 301-475-9791
December: Santa & Mrs. Claus on the Square, 301-475-9791

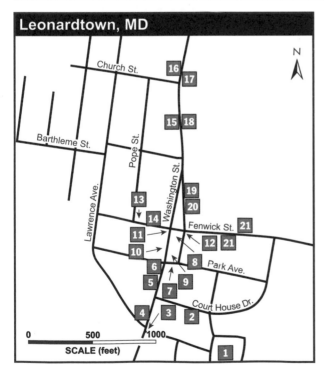

POINTS OF INTEREST

1 TUDOR HALL, Tudor Hall Road; this Georgian-style Mansion is home of the Historical Society.
2 OLD JAIL, Town Square, 1858; rebuilt in 1876, now a museum.

3 ST. MARY'S COUNTY COURTHOUSE, 41605 Courthouse Drive,
   1710, 1832, 1901, 1957
4 SPAULDING/CAMALIER HOUSE, Washington Street at Park
   Avenue, 1858; Greek Revival, one of the earliest homes
5 LEONARDTOWN BANK OF THE EASTERN SHORE,
   Washington Street, 1913; Classical Revival
6 BELL MOTOR COMPANY, 22675 Washington Street,1923,
   1939; second oldest Chevrolet dealership in the world
7 MERCANTILE BANK OF SOUTHERN MARYLAND
   (1ST NATIONAL BANK), 5 East Park Avenue, 1921
8 WORLD WAR I MEMORIAL, Town Square;
   site of annual veterans' day parade
9 WORLD WAR II DECEASED VETERANS MEMORIAL,
   200 Town Square
10 THE NEW THEATER, 1925, just north of Park Avenue
   and Washington Street on the east side;
   undergoing restoration as a banquet room
11 UNION HOTEL (THE CAROUSEL), 1850,
   409-413 Washington Street
       Renamed the Fenwick Hotel, in its heyday it could
       accommodate one hundred guests and had a stable
       of two hundred horses.
12 DUKE'S FOUNTAIN-BAR-RESTAURANT, on the Town Square, c.
   1920s; houses a restaurant and a variety of retail businesses
13 THE PICTURE BOX, 22 Fenwick Street, 1938;
   now a real estate office

14 THE FIRST ST. MARY'S HOSPITAL, 1912, Fenwick Street, on the east side of The Picture Box

15 HENDERSON HOUSE, North Washington Street, c. 1910; now an office building

16 ST. PETER'S CHAPEL, Lawrence Avenue, late 1860s; now law offices

17 ST. ALOYSIUS CATHOLIC CHURCH, 22800 Washington Street, 1846, 1859, 1962; the congregation dates back to 1710

18 ST. ALOYSIUS CHURCH RECTORY, 1870, 1933; next door to the church

19 LEONARDTOWN NAZARINE CHURCH, 1915, 340 Washington Street

20 THE LEONARDTOWN MURAL, just east of Washington Street
Designed and painted by Tim Scheirer, Carla Tomaszewski, and Clarence Schumaker, this mural depicts various periods in Leonardtown's history.

21 THE JOHNSON HOUSE, north side of Fenwick Street, just east of intersection of Fenwick and Washington Street, 1919

Lexington Park
2010 Census Population: 11,626

N. 38 15' W. 76 27'

Lexington Park was first known as Cedar Point, and then Jarboesville, after the local postmaster. In 1943, the U.S. Navy appropriated 6,000 acres for naval aviation testing and evaluation. The area surrounding the Patuxent Naval Air Station was named Lexington Park for the aircraft carrier *Lexington*, which was lost during the Battle of the Coral Sea. About a quarter of the county's population can be found in the vicinity of the naval station, known simply as Pax River. The naval facility accounts for one-third of the county's jobs. Its growth continues as the primary center for naval testing. Mattapanny, an early nineteenth century brick house, serves today as the residence of the base's commanding officer. The Thomas Johnson Memorial Bridge connects the area with Solomons Island.

The Patuxent River Naval Air Station is the location of Mattapany-Sewall archeological site not quite one thousand feet south of the river on Saufly Road. Records indicate that Mattapany-Sewall, a seventeenth century manor, was occupied from 1666 to 1684 by Maryland's Catholic Proprietor, Charles Calvert, the third Lord Baltimore. The colony's government used the manor for meetings and as an arsenal. It became a scene of battle in 1689 during the Protestant Revolution that overthrew Maryland's Proprietary government. The manor was listed on the National Register of Historic Places in 1985. Naval history has a place in the area as well. Permission must be sought in advance to visit sites inside the Patuxent Naval Air Station. The Patuxent Naval Air Warfare Center Museum is located on the naval base property, but is readily accessible from Route 235.

⬛ MARINAS
• None, but the Navy maintains a center for search and rescue.

🏨 LODGING
• A & E Motel, Great Mills Road, 301-863-7411
• Best Western, 22769 Three Notch Road, 301-862-4100
• Days Inn, Three Notch Road, 800-428-2871
• Extended Stay America, Route 235, 1-800-EXT-STAY
• Hampton Inn, Route 235, 301-863-3200

🍽 RESTAURANTS
• Aloha Restaurant, Route 215, 301-863-4838
• Hong Kong Chinese Restaurant, N. Shangri-La Drive, 301-862-4776
• Linda's Café, 27 Tulagi Place, 301-862-3544
• Mattie's Seafood & Steaks, 19661 Three Notch Road, 301-863-2718
• Nocolletti's Pizza, Route 235, 301-863-2233
• Northridge Restaurant & Pub, Route 235, 301-862-3644
• Peking Restaurant, Great Mills Road, 301-863-6190
• The Roost Restaurant, 21736 Great Mills Road, 301-863-2718
• Showtime Deli, Coral Drive, 301-863-2555

SPECIAL EVENTS AND ACTIVITIES
Please check the internet or call ahead, as dates, times, and locations may change.
October: Oyster Festival, Lexington Park, 301-863-5015

Lexington Park, MD

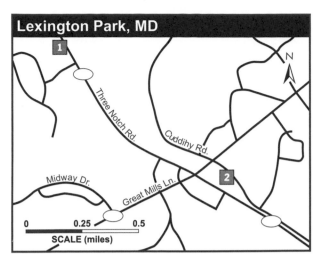

1 Patuxent Naval Air Warfare Center Museum, 22119 Three Notch Road (Route 335)
2 Site of St. Nicholas Church Marker, Three Notch Road (Route 235) just south of the Naval Air Station entrance gate; actual chapel site is located inside the Naval Air Station

ST. MARY'S COUNTY

Piney Point
2010 Census Population: 864

N. 38 08' W. 76 30'

Piney Point is a small unincorporated town on the Potomac River. Its history goes back to the earliest days of Maryland's settlement as a province belonging to the Catholic Calverts or Lords Baltimore. One of its earliest settlers was a Protestant firebrand by the name of John Coode, who led a Protestant rebellion in 1689. The so-called revolution ended the proprietorship of the Calverts and the Catholic dominance of Maryland, which became a royal colony subject to the King of England. A result of the rebellion was the move of Maryland's capital from St. Mary's City to Annapolis. Today St. Mary's City is an historic site. Piney Point and the surrounding area are largely rural, but with considerable activity on its waterfront.

In 1940, the area became the site of a U.S. Navy torpedo test range and led to a surge in population. When the station closed in 1954, a marina was opened on the site. Eventually Steuart Petroleum bought the site and, then, sold it to the Seafarer's Union. Today it is the site of the Harry Lundeburg School of Seamanship, which trains men and women for the merchant marine. At one time, President Munroe had a cottage at Piney Point, but it was swept away by the devastating hurricane of 1933. During World War II, a German submarine, the *Black Panther U-1105*, was sunk nearby in the Potomac River. The location became Maryland's first historic shipwreck preserve in 1994.

▣ MARINAS
• Curley's Point Marina, Clarke Road, 301-994-0352

▣ LODGING
• Swanns Resort Properties, 17220 Piney Point Road, 301-994-0774

▣ RESTAURANTS
• Evans Seafood Restaurant, 16688 Piney Point Road, 301-994-9944
• Oakwood Lodge, Lighthouse Road, 301-994-2271

SPECIAL EVENTS AND ACTIVITIES
Please check the internet or call ahead, as dates, times, and locations may change.
May: Piney Point Lighthouse Waterfront Festival, Piney Point Lighthouse, 301-994-1471

Piney Point, MD

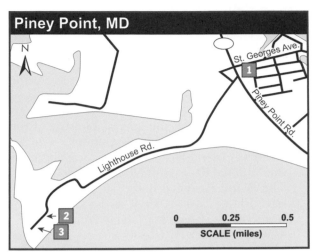

SCALE (miles)
0   0.25   0.5

POINTS OF INTEREST

1 HARRY LUNDEBURG SCHOOL OF SEAMANSHIP,
   45353 St. Georges Avenue
2 PINEY POINT LIGHTHOUSE MUSEUM,
   44701 State Highway 498; worth the visit!
3 PINEY POINT LIGHTHOUSE,
   44701 State Highway 498

St. Clements Island

2010 Census Population: 0

N. 38 38' W. 76 43'

Once named Blackiston Island for former inhabitants, St. Clements Island was the site where Leonard Calvert, younger brother of Lord Baltimore, led Maryland's first settlers ashore on March 25, 1634. The name was chosen in honor of the sainted Pope Clement I, patron saint of sailors. The date is still observed in the state as Maryland Day. Father Andrew White, one of the group's leaders, wrote: "In this place we first offered [mass], erected a cross, and with devotion took solemn possession of the country." The colonists decided that the island wasn't suitable for a settlement and moved south to create St. Mary's City on the mainland. On the 300th anniversary of the landing, a large cross was erected on the island to commemorate the event. Today, erosion has diminished the island from four hundred to forty acres, but that has not interfered with the annual Blessing of the Fleet, in the first week of October. The St. Clements Island Historic District was listed on the National Register of Historic Places in 1972. The island has been designated St. Clements Island State Park. A ferry to the island leaves from the St. Clements Island-Potomac River Museum. A dock for visitors who come by water and the Maryland Dove is available, but with no facilities.

SPECIAL EVENTS AND ACTIVITIES

Please check the internet or call ahead, as dates, times, and locations may change.

March: Maryland Day, St. Clements Island Museum, 301-769-2222

July: Black Eyed Susan Day, St. Clements Island Museum, 301-769-2222

October: Blessing of the Fleet, St. Clements Island Museum, 301-769-2222

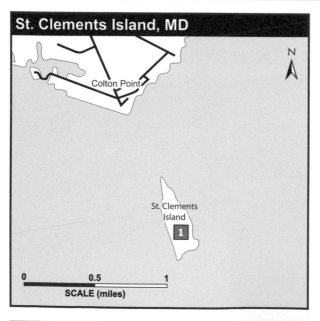

St. Clements Island, MD

Colton Point

N

St. Clements Island

1

0   0.5   1
SCALE (miles)

POINTS OF INTEREST

1 ST. CLEMENTS ISLAND

Located across from Coltons Point, St. Clements Island is a state park. Its chief landmark is the stone cross erected in honor of Maryland's first settlers led by Leonard Calvert, the colony's first governor.

St. George Island

2010 Census Population: 257

N. 38 08 W. 76 29'

St. George Island is located in St. Mary's County. Its history goes back to the founding of Maryland in 1634, when it was part of the St. Indigoes Manor grant to the Jesuits who came with the first settlers. During the American Revolution, the island was the scene of the first confrontation between the Maryland colonists and the British. In July 1776, a fleet of armed galleys carried Lord Dunmore, the royal governor of Virginia, and his fellow Loyalists to the island where they sought refuge from the rebel militia. On July 26th, Captain Nicholson of Maryland's first and only warship, the *Defense*, managed to recapture her after she was taken by the British. She remained in the state's navy and was captured again by the British during the War of 1812. In 1851, the Jesuits sold the island to Ennels Rozell and John H. Robrecht. Thereafter, it developed as a community of fishermen from Tangier Island and the Virginia Eastern Shore. It has remained a community of watermen, year-round residents, and those who have vacation homes.

ACTIVITIES

Please check the internet or call ahead, as dates, times, and locations may change.

🛏 LODGING

• Camp Merryelande B&B and Cabins, 15914 Camp Merryelande Road, 800-382-1073

St. George Island, MD

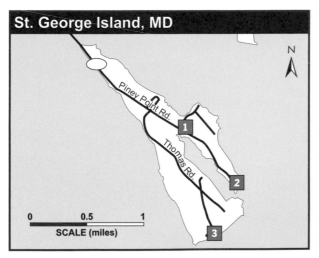

N

0   0.5   1
SCALE (miles)

POINTS OF INTEREST

1   FRANCIS XAVIER CHAPEL,
    19212 St. George Road
2   CHESAPEAKE BAY FIELD LABORATORY,
    16129 Piney Point Road
3   WINTER BEACH AT CAMP MERRYELAND,
    15914 Camp Merryeland Road

St. Mary's City

2010 Census Population: Not available

N. 38 11' W. 76 26'

St. Mary's City was founded in 1634 by a group of English settlers who came with Leonard Calvert, brother of Lord Baltimore and Proprietor of the Maryland colony. They arrived in two ships, the *Ark,* and her tender, the smaller *Dove.* The Calverts laid out a city, but the most of the settlers chose to buy plantation land and grow tobacco. In the second half of the seventeenth century, however, St. Mary's City grew as an important port in the tobacco trade. As the capital of the Maryland colony, the town soon had a brick State House and the community around it included a Jesuit chapel, a jail, an inn, several other public buildings, and private houses. By 1695, the Calverts had lost the colony to the king, and Francis Nicholson, the royal governor, decided to move the capital to a more-centrally located town, which he named Annapolis.

The St. Mary's State House subsequently became a protestant church that served the remaining residents who did not move north with the government. Because most of those who stayed in the area were farmers, the city began to fail and its buildings left to deteriorate. By the twentieth century, most of Maryland's first capital came back to life with the reconstruction of the State House and archaeological excavations that began in 1971. Archaeologists continue their exploration to the present day. A museum was established the same year. The community now is the home of St. Mary's College and Historic St. Mary's City, which runs a tourist center and one of the premier archeological sites on the East Coast. Although much of the old city has been found, including the sites of a seventeenth-century inn and a printing house, there is still much to be discovered as visitors learn when they tour St. Mary's City, which also includes recreations of a Woodland Indian Longhouse and Garden and seventeenth century taverns.

▣ LODGING

- Brome–Howard Inn, 18281 Rosecroft Road, 301-866-0656 (*Also includes a restaurant*)

▣ RESTAURANTS

- Brentland Farm Visitor Center, Rosecroft Road

SPECIAL EVENTS AND ACTIVITIES

Please check the internet or call ahead, as dates, times, and locations may change.
March: Maryland Day, 240-895-4990
June and July: St. Mary's College of Maryland River Concert Series, 240-895-4107
July: Tidewater Archeology Weekend, 240-895-4990
August: St. Mary's College of Maryland Governor's Cup Yacht Race, 240-895-3039
September: Woodland Indian Discovery Day, 240-895-4990
   Riverfest, 301-737-2903
November: Hearth & Home in Early Maryland, 240-895-4990

St. Mary' s City, MD

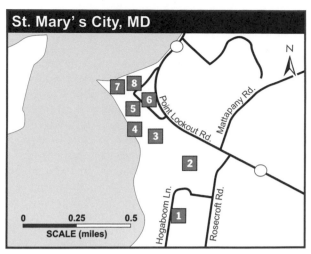

POINTS OF INTEREST

Note: All sites are part of the museum exhibit at 18751 Hogaboom Lane.

1 ST. MARY'S CITY VISITOR CENTER AND MUSEUM
2 18TH CENTURY BARN
3 LAWYER'S LODGING SITE, Town Center
4 MARGARET BRENT GAZEBO & MEMORIAL GARDEN
5 FARTHING'S ORDINARY & GARDEN; Scent & Medicine
6 RECONSTRUCTED STATE HOUSE; original built in 1676
7 ORIGINAL STATE HOUSE SITE; next to Trinity Church
8 TRINITY EPISCOPAL CHURCH, 1829

Scotland (Scotland Beach)

2010 Census Population: Not available

N. 38 05' W. 76 22'

Scotland is a small town near the southernmost point of Maryland. Early records indicate that a tract of land called "Scotland" was willed to William Jones from Solomon Jones in 1710. According to tradition, the area was named for a group of Scottish soldiers captured during the unsuccessful rebellion of Scotland's Bonnie Prince Charley against England. The captured soldiers were shipped to Maryland to be sold as indentured servants.

The Scotland post office is the only one of the original three on the peninsula to survive. Erosion has eaten away hundreds of feet of the town's waterfront. A dramatic example and reminder is the road to Point Lookout. It is now a hundred feet offshore. In the early years, vacationers arrived by steamship or via the road from Leonardtown to fill a thriving hotel. It burned in 1909, as did the original post office. A monument and houses survive from the time of the Civil War, which is commemorated during June's annual Blue & Grey Days at Point Lookout State Park.

⛴ MARINAS

• Rick's Marine, 11762 Point Lookout Road, 301-872-5156

🛏 LODGING

• Hale House Bed & Breakfast, 49644 Potomac River Drive, 301-872-4558
• St. Michael's Manor B&B, 50200 St. Michael's Manor Way, 301-872-4025
• Wide Bay Cottage, Route 5, 301-872-0057

SPECIAL EVENTS AND ACTIVITIES

Please check the internet or call ahead, as dates, times, and locations may change.
June: Blue & Grey Days, Point Lookout State Park, 301-872-5688
September: Lighthouse Challenge, 301-872-5688

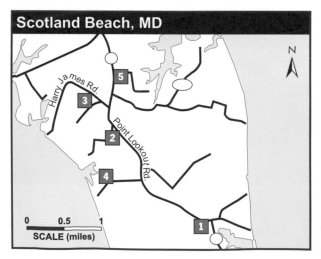

Scotland Beach, MD

0   0.5   1
SCALE (miles)

POINTS OF INTEREST

1 CIVIL WAR MONUMENT,
   11175 Point Lookout Road

2 KIRK HOUSE, seen west from Route 5/Point Lookout Road; four-level, telescope-style house
3 BRADBURN HOUSE (HOLLY GROVE), 15515 Holly Grove Farm Lane
4 CAMP BROWN, 49300 Camp Brown Road; camp for challenged youth
5 ST. MARY'S EPISCOPAL CHAPEL, c. 1889, Route 5/12960 Point Lookout Road

bibliography

EASTERN SHORE RESOURCES

A Century of Betterton 1906-2006, Tour Guide. Betterton, Maryland: Betterton Community Development Corporation, 2006.

A Guide to Cruising Chesapeake Bay. Annapolis, Maryland: Chesapeake Bay Magazine, 2007.

Adkins, Leonard. *Maryland, An Explorers Guide*. Woodstock, Vermont: The Countryman Press, 2003.

Army Engineers Waterways Experiment Station, Vicksburg, Mississippi; Experiment Station, Accession Number ADA111812, 1981.

Arnett, Earl, Robert Brugger, and Edward Papenfuse. *Maryland, A New Guide to the Old Line State*. Baltimore, Maryland: Johns Hopkins University Press, 1999.

"Bivalve, Wicomico County, Maryland," MDGenWeb, www.bivalve.net

Bowen, John. *Adventuring in the Chesapeake Bay Area*. San Francisco, California: Sierra Club Books, 1999.

Bunting, Elaine and Patricia D'Amario. *Counties of Maryland, Lower Eastern Shore*. Centreville, Maryland: Tidewater Publishers, 2003.

Calendar of Events, Queen Anne's County Office of Tourism, 107 N. Liberty Street, Centreville, Maryland, 410-604-2100

Cambridge Historic Walking Tour, Dorchester County Department of Tourism, 1-800-522-8687

Caroline Calendar of Events, Caroline County Office of Tourism

Caroline County Accommodations, Caroline Economic Development Corporation, Office of Tourism

Caroline County, Maryland, Caroline Office of Tourism

Cecil County Visitor's Guide, Cecil County Tourism, www.SeeCecil.org

Chesapeake Life Magazine, July 2002

Corddry, Mary U. *Maryland's Eastern Shore*. Chestertown, Maryland: Literary House Press, 1984.

"Discover Kent County," *Kent County News*, Chestertown, Maryland

Deringer, H. Hurtt. *Visitor's Guide, Kent County, 1993*. Chestertown, Maryland: Kent County News, 1993.

Diggins, Milton. *National Register Listings in Maryland, Inventory CE -112*. Principio Furnace, Maryland: Historical Society of Cecil County, 2000.

Eastern Shore Magazine, September 2009

Events and Festivals. Centreville, Maryland: Queen Anne's County Department of Business and Tourism, 2008.

Foley, A.M. and Freddie T. Waller. *Elliott's Island, The Land That Time Forgot*. Elliott Island, Maryland: Dogwood Ridge Books, 1999.

"Guide to Cruising Chesapeake Bay," *Chesapeake Bay Magazine*, Annapolis.

Hall, Marion. *Oriole and its Satellites, Somerset County*. Somerset, Maryland: self-published, 1964; www.rootsweb.ancestry.com/tildamdsomers/history/oriolehx.html

Hedeen, Robert A. *Naturalist on the Nanticoke*. Centreville, Maryland: Tidewater Publishers, 1982.

Historic Princess Anne, A Self-Guided Walking Tour, Somerset County Tourism, 1-800-521-9189

Historic Sites Consortium of Queen Anne's County, Centerville, Maryland.

Historic Stevensville, A Walking Tour. Stevensville, Maryland: Kent Island Heritage Society, 2008.

Holly, David. *Steamboats on the Chesapeake*. Centreville, Maryland: Tidewater Publishers, 1987.

Johnson, George. *History of Cecil County Maryland*. Reprint: Baltimore, Maryland: Regional Publishing Company, 1989.

Kaminkow, Marion J. *Maryland, A to Z*. Baltimore, Maryland: Magna Carta Book Company, 1985.

Keatley, J. K. *Placenames on the Eastern Shore of Maryland*. Queenstown, Maryland: Queen Anne Press, 1987.

Keiser, RJ, PJ Horsey and WA Biddle. *Postcard History Series*. Charleston, South Carolina: Arcadia Publishing, 2005.

Kenny, Hammil. *The Placenmames of Maryland, Their Origin and Meaning*. Baltimore, Maryland: Maryland Historical Society, 1984.

Kent County Guide. Chestertown, Maryland: Kent County Bicentennial Committee, 1977.

Kent County Office of Tourism, Kent County Visitor Center, 122 N. Cross St., 410-778-0416

Kent County Tourism and Economic Development Office (tourism@kentcounty.com)

Lake, Matt. *Weird Maryland*. New York, New York: Sterling Publishing Company, 2006.

Linda Hall, author contact, April 2008

Map of Talbot County, Department of Transportation, State of Maryland, 1981

Maryland Calendar of Events, 1-877-333-4545, www.visitmaryland.org

Miller, Alice. *Cecil County, Maryland: A Study in Local History*. Port Deposit, Maryland: Heritage, 1949.

Moose, Katie. *Eastern Shore of Maryland, The Guidebook*. Annapolis, Maryland: Conduit Press, 1999.

Oxford, Maryland, Oxford Business Association, 410-226-5730

Preston, Dickson J. *Talbot County, A History*. Centreville, Maryland: Tidewater Publishers, 1983.

Queen Anne's County Calendar of Events, 2007. Queen Anne's County, Maryland: Queen Anne's County Office of Tourism; www.Centreville.com

Queen Anne's County Visitors Guide. Queen Anne's County, Maryland: Queen Anne's County Department of Business and Tourism, 2008.

Rhodes, Jason. *Crisfield: The First Century*. Charleston, South Carolina: Arcadia Publishing Co., 2006.

Robert, J. H. *Chestertown, An Architectural Guide*. Chestertown, Maryland: Town of Chestertown, 1985.

Rock Hall, Maryland, The Pearl of the Chesapeake. Rock Hall, Maryland: The Greater Rock Hall Business Association, 2007.

Savin, Nancy and Esther Perkins. *Backroading Through Cecil County Maryland*. Dover, Delaware: Dover Graphics, 1977.

Self-Guided Driving Tour, Maryland History.

Shellenberger, William H. *Cruising the Chesapeake*. Camden, Maine: International Marine, 2001.

Shellenberger, William H. *Cruising the Chesapeake: A Gunkholer's Guide*. New York, New York: McGraw Hill, 2001).

Shomette, Donald G. *Lost Towns of Tidewater Maryland*. Centreville, Maryland: Tidewater Publishers, 2000.

Singewald, J.T. Jr. "Report on the Iron Ores of Maryland." *Maryland Geological and Economic Survey Special Publication, Volume IX, Part III*. Baltimore, Maryland: The Johns Hopkins Press, 1911.

Smith, Elizabeth Adams. *Guide to Chesapeake Bay Marinas*. New York, New York: Jerawion Publishing, Inc., 2006.

Smith Island, Maryland. Chrisfield, Maryland: The Crisfield and Smith Island Cultural Alliance, 2008.

Snow Hill Calendar of Events, Town of Snow Hill, 103 Bank Street, 410-632-2080.

Snow Hill Historic Walking Tour, brochure.

Somerset County Tourism, 1003 Main Street, 410-968-1543

Talbot County Visitor's Guide and Map, Talbot County Chamber of Commerce, 410-822-4606

Tidewater Times. Easton, Maryland: David C. Pulzone, January 2006.

Touart, Paul Baker. *Somerset, an Architectural History*. Annapolis, Maryland: Somerset County Historical Trust, 1990.

BIBLIOGRAPHY

Visitor Guide 2007, www.tourdorchester.org, 410-228-1000

Visitor's Guide 2007-2008, www.stmichaelsmd.org, 800-808-7622

Visitor's Guide, Department of Business and Tourism, 425 Piney Narrows Road, Chester, Maryland, 410-604-2100 or www.tourism@qac.org

Visitor's Guide to Kent County. Chestertown, Maryland: Kent County Office of Tourism Development, 2007.

Weeks, Christopher. *Between the Nanticoke and the Choptank, An Archeological History of Dorchester County.* Baltimore, Maryland: The Johns Hopkins University Press & the Maryland Historical Trust, 1984.

Welcome to Caroline County, Caroline Office of Tourism, www.tourcaroline.com

Welcome to Crisfield, Chamber of Commerce, 410-968-2500

Wennertsten, John R. *Maryland's Eastern Shore: A Journey in Time and Place.* Centreville, Maryland: Tidewater Publishers, 1992.

Wicomico County Convention & Visitors Bureau, www.wicomicotourism.org

www.baydreaming.com/TilghmanIsland

www.cecilcounty.wordpress.com (blog by Brent McKee)

www.Furnacetown.com

www.shipjacks.com

WESTERN SHORE RESOURCES

Arnett, Earl, Robert Bruger, and Edward Papenfuse. *Maryland, A New Guide to the Old Line State.* Baltimore, Maryland: Johns Hopkins University Press, 1999.

Atlantic Cruising Club. *Guide to Chesapeake Bay Marinas.* Rye, New York: Jerawyn Publishing, Inc., 2006.

Baltimore County Visitor's Guide, Marine Trades Association of Baltimore County, 410-687-1002

Baltimore Visitor's Center, 401 Light Street, Inner Harbor West Shore, www.baltimore.org

Brugger, Robert J. *Maryland: A Middle Temperament, 1634–1980.* Baltimore, Maryland: Johns Hopkins University Press, 1988.

Calendar of Events, Largo, Prince Georges County, 301-925-8300

"Calendar of Events," *Maryland Life Magazine,* 800-0357-9554

Calvert County Calendar of Events, Calvert County Department of Economic Development, 800-331-9771

Calvert County Visitor's Guide, Calvert County Department of Economic Development, Prince Frederick, 410-535-4581

Charles County Economic/Tourism Department, La Plata, 800-766-1341

Chesapeake Bay Magazine, October 2001 and September 2007, Annapolis, Maryland; 301-263-2662

Chesapeake Bay Embassy Guide, first edition, Maptech, Amesbury, Massachusetts; 978-792-1068

Cronin, William B. *The Disappearing Islands of the Chesapeake.* Baltimore, Maryland: The Johns Hopkins University Press, 2005.

"Guide to Cruising Chesapeake Bay," *Chesapeake Bay Magazine,* Annapolis, Maryland; 410-263-2662

Hammett, R. C. *History of St. Mary's County, 1634-1990.* St. Mary's, Maryland: self-published, 1991.

Harford County Visitor's Guide, Harford County Tourism Council, 410-272-2325

Historic Leonardtown, Maryland, Calendar of Events, Commissioners of Leonardtown, 301-475- 9791

Historic Leonardtown Walking Tour, St. Mary's County Division of Tourism, 301-475-4200

History of Charles County, Tercentenary Year, 1958. Baltimore, Maryland: George W. King Printing Company, 1958.

"Inventory of Historic Sites in Calvert, Charles & St. Mary's Counties," Maryland Historical Trust, 1980.

Johnston, George. *History of Cecil County, Md, and the Early Settlements Around the Head of Chesapeake Bay and on the Delaware River*. Baltimore, Maryland: Regional Publishing, 1881; reprint 1972.

Kaminkow, Marion. *Maryland, A to Z*. Baltimore, Maryland: Magna Carta Book Company, 1985.

Kenny, Hamill. *The Placenames of Maryland, Their Origin and Meaning*. Baltimore, Maryland: Maryland Historical Society, 1984.

Kihl, Kim R. *Port Tobacco, A Transformed Community*. Baltimore, Maryland: Maclay & Associates, 1982.

Klapthor, Margaret Brown. *The History of Charles County, Maryland*. La Plata, Maryland: Charles County Tercentenary, Inc., George W. King Printing Company, 1958).

London Town News, winter 2011, et al. Edgewater, Maryland: Historic London Town & Gardens.

Maptech Embassy Guide, Chesapeake Bay. Andover, Massachusetts, no date.

Maptech, Inc., 10 Industrial Way, Amesbury, Massachusetts, 01913

McWilliams, Jane Wilson. *Annapolis, City on the Severn*. Baltimore, Maryland: John's Hopkins University Press & Crownsville: the Maryland Historical Trust for Preservation, 2011.

Moose, Katie. *Maryland's Western Shore, The Guidebook*. Annapolis, Maryland: Conduit Press, 2001.

The Official Visitor's Guide, Annapolis and Anne Arundel County. Annapolis, Maryland: Anne Arundel County Conference and Visitor's Bureau.

Prince Georges Calendar of Events, Maryland Conference & Visitors Center, Largo, 301-952-9554

Prince Georges Fall and Winter Travel Planner, Largo, Prince Georges County, 301-925-8300

Russell, Donna Valley. *Historic London Town, Maryland*. Edgewater, Maryland: London Town Foundation, 2006.

Shellenberger, William H. *Cruising the Chesapeake*. Camden, Maine: International Marine, no date.

Shomette, Donald. *London Town: A Brief History*. Edgewater, Maryland: London Town Publik House Commission, 1978.

Shomette, Donald C. *Lost Towns of Tidewater Maryland*. Centreville, Maryland: Tidewater Publishers, 2000.

St. Clements Island-Potomac River Museum; somd.com

St. Mary's County Department of Tourism, Leonardtown, 301-475-4200

St. Mary's County Destination Guide, St. Mary's County Tourism Division, 301-475-4200

St. Mary's County, Maryland Begins Here. St. Mary County, Maryland: St. Mary's County Department of Economic and Community Development, 1-800-327-9093

St. Mary's, Maryland, Attractions Map & Guide, St. Mary's County Division of Tourism, 800-327-9093

Stein, Charles Francis. *A History of Calvert County, Maryland*. Baltimore, Maryland: Calvert County Historical Society, 1977.

Touring Charles County, Charles County Comissioners

U.S. Geological Survey & U.S. Census Bureau

BIBLIOGRAPHY

Visitor's Guide, Charles County Office of Tourism, La Plata, 301-645-0558.

Visitor's Guide, Harford County Tourism Council, www.harfordmd@msn.com

Walking Map, 2007. Antique Group of Havre de Grace, Visitor's Center, 450 Pennington Avenue, 410-939-2100

Waterfront Guide, Life Along the Chesapeake. Marine Trades Association of Baltimore County, 410-687-1002

Wright C. Milton. *Our Harford Heritage.* Glen Burnie, Maryland: French-Bray Printing Company, 1967.

www.campmd.com

www.historiclondontown.org

www.leonardtown.somd.com

www.townofeagleharborinc.org

www.visitprincegeorges.com

index